Between the Body and the

●

Between Men - Between Women
Lesbian and Gay Studies
Lillian Faderman and Larry Gross, Editors

Between the Body and the Flesh

•

Performing Sadomasochism

Lynda Hart

Columbia University Press
New York

Columbia University Press
Publishers Since 1893
New York   Chichester, West Sussex
Copyright © 1998 Columbia University Press
All rights reserved
Library of Congress Cataloging-in-Publication Data
Hart, Lynda, 1953–
     Between the body and the flesh : performing sadomasochism /
Lynda Hart.
          p.   cm. — (Between men—between women)
     Includes bibliographical references and index.
     ISBN 978-0-231-08402-4 (cloth : alk. paper)

     ISBN 978-0-231-08403-1 (pbk. : alk. paper)
     1. Sadomasochism.   2. Lesbians—Sexual behavior.
3. Lesbianism.   I. Title.   II. Series.
HQ79.H36   1998
306.77'5—dc21   97–26544

Casebound editions of Columbia University Press books are printed
on permanent and durable acid-free paper.
Printed in the United States of America

For Clara

His books take hold of us as soon as we become aware that for all their repetitiousness, their platitudes and clumsiness, he is trying to communicate an experience whose distinguishing characteristic is, nevertheless, a tendency to be incommunicable.

—Simone de Beauvoir, introduction to the Marquis de Sade's
One Hundred and Twenty Days of Sodom

I don't have any documentation for this. I don't have any statistics to quote or studies to put in a footnote. Either you know what I'm talking about or you don't. . . . You either see yourself in the cathode ray tubes of what's laughingly called civilization, or you know you are a ghost in the machine, and that invisibility is one of the very few things that might guarantee your safety. . . . We are glitches in the horizontal hold, pixels that are the wrong color, viruses tormenting a hard-drive, songs played backwards, piggy-back programs chipping fractions of a cent off the bourgeoisie's ATM deposits.

—Pat Califia, introduction to *Forbidden Passages*

Contents

Acknowledgments

I have written this book with more than a little help from my friends. Some of this writing demanded more of me than I could find alone, and I have been fortunate to be supported by an extraordinary group of people who had the courage not to abandon me when I faltered on the way. Una Chaudhuri and her family; Gabrielle Cody, David Boyd, and Larry Helfer; Bob Vorlicky, Pamela Rhea, Deb Margolin, Catherine Keller, Mary DeShazer, Anita Helle, Elena DiLapi, Ruth Kauffman, Leslie Thrope, Amy Robinson, Anne Cubilié, Jim Downs, Chris Straayer, and Terry Lawler; and my sister, Kerry Hart. To enumerate their individual gifts would constitute another volume, so I will simply say that each in her or his own way gave me something absolutely indispensable, for which I am forever deeply grateful.

Chera Finnis has had the patience and persistence to watch and teach me how to trust myself, a formidable task. Her loyalty and wisdom have led me through many dark passages.

Peter Stallybrass has been heroic in his support. Other colleagues at the University of Pennsylvania have also been consistently and unflaggingly present at various stages in this writing, especially: Maureen Quilligan, David DeLaura, Eric Cheyfitz, Stuart Curran, Houston Baker, Jean-Michel Rabaté, and Phyllis Rackin. Carroll Smith-Rosenberg prompted me to make this work public and gave me my first forum for doing so. Betsy Erkkila has remained faithfully in touch with and supportive of my work.

An abbreviated version of "Doing It Anyway" was published in Elin Diamond, ed., *Performance and Cultural Politics* (New York: Routledge, 1996). A short version of "Death and the Referent" was published under the title "Blood, Piss, and Tears," in *Textual Practice* 9, no. 1 (Spring 1995). Sections of chapters 3 and 4 were published under the title "That was Then, This Is Now: Exchanging the Phallus," in *Postmodern Culture* 4, no. 1 (September 1993).

Outside my immediate academic environment a number of people have fostered this project by offering me various venues for airing my ideas, reading drafts of chapters-in-progress, donating their time to discuss these ideas with me: Elin Diamond, Jill Dolan, Janelle Reinelt, José Muñoz, Alan Sinfield, Jody Greene, Roxanne Hamilton, Liza Yukins, Geeta Patel. Pat Califia and Gayle Rubin both communicated with me very generously. Special thanks to Lauren Berlant and Eve Sedgwick for offering me abundant portions of their wisdom and understanding that I could not incorporate it all. Aralee Strange showed me how to write from a different perspective.

Valerie Savage's wily wit carried me through many difficult months and across an ocean. When I arrived on the other side, I found another community of people, who have carried me through the repetitions that this book has elicited: Sally Munt has been a source of consistent loyalty and stimulation, as well as a good bit of highly productive aggravation, which she alone could dare. Paul Heritage's devotion and intellect have sustained me through nearly twenty years of thinking about theater. Lois Weaver, Kerry Moore, Charlie Spencer, Emma Field-Raynar, Sue O'Sullivan, Jonathan Dollimore, Lorna Hutson, Lisa Jardine, and David Mayer have all given me significant portions of their time and offered provocative dialogue.

I owe a very special debt to Cherry Smyth, who not only gave this book one last very tough reading—as only she could—but also worked with me diligently through the last stages of preparing the manuscript for the press. I also owe special thanks to Anjali Arondekar, whose biting wit, sharp intellect, and endless warnings against the perils of too much Diet Coke made the last stages of the writing pleasurable. Once again, I cannot enumerate the delicate and generous acts these people performed. I can only say that without them I could not have managed.

Susan Heath braved the wilds of the book's transformation from manuscript to book; Ann Miller faced the tempests of my moods; LeAnn Fields performed the precarious balancing act of friend and editor; Ken Wissoker extended his hand to steady me during a final falling.

Since the book's first incarnation Peggy Phelan has been a most faithful reader and commentator. Her companionship, her intellectual acumen, and her presence as a fellow traveler through the labyrinthine paths of this journey are inscribed throughout.

In the entrance to the Tate Museum in London stands Jacob Epstein's monumental sculpture of Jacob wrestling with an angel. Jacob and the angel grip each other in an inextricable bond, their gazes locked. The first time I saw this sculpture, I read their embrace as sexual—then I saw the angel's wings. What I missed in my initial interpretation of this work of art added depth to my subsequent "right" reading. Where I was "wrong" I best understood the "meaning" of the sculpture. And my misreading informed my own struggle to complete this book. Perhaps Jacob, too, missed the angel's wings as he strove to fend it off. Locked in a perpetual combative embrace, Epstein's Jacob will never let go of his angel. Their arms will never fall to their sides, but the sculpture has helped me to see how to let go, to "finish" without ending.

> Angel: suppose there were a place that we know nothing of,
> And that in it lovers—
> who never did find their fulfillment here below—
> performed their showy, daring acts upon
> the heart's trapeze, and built their towers of pleasure
> from ladders each propped only by the other's
> and standing, ever-swaying, where no ground is.
>
> (Rilke, "The Fifth Elegy")

Between the Body and the Flesh

•

Introduction

Pat Califia's and Robin Sweeney's long-awaited sequel to *Coming to Power,* *The Second Coming: A Leatherdyke Reader,* addresses the problems of naming that I too have wrestled with in writing this book. Keenly aware of the volatile constructions of my topic(s), I could, perhaps, have circumvented some potential controversy by avoiding using the words *lesbian* and *sadomasochism.* Both words have become so overdetermined that they are lightning rods in lesbian-feminist communities, especially when they are conjoined. The issue always of course is fundamentally about to whom and to what these words refer.

Califia and Sweeney choose the word *leatherdyke* in their subtitle deliberately "to carve out an area for ourselves in the world of identity politics in which the leather community currently finds itself."[1] Throughout *The Second Coming,* but especially in part 2, "Who is My Sister? Challenging the Boundaries of the Leatherdyke Community," the issue of reference is continually evoked, by transgendered, transsexual, bisexual, pansexual, heterosexual, homosexual, lesbian, and a host of other self-nominated writers. No one comes to any theoretical conclusions; everyone, however, makes a choice, states her preference.

There is a danger of becoming mired in this litany, a tendency toward creating so many categories that there is no way left to speak of communities at all, much less *a* community. The shift from the 1981 subtitle of *Coming to Power: Writings and Graphics on Lesbian S/M* to the 1996 subtitle, *A Leatherdyke Reader*, speaks worlds that had I world enough and time I might attempt to address more fully. That, however, is not the aim or intention of this book. I can only simply reiterate here the position that I have taken and continue to hold from earlier writing. My position on identities and their politics is a fairly simple psychoanalytic one. Identities are necessary in order to function in "reality." I see them as prosthetic devices, which is not to say that they are any less "real" than anything else. They are, however, in a conflicted relationship with sexuality and its practices. In some sense, a sexual identity, any sexual identity, is a fundamentally unstable concept. For, as I understand sexual desires, they are always mutable, shifting, contextual, changeable, and anti-ontological.[2] The essays in *The Second Coming* testify to this. That is not to say that some people do not experience their sexual identities as cohesive, continuous, stable, and determining of which sexual practices they will or will not explore and enjoy. This position too, however, seems to me to be yet another *one* of the myriad ways in which we locate ourselves in our sexual beings and becomings. We are all enjoined to select names, to nominate ourselves.

I have decided to use the words *lesbian* and *sadomasochism* in this book for a variety of reasons. First, I do have an affinity with these words if not always (which is *not* to say *not ever*) an identity. I *use* them with the awareness that their referents are elusive, but some of the structures of feeling that have become attached to them are persistent with me. I decided finally, that I would be cheating more by avoiding them than by using them. I'm bound to be caught cheating anyway. One always is. After selecting various phrasings that were less nominative and more elusive, I realized that there was a pattern emerging as I gave talks from this book in a variety of venues—from the International S/M Pride Conference in London to American universities where I was being surveyed for possible academic positions. It was abundantly clear (albeit, belatedly and retrospectively, which is only when clarity can emerge) that I was using terms like *dominance and submission, power plays*, and *the eroticization of power*, in a descending (or ascending) order according to my expectations of the particular audience's ability to absorb this language without relegating me to the fringes of "sex radicalism." In short, I was censoring myself by suppressing words that I *do* feel are descriptive of (some of) my selves. At the same time, I am concerned by the iconicity of these words; the ways in which they so easily proceed from many things to a singular set of ideas. I hope that the actual content of this writing will sometimes succeed in bypassing that problem. My primary interest here is *not* in writing about "identities," though they will unavoidably resurrect in the writing. Most writing by academics on the subject of s/m has tended to focus primarily on identity formations. I wanted to explore what it means to engage in some of these practices—to perform them. My readings cannot be other than individualistic on one level; and though I am not claiming to speak for any particular community, I also see this book as participating in an ongoing series of dialogues, and hope that some readers will find various ways into this book.

Luce Irigaray suggests that rather than remaining mired in "the exhausting labor of copying, miming. Dedicated to reproducing that sameness in which we have remained for centuries, as the other," we search for other ways to love, restaging that commerce through a love that is "neither gift nor debt."[3] Utopian? Yes, perhaps. But I cannot stop seeking it. I do not expect to find it through "sadomasochism," but I don't expect to find it by avoiding what I think is a certain, inevitable power struggle within any erotic relationship. This is a book of prayers and despair, a wildly optimistic book, and occasionally a coldly cynical one. I have not tried to force my various attitudes toward these subjects into a cohesive whole, leaving them rather to be "subjects" very much in the making.

However my readings are received, I know that this is a book of flesh and blood and bones. Like Lot's wife, I cannot always resist the urge to turn and look backward; I hope not with nostalgia but with insatiable curiosity. Flesh: not "too too solid" (or was it "sullied"?) to melt, but flesh already in that liminal state between solid and liquid. In part, I wrote this book desiring to make a narrative about the fantasies and practices that have concerned (and sometimes consumed) me since my earliest memories. And yet, of course this book is not a narrative. It could not have been. I am not yet at that place where a coherent story can be told (see chapter 4), nor do I expect ever to arrive there. Nonetheless, there are some things that must be spoken with the full awareness that the words will inevitably miss their cue, arriving too late or too soon, or not even finding the theater. Although I make no claims to speak for a community, I am also not an outsider looking in. The outside/in relationship does exist in my writing, because I inhabit both these spaces, sometimes simultaneously, but not always. And they are always (con)fusing. Mostly, I have written it in conversation with one primary other, with whom I have only recently become acquainted. I have written it for her, listening to her voice as it grew increasingly audible and commanding.

In chapter 1 I bring together four rather unlikely partnered texts: an essay by Anna Freud in which she discusses her father's essay "A Child is Being

Beaten," which she found illuminating in a case she was working on with a fifteen-year-old girl troubled by beating fantasies; Janice Radway's important, ground-breaking feminist book, *Reading the Romance*, which studies the responses of a women's community who gave over most of their (little) leisure time to reading romance novels; Dorothy Allison's short story "Private Rituals," first published in the anthology *High Risk*, a story that clearly is a kind of blueprint for her acclaimed novel, *Bastard Out of Carolina*; Daphne Merkin's essay, "An Unlikely Obsession," published in *The New Yorker* in a special Women's Issue in 1995, in which Merkin confesses her own masochistic desires and traces them through a number of experiences searching for a cause, which she (in my opinion most unfortunately) finds. At first, these were simply four texts that I found absorbing, or at least engaging. They seemed to partake in a common theme, "the problem" of women's masochistic fantasies. As I read them separately, together, repeatedly, and in different combinations, I caught myself aware of my first impulse—to argue for a certain sameness between them, and to mitigate the cultural horror (and fascination) with a certain kind of desire. These texts proved strongly resistant to that impulse, and I have learned from them both how strong the desire is to elide differences and how powerful the internalized mandate is to do so—as well as how gratefully impossible it is to do.

Chapter 2, "To Each Her Other: Performing *Lesbian* Sado-Masochism," takes another look, along with as many of the others that have been taken that I could incorporate, at the last couple of decades of the "sex and culture wars" in relation to feminist debates, concerns, and opinions. The sweep of this section is narrowed by not attempting an historical survey—referring readers rather to the fine ones that have already been written—and by focusing on one particular nodal point within these debates: lesbian sadomasochism. My argument here attempts to shift the terms of these debates in reference to s/m by standing back and asking a question that is often unarticulated but nascent prior to the debates: why what has been referred to, for better or for worse, as *lesbian sadomasochism* has been such a vexed site in these "wars." In this section then, my question is not so much about *what* lesbian s/m *is*, as it is *why* lesbian s/m has become the marginal center, the paradoxical *place* around which much of this controversy has circled.

In chapter 3, "Doing It Anyway: The Impossible-Real," I engage with a number of theorists—Leo Bersani and Kaja Silverman in particular—who have written about masochism and its liberating possibilities. My concern is to show how the reclamation of "masochism" as a privileged sexuality for the production of a "new male" (both homosexual and heterosexual) leaves the psychoanalytic construction of "feminine masochism" intact, effectively participating in and perpetuating the notion that a "feminized *feminine* masochism" remains *necessarily* impossible in order for this sexual "revolution" to take up its place in fantasy. This chapter also reconsiders debates about the meanings and uses of dildos among lesbians: their racialization, their function as prosthetic devices, and, unavoidably it seems, their associations and disassociations with the phallus and/or penis.

In chapter 4, "Death and the Referent: The Queer Real," I discuss the work of artists such as Anna Munster, Bob Flanagan, Ron Athey, and Bill T. Jones, in reference to the ways in which their work has become implicated in a discourse that seeks to mark a clear border between the "real" and the "phantasmatic." The overriding question that this section engages concerns the social and theoretical implications of that marking as it is attached to queer performances. I move from discussing the "performativity" of s/m within theoretical, fictional, and cultural accounts, to looking at performativity *within* performance per se. Whereas one would think that within discourses already marked as "theatrical" the perplexing distinction between the "real" and the "performative" would not be at issue, I have found that this is scarcely the case. At least such is not the case in many contemporary accounts of queer performativity. Hence what I pursue in this chapter concerns an unarticulated—and perhaps mostly unconscious—link between the desire to demarcate the boundaries of fantasy and reality and entrenched cultural presumptions about the very constitution of queer sexualities— inside and outside the theater.

In chapter 5, "Bearing (to) Witness: The Erotics of Power in *Bastard Out of Carolina*," I return to Dorothy Allison, to end the formal part of this book with a discussion of her novel, *Bastard Out of Carolina*. This section begins to work through connections between sexual abuses (and memories of them) and sadomasochistic sexualities. Although this chapter marks the (formal) ending of the book, it is in many ways both a prelude and a return to questions that have been implicit throughout earlier chapters. Specifically, chapter 5 explores what it means to be a spectator, here conceptualized in the particular form of a witness; the ways in which writing is an attempt to form, formulate, or formalize a bond with a community by presupposing a collective of readers; and the risks one unavoidably takes in order to speak "the truth" of one's experience—a project destined to fail, but a failure that need not be a loss. This chapter is also *about* the perils of passionate identifications. At the same time, it *performs* my own in relation to Allison, whose writing moves me to the edge of a kind of blindness, where I can only see in the dark.

The analytic work of chapter 5 lays some ground for the epilogue, *Crows 111*, a piece of writing in which I hope to perform some of what I have described in the book's main body. It is also a way into this book for readers who do not find other theories and ideas particularly interesting or compelling, and it could be read first, for it is also another beginning.

Perhaps *Crows III* is better described as a way of braking myself while I am yet learning how to ride. My father taught me how to ride a bicycle. He also taught me that I could write. I was afraid to ride until I was sure that I knew how to stop the bike and get off. He coaxed me to understand that it was impossible to know how to stop before one began, and promised to catch me if I fell. Sometimes he did. But not always. One time I was especially hurt and furious when he looked away, distracted just as I was crashing into the curb. He picked me up after it was too late, and burst out laughing. So did I. Both of us were humiliated. Deleuze argues that "the formula of masochism is the humiliated father."[4] He also argues that the masochist is a great humorist, and that "humor is the triumph of the ego over the superego."[5] Writing, like riding, is a kind of surrender. Hence my epilogue is an attempt to capture the irony, the terror, and a certain divine comedy of writing a book that has said what it wanted to despite my struggle for control. I can only hope that readers will find the humor in catching me where I will most assuredly fall, and that for some of you there will be resonances of your own experiences.

"Crows III" is "autobiographical" *only* in the sense that Shoshana Felman elaborates in *What Does a Woman Want?* Felman argues that "women's autobiography is what their memory cannot contain—or hold together as a whole—although their writing inadvertently inscribes it."[6] My struggle to write this book has entailed my most conscious awareness that to write is to testify to a kind of dying; for to end is to surrender to a memorial of what one has become. But testimony, as I argue in my final chapter, is not confessional. Again, to cite Felman: "insofar as any feminine existence is in fact a traumatized existence, feminine autobiography *cannot be* a confession. It can only be a testimony: to survival. And like other testimonies to survival, its struggle is to testify at once to life and to the death—the dying—the survival has entailed.[7] My book is thus written with the humility and the humor of knowing that I *cannot* know what it is that I have written until I see it reflected in the desire of others. In this sense, it is my "femininity" that has guided my hands.

What unites this book above all is a persistent focus on the ways in which s/m sexual practices have been variously caught up in a theatrical discourse. Throughout the book I return again and again to the vexed distinctions (and lack of them) between fantasy and reality, the "real" and the "performative."

A turning point in the erotic power struggle between Wanda and Severin in Leopold von Sacher Masoch's *Venus in Furs* serves to introduce the issues that are a central focus throughout my book. Narrating the story of his passionate idolatry for Wanda, his "Venus in Furs," Severin has finally begun to awaken in her all of the supersensual cruelty that he is convinced is already in her "nature." Wanda warns him that his plea to become her plaything is arousing dangerous tendencies in her and that, should he persist, she may well become the ideal of his fantasy. But Severin is undaunted in his desire to be enslaved by a beautiful and tyrannical mistress.

"Tread on me!" I cry, throwing myself before her.
"I dislike playacting," says Wanda impatiently.
"Then hurt me in earnest."
A disturbing silence.[8]

The disturbing silence that punctuates this philosophical debate between Severin and Wanda is in some sense the "subject" of this book. Debates about the constitution of sadomasochistic sexuality frequently turn on precisely the moment that Sacher-Masoch captures here: is it "real" or "phantasmatic?" If the emphasis is on the phantasmatic, the language in which it is couched is often derived from theatrical discourse—*play, acting, scene, spectacle, scenario, staged*—or its discursive close cousin and sometimes theorized origin—*ritual*. Wanda initially responds to Severin's desire to be enslaved by her with scorn for his "modern view" of women's love as a hostile force that he endeavors to defend himself against and is yet drawn to irresistibly. Throwing himself willingly headlong into the breach, Severin desires to *choose* the inevitable by *performing* it and thereby risking the repetition, as Wanda warns him, that could make her cruelty real. Wanda begins to resist the ways in which Severin desires to retain control of his submission to her. She is contemptuous of his ideal, which she describes as "the love preached by Christianity and our modern knights of the spirit," and she refuses to partake in that "alien and hostile" struggle of the "spirit against the senses." Detesting "playacting," Wanda desires the "real" as opposed to Severin's fantasy. Severin sees his task as persuading Wanda to forego her "paganism"—her admiration for the "serene sensuality of the Greeks—pleasure without pain."[9]

Wanda and Severin seem to make opposite uses of their gods. Emulating the Greeks, Wanda initially represents what Nietzsche describes as the "race of noble and proud beings, in whom man's animal self had divine status and hence no need to lacerate and rage against itself." Like Nietzsche's Greeks, Wanda uses her gods "to keep bad conscience at a distance."[10] In what appears to be stark contrast, Severin seems to be Nietzsche's "mad, unhappy animal" who wills himself guilty, believing that he "might be punished to all eternity without ever expunging his guilt" and thus "cut[s] off once and for all his escape from this labyrinth of obsession" by erecting an ideal (God's holiness) "in order to assure himself of his own absolute unworthiness."[11]

Venus in Furs could be read as an allegorical confrontation between Christian guilt and Hellenic pleasure in which the former's triumph leads to the abjection of both contestants. Allegory, however, is not oppositional. A form that creates the illusion of opposition (as "playacting" most often refers to theatrical realism, a form that creates the illusion of non-illusionism), allegory, as Ronald Schleifer has argued, is a "way of saying . . . in which truth comes to inhabit time and things speak. But it is more than this, this dialogue: it is the way time comes to inhabit truth."[12] For Geoffrey Hartman, "allegorizing, though driven by a desire for transcendence, remains skeletal, grimacing, schematic . . . the no man's land between what can and cannot be represented."[13] And as Joel Fineman notes: allos, other; agoreuein, to speak—allegory etymologically signifies the "discourse of the Other."[14]

The allegorical contest between Christianity and "paganism" in Wanda's and Severin's erotic dance takes the form of a struggle between the "real" and "playacting"; but just as Hellenism and Christianity are neither wholly different nor wholly distinct cultural or theological orders, so Wanda's "real" and Severin's "play" are not separate psychic orders. They do, however, manifest themselves differently. Severin's desire for continuance is represented as fidelity. His desire to evade death makes its appearance as an obsession to extract a promise from Wanda, a guarantee that she will not abandon him. "To breed an animal with the right to make promises—is not this the paradoxical problem nature has set itself with regard to man? And is it not man's true problem?" Nietzsche asks in The Genealogy of Morals.[15]

Wanda and Severin argue over truth's relationship to eroticism. Wanda rebukes Severin: "no permanence can ever be imposed on love; it is the most changeable element in our transient lives."[16] Her desire is the desire for desire to be unmediated by time—the desire to remain forever in the present—Eros purified of the exigencies of time. Severin's desire, on the other hand, passes through the intervening agency of the death instinct, his love "like a bottomless abyss into which [he] seems to be sinking deeper and deeper and from which nothing can save [him]."[17]

While Wanda cannot imagine her love enduring for more than a month or two, Severin is obsessed with constancy, willing to do anything to make Wanda his forever, agreeing to undergo any torture she can inflict upon him in order to command her perpetual return. But both these passionate opposites share the goal of renewal. For Wanda that renewal is achieved by changing the object, which she believes will endlessly repeat the desire *for* desire. Severin's desire is to possess and retain the singular object of his desire. In order to do this, he must find a way to insure that Wanda *remains* what he already imagines her to be: a cool, indifferent, cynic whose passion burns brilliantly but fleetingly. Severin's task is then, paradoxically, to capture Wanda's transience *outside time.* She warns him that the achievement of his desire is death (but whose death?). Severin's aim is to corrupt Wanda into constancy. Thus he is always contemplating endings and languishing in the pleasurable suffering of anticipating—thereby thwarting the finish. As he begins to "awaken dangerous forces lurking within [her]," Severin appears to be winning the game. If Wanda detests "playacting," Severin desires the cruelty of the real. Neither want theater. Both demand truth. Each yearns for something that is before and beyond "performance," but they seek it differently: she through a desire for authenticity sought in spontaneity and transience; he in ritual and repetition that would promise constancy. If her passion is "paganistic," his is theological. Although it is his body that is the proposed site where this yearning for truth is to be inscribed, the marks he seduces her into inflicting upon him are, for him, a means toward spiritual transcendence. Severin wants Wanda to leave her pagan body behind and join his spirit by traveling through his flesh. While neither of them will achieve the end that their desire aims for, the struggle between them is powerfully erotic. Sacher-Masoch's narrative must end. But Wanda's and Severin's two seemingly disparate desires could, theoretically, continue to occupy the same phantasmatic place. For despite his rush for the future and her lingering in the present, the erotic dynamic between them is not realized in the accomplishment of either of their goals—neither in his quest for the spirit traversing the flesh nor in her fixation on the body. *Venus in Furs* gives us a debate on the philosophy of erotic love that takes its place, that can *only take place*, in the impossible, unrepresentable space *between* these lovers locked into performing the "real" of their differences.

If desire is always in some sense "theatrical," it is so, as I understand it, in much the same way that the "play" always takes place in the space between the spectators and the performers. In a way, then, we can understand the "theatrical" as intrinsically "traumatic," for the ontology of performance takes place neither on the stage nor in the stalls. No matter how one arranges the architecture of the theater, there is always a space in between—a gap, a space of fantasy that cannot be filled with content, where the play *must* take place. To enter fully into the performance, one must be willing to risk leaving the security of one's "self" behind and step into this void, trusting that others will be found there as well. Desire, like theater, takes place in the fantasy one constructs with others, and like any communal experience, requires a relinquishing of control. We love, and we play, in order to learn how to survive letting go.

The "body" of my title might be understood as the cultural constructions, the architectures, the fixed, stabilized sites that we know are inventions of reality, but that we disavow as such in order to survive the disequilibrium of our desires for the "real" of our fantasies. The "flesh" is that phantasmatic "object" of our desires, as well as our longings for and resistances to merging the distinctions between the real and the phantasmatic. Both the "body" and the "flesh" are illusions. Both are phantasmatic constructs. But they serve different ends, purposes, and desires. The "body" keeps us anchored in the worlds we have constructed in "reality." The "flesh" is a place toward which we reach that always exceeds our grasp, that indeed *must* elude us for it is the site beyond (or before) the "body" that permits us to continue *making* reality even as our desire disavows it. The temporality of this writing is the past—anticipated, prolonged, repetitive, and paradoxically "impossibly" present. The tense in which I argue s/m sexual performances seek, while forever failing, to hold. The moments I strive to capture are beyond my grasp—always either before me or behind me, except in those rare altered states where time and space lose their naturalized meanings. Sex and performance are two locations where I sometimes feel this loss. Marilyn Hacker's poem, "Somewhere in a Turret," articulates this longing to cross the threshold.

> Nobody lives in the present, time
> has textures past and future that
> tongues taste at, fingers feel for.
> The present happens in rooms
> I am not in; past rooms
> are only momentarily
> empty, if I knew how
> to turn around, I would cross the threshold smiling.
> No one would ask me to leave, no one would send me away.[18]

Theater takes place in that space *between* the watchers and the watched; so desire I place *between the body and the flesh.*

1 • Knights in Shining Armor and Other Relations

> Identity is a mere outer skin that constantly distorts one's relations
> with others. Yet there is no other way to have relations with others,
> since without identity there is no language . . . no social life, only an
> autistic existence . . . one needs this knight in shining armor.
>
> —Catherine Clément, *Lives and Legends*

In the final chapter of this book, I use Dorothy Allison's novel, *Bastard Out of Carolina*, as a way of concluding and extending the discussion of many of the questions that inform this entire work. It is the only chapter that focuses on one self-contained text. But it is not a reading of Allison's novel per se. The questions that I raise about the generic status of Allison's novel—particularly in relationship to the narrative possibilities and impossibilities, likenesses and differences between testimonials, autobiographies, confessionals, and fiction—bring me back to the beginning. As I write my first chapter last, I can see more clearly now how origins are effectively— and affectively—belated. To begin is to end again—from an ending that is entirely arbitrary, a beginning that repeats this movement ceaselessly. Allison undoubtedly had to write *Bastard Out of Carolina* many times before the novel made its appearance. Before, that is, she let it go—off on its own, into the gaze of other readers.

One of Allison's stories, "Private Rituals," which was a precursor to *Bastard Out of Carolina* and contains many of the same passages that appear in the novel verbatim, tells us some of what she kept and what she discarded to make her novel. In some ways *Bastard Out of Carolina*, a novel that has been widely read and recognized, is more "private" than her short story, which she names "*Private* Rituals." This is another way to point out what I mentioned in my introduction; that nominations, which function as identity markers, appear to be revelatory, when in fact they are complex negotiations *between* the public/private divide. They do not reveal a "secret"; rather, they present an appearance of openness, that is, they create an illusion of standing in contrast to—con(against)cealing—when in fact they seal *together* oppositional and hierarchical dualisms.

In an interview, Allison says that she did not want to censor herself in writing this book:

> I did not want to lie. In the process of writing the book, the first thing I did was write "Private Rituals," which is kind of an abstract. It's only about sex, about the sexual fantasies of Bone, the main character—whereas I think it is possible to read *Bastard* and avoid the sexual stuff. It's really possible to read *Bastard* as a working class novel and sidestep the sexual and violence issues. I was afraid in going to mainstream publishers that once they got a look at what I had, they would push me to lessen the sexual content, to soften it or even to make it more traditionally sexual.
>
> Most novels about incest have this really offensive tone where the sex becomes a kind of fetishized dwelling on the interaction between the perpetrator and the victim, with enormous detail to the sexual violence. I was afraid they would push me into more of that because that stuff sells.[1]

The struggle that we see enacted by Allison here is not just about "sex" but also and always about class—about "high" and "low" cultures and the ways in which they are constituted in the complicated nexus of class and sexuality. The censorship and self-censorship issues encapsulated here are enormously complicated. In her introduction to *Forbidden Passages*, Pat Califia speaks eloquently and boldly to these issues:

> The loss of our creative potential is one of the least-visible consequences of censorship. We are intimidated by the grand scale of what we see in the mass media, and we never get to see how this stuff is produced. The creative process has been mythologized, and so has the process of finding an audience. I suspect it is also because our hearts have been broken once too often. . . . It is internalized self-censorship which has made it possible for industrial capitalism to create a consumer class.[2]

While I suppose it is possible to read Allison's novel as a working-class novel and to avoid the issue of sex and violence, it is not possible for *me* to do so. The network of censoring and self-censoring spins in and around our control: Califia's writing is subjected to constant censorship efforts (see Califia's and Janine Fuller's introduction to *Forbidden Passages*). Allison writes "Private Rituals," then tones down the sex and violence and writes a novel that is nominated for a national book award and ends up on the syllabi of university professors. She is dismayed by this success and responds initially with the feeling that she must have done something wrong. But earlier, in the same interview, she says that she toned down the sex and violence because she wanted to avoid a fetishistic, prurient display of incest. She also says, however, that she was worried about the whether a mainstream publisher would take the novel. Then feminist academics, like myself, write about Allison's novel (not about "Private Rituals," nor do many of us write about Califia's work and other graphic writings about lesbian sexuality). And not without running into our own peculiarly academic modes of censorship.

A relevant aside: I am giving a talk from this book at a "cocktail seminar" at Gay Sweatshop in London. I have given the same talk at prestigious American universities. After I have finished, a member of the audience identifies herself as an active participant in the U.K. s/m subculture. She is polite but clearly annoyed. "Why do you have to talk like that?" she asks me. "Talk like what?" I respond. "Speak to *them*, for *them*," she answers. I have fielded this question many times. This time I try to keep it simple: "I *am* one of *them*," I answer. Unsatisfied, she retorts, "But why must your language be so theoretical, so inaccessible?" Finally I arrive at the answer that I should have made long ago: "I like theory," I tell her, "it is a kind of fetish for me; it turns me on." She asks me after the seminar to contribute an essay to the new s/m lesbian magazine she has just started. I get invited to the International S/M Pride Celebration to participate in a series of queer performances. It is not easy to bridge these gaps, but it is not impossible.

As a critic, I choose my "subjects" largely on the basis of powerful identifications or disidentifications. As Wendy Steiner admits openly, with great relief for many of us, appreciating literature and art is about what one likes:

I was naive, no doubt, to look to semiotics for a scientific paradigm of art. The result was a parody of academicism: endless essays coining terms, proliferating typologies, using art merely to justify or exemplify the emergent categories. I have given up on being such a scientist. It has taken me a long time to admit that the thrust of criticism is the "I like," and whatever expertise I have accumulated conspires in this admission. The authority of one's institution of higher learning, one's academic credentials, one's ever-increasing experience may establish "objectively" one's claim to being an expert, but at the heart of any critical act is a subjective preference. To like, to find important, at this time and in such-and-such a situation: this is the essence of the critical act.

Somehow our culture has forgotten that fact.[3]

In this complex network of identifications, power, hierarchy—some of it pleasurable and some of it painful—I think even more about the ways in which *I* am censored and self-censor in writing this book. Is the language I employ in writing it—what some critics on both "sides" (obviously there are many more sides than the two I keep referring to) call "jargon" or "opaque prose" or simply "theory," a form of masking what I *really* want to say? Or is it what I really want to say? Of course one never can say what she really *wants* to say—that is why we keep writing. It's also why we keep having sex. Roxanne, in Califia's "The Calyx of Isis," never has that one great orgasm that would put the desire for all other orgasms to rest (see chapter 3). But she keeps trying, even though she knows it is impossible, indeed *because* she knows it is impossible.

Returning to these issues as they get played out in writing and publication, in Allison's widely acclaimed novel, Bone appears to be alone with her fantasies, alone in her struggles, her shame, her self-doubt, her rage, her solitary pleasures and pain. Significantly, Bone's little sister Reese does not appear in the novel as Allison once saw her in "Private Rituals." "Private Rituals" is a story in which Bone has a companion, a secret survivor who travels a path that takes a different form than the narrator's, who nonetheless crosses or intersects with her in highly charged moments. In the novel Bone's sister Reese's presence is spare, because she is presented as if she had been spared. Bone has little affinity with her. Reese is the one who "gets away," while Bone becomes the singular target of her step-father, Daddy Glen's, raging jealousies and insecurities. In *Bastard Out of Carolina*, Allison does include a scene in which Bone becomes aware that Reese also masturbates, but she knows little or nothing else of her sister's private rituals, and the readers must come to the conclusion that Reese has been exempted from the agonizingly pleasurable sexual fantasies that Bone engages in. The novel also shows us little concerning how Bone puts these fantasies into practice.

Such is not the story of "Private Rituals." Collected in the anthology *High Risk*, surrounded by other writers whose sexual fantasies challenge normative inscriptions of sexuality, Allison's narrative "I," who will later become Bone, not only fantasies about the fire in the haystack, fetishizes the belts that Daddy Glen uses to whip her, and masturbates to the re-membering of the beatings, as she does in the novel. She also acts out her masochistic pleasures in much more graphic detail than in the novel. The games she had dreamed about for so long become her own private reality, her way of bearing the secret of being "different": she uses scraps of worn belts and her mother's clotheslines to tie herself down to the bed; she finds a link of broken chain, cleans and polishes it and locks it around her hips, pushing the links inside her; she wears layers of thick cotton panties and sleeps with her arms spread-eagled so that she wouldn't sin—but it was "a joke on Jesus"[4] as well as herself that she began to have orgasms in that position; she uses screwdrivers, hairbrush handles, rocks, letter openers, and pine cones to replace the test tubes she first discovered in her chemistry set and manipulated into dildos. And, in "Private Rituals," Allison's "I" has sex with her beloved Uncle Earle, who gives her dollar bills to let him rub up against her backside. She enjoys it so much that she begins to initiate the sex, until Earle gets frightened and withdraws from his niece's precocious voluptuousness. Allison chose not to risk these details in her novel, knowing that a wider audience might read it and aware that few people outside of s/m subcultures can tolerate or fathom these differences from sexual "norms." The story also tells us much about what can be said and done within a community of similarly-minded writers, compared to the constraints of the novel as a singular form.

Allison's nascent Bone is already beyond the kind of intervention some readers might desire for her. Furthermore, she has, in her own ways, solved the problem of the horror of her daily existence by constructing these fantasies. These private rituals are not "evidence" of an irremediably wounded child. On the contrary, they are her remedy and they exist for her as luxuriously pleasurable. What haunts her in these moments are her feelings of guilt and shame. Not so much because she is doing something that she knows to be somehow "different" but mainly because she feels so alone in this difference. Her shame is not caused by the memory of the acts she endured without her consent; rather, it is produced by her isolation. It is the loneliness that makes her pain endure. She is thus incredibly relieved when she makes the simple recognition that her little sister masturbates as well. She hears Reese in the night, curled up on her side of the bed, rocking its frame, trying to remain still and silent. And she knows that she is not the only one. Still she thinks that Reese probably never went so far as to tie herself up.

There is one particular scene in "Private Rituals" that makes a compelling, if implicit, comparison. The not yet not quite Bone is watching her sister from her perch in a tree. Reese cannot see herself being seen as she acts out her fantasies in the woods:

> I watched her one afternoon from the top of the tree Mama hung her bird feeder on. Reese hadn't seen me climb up there and didn't know I had a clear view of her as she ran around wearing an old sheet tied to her neck as a cape. It looked like she was fighting off imaginary attackers. Then she dropped to the ground and began rolling around in the grass and wet leaves, shouting, "NO! NO!" The haughty expres-

sion on her face was replaced by mock terror, and she threw her head back and forth wildly like the heroine in an adventure movie.[5]

Or, like the heroine in a romance novel?[6]

Reese might grow up to be one of those middle-class, middle-aged, ubiquitous, and for the most part anonymous females who devour romance novels in spectacular proportions. Ann Douglas theorizes:

> Admittedly incomplete surveys of readers suggest that Harlequins . . . are consumed not only by schoolgirls but by "normal" active women in their 30s, 40s, and 50s. If true, this statistic hardly assures us that the Harlequins are harmless . . . but provokes instead a serious concern for their women readers. How can they tolerate or require so extraordinary a disjuncture between their lives and their fantasies? [They] are enjoying the titillation of seeing themselves, not necessarily as they are, but as some men would like to see them: illogical, innocent, magnetized by male sexuality and brutality.[7]

I do not mean to single out Douglas here; her comments are representative of many feminists who held such opinions about the sexual fantasies of other women in the late 1970s and early 1980s. Unlike most other academic discourses, feminism tries to avoid making the spurious claim to "objectivity." Nonetheless, we succumb to self-censorship by writing in ways that suggest we have authority, which can sound very much like having discovered "the truth." It is also important to keep in mind that Douglas's comments were produced in a time when many feminists were engaged in tasks that narrowed or elided our differences due, in part, to the overwhelming fear of the violence that permeates even the most mundane daily activities of women. Despite the pronouncements of the new right's happy spokeswomen, such as Camille Paglia and Katie Roiphe, the violence in women's lives has changed very little—if indeed it has not increased in some areas. What has changed, but not nearly enough, is the understanding between and among feminists that we must attend much more closely to each others's differences and resist one of the impulses of identification, which can lead us too often to incorporate those differences into our own psychic locations.

We are also beginning to understand, but not without an immense struggle, that identitarian politics, which channel differences into identity categories—class, race, nationality, sexual orientation, etc.—can repeat and perpetuate the same movement that occurs in psychic identifications. That is not to say, however, that all identifications are self-incorporating, or that identity politics are hopelessly retrograde and damaging to political interventions. One of the first and most successful academic books to take on these challenges was Janice Radway's *Reading the Romance*, which combines an ethnographic analysis with a literary/theoretical one.

Radway takes critics like Douglas to task for failing to explore the motivations and pleasures of real women who read the romance. Radway critiques opinions like Douglas's for their locations—the space of fantasy: from the outside looking in, Douglas presumes to read the unconscious of these women who blindly stumble into a pleasure that is in fact "bad" for them if they were only to open their eyes and see—as she can see—that the pleasures in which they participate are in fact internalized renditions of their own abjectness under patriarchy. This is precisely the kind of theorizing, in both form and content, that has been, and continues to be, directed against women whose sexualities are "deviant." The romance readers are critiqued for being "normal" women, who are, paradoxically, deviating from that "normality" by entertaining the pleasures of fantasies that arise from a reading that is, unknown to them, a coded repetition of patriarchal attitudes toward women. Both groups then are charged with complicity in the maintenance of "violence" against women.

What distinguishes attitudes toward the two groups is a matter of the degree to which they keep their fantasies and activities private. The romance readers are treated with gentle condescension, since they are presumed to lack the tools for understanding their own engagement with harmful material. Women who are openly, defiantly, and proudly sexually "deviant" are also charged with a lack of understanding; but their public stance generates a hostility toward them that incites a desire to police their activities. Hence the governing regulations of the various states collides with and finds collusion in the feminist derision of "perversions." It is interesting to note that Douglas bases her critique not on the fantasies per se contained within the pages of typical romance novels but on the presumption that the fantasies and the "reality" of the readers' lives are *disjunctive* and, therefore, *intolerable*. Certainly for these readers, as Radway has shown and as we might surmise anyway, the reading and fantasizing is not at all intolerable. On the contrary, whether the disjunction exists or not, the reading and fantasizing is altogether pleasurable. Douglas not only presumes the disjuncture, which Radway's analysis goes far toward suturing, but, more important, it is clearly Douglas herself, as spectator, who cannot tolerate it.

This is a rather odd and certainly counterintuitive argument. The most common understanding of fantasy is that it is always disjunctive with reality—indeed it is most often understood as a retreat, or escape, from reality. Disjunction is at the very core of the difference between fantasy and reality in the most popular understanding of their differences. What this intolerance reveals, among other things, is that the spectator/reader's *own* psychic identifications and desiring-fantasy structures are challenged by the site/sight of pleasures that appear to her as inexplicable. It also points out that the popular understanding of fantasy as an *escape* from reality is inaccurate; for if we truly believed that fantasy was something like a vacation—a temporary retreat that removed us from the social realities of our daily lives—we would not be so concerned with it. Is it then the disjuncture that is really so troubling, or the possibility that the disjuncture does *not* divide fantasy from reality? Perhaps the disjunctive theory is merely a way of avoiding the fear that fantasies can indeed not only affect reality but even constitute it.

The idea that women, in particular, should seek to make their sexual fantasies and their "reality" consonant is a curious enjoinder. It is based, I think, on a feminist ideal that, given the oppressiveness of most women's lives under a heteronormative, patriarchal regime, we should be working to change reality (which of course we *should*). But the notion that the place of fantasy has no relation to the changing of reality is what is most problematic. It strikes me as odd, to say the least, that we can at once theorize that reality is produced from and by a masculinized imaginary, and hence allot a tremendous amount of credence and power to male fantasies, even so much as the power to determine women's social realities; while at the same time "we" deny, even prohibit, the power of women's fantasies. It is as if there is only one fantasy, just as there is presumably only one sex or gender or sexuality—and it is masculine.

Radway seeks to intervene in some of that theory by closely studying and interacting with a community of women who have given over a considerable portion of their leisure time to read the romance. Radway's Smithton community not only read the romance, they categorize, classify, and rate these novels on a meticulously constructed scale that accords with the pleasures they experience in the consumption of these novels. They even have a leader, Dot, who performs for them some initial screening of these novels so that they can attain the maximum pleasure in the least amount of time, an experience not unlike reading pornography.

Radway performs a precarious balancing act: on the one hand, she insists upon recording the voices of the actual readers and discrediting the theories of scholars who perceive the readers as "untrained and self-deceptive . . . women who either do not know what the novels really say or who refuse to admit that meaning to consciousness." The pleasure these women experience then becomes reduced to "mere rationalizations and justifications, false consciousness," while the trained literary scholar is able to "discern the nature of the connection between these tacit meanings and the unconscious needs and wishes that readers have but cannot acknowledge." Radway argues that these theorists repeat and perpetuate the analytic strategy that generates conclusions about the "ideological function of the genre upon the people who read it," and that they are thereby able to deplore the form by showing how "the consciousness created by popular literature reconciles readers to a social order dominated by others."[8]

Ethnographic analysis is often proposed as the solution to this problem. It is also, however, a problem in itself. Most obviously, the anthropological bent of ethnographical analysis is virtually impossible to erase entirely; for no matter how closely one listens and faithfully records, such recording, as we know, will always bear the trace of the spectator's own subjectivity. Radway's book exemplifies this problem, wrestles with it admirably, and to some extent overcomes it. But finally Radway ends up more aligned than she would have initially desired with theorists like Douglas, whom she sets out to challenge. Although she continues until the end of her study to emphasize that the Smithton readers' testimony about their own experiences cannot be ignored, and stresses that hers is *not* the only view that one can take, she nonetheless arrives at this position:

Women's domestic role in patriarchal culture, which is simultaneously addressed and counter-valuated in the imagination through a woman's encounter with romantic fiction, is left virtually intact by her leisure-time withdrawal. Although in restoring a woman's depleted sense of self romance reading may constitute tacit recognition that the current arrangement of the sexes is not ideal for her emotional well-being, it does nothing to alter a woman's social situation, itself very likely characterized by those dissatisfying patterns. In fact, this activity may very well obviate the need or desire to demand satisfaction in the real world because it can be so successfully met in fantasy.[9]

Although I may well agree with Radway's readings of the romance novel, there is nonetheless a fundamental theoretical problem in her valuable and engaging study. For if we are to take Radway's conclusions seriously, then it would seem that engagement in *any fantasy*—as opposed to the "real" of social life—could turn out to be a paralyzing gesture. That is, according to this theory, how could one argue that women who read fiction or theory that is unquestionably marked as feminist are empowered to activism through its consumption? Might not this material just as well satiate the need or desire to activate its principles in the social sphere?

Ethnographic analysis is not a solution to the problem of the split between fantasy and the real—or to the schism between "theory" and "practice." The notion that some of us are "really doing it," while others of us are merely observing "it" or talking/writing about "it" is a specious and persistent dualism that misunderstands the relationship between fantasy and the real. Marking them as *separate* locations (indeed the frequent marking of the real *as* spatial and fantasy as the *nowhere* of the social) reproduces the split between the mind and the body that is, arguably, the most efficient and tenacious binary. Although most of us are quite adept by now at challenging binary constitutions, the mind/body dualism has resisted nearly all efforts to complicate or undo its fortifications. As Elizabeth Grosz points out:

> The major problem facing dualism *and all those positions aimed at overcoming dualism* [emphasis mine] has been to explain the interactions of these two apparently incompossible substances, given that, within experience and everyday life, there seems to be a manifest connection between the two in willful behavior and responsive psychical reactions. How can something that inhabits space affect or be affected by something that is non-spatial?[10]

To return to Allison's "Private Rituals," and another tenacious binary, it is meaningfully ironic that it is in this space marked "private" that she is more *public* about her fantasies than she is in her award-winning novel. In this short story the narrator observes Reese acting out her masochistic fantasies within the relatively safe space of the "popular romance" and takes pleasure in her voyeuristic positioning, a pleasure that is akin to the "narrative" pleasure that Laura Mulvey has so famously denounced in her essay, "Visual Pleasure and Narrative Cinema."[11]

The pleasure "Bone" takes in watching her sister act out her sexual fantasy is much like the pleasure of the Smithton women, who simultaneously identify and disidentify with the heroines whom they observe. As Radway continually asserts, the "ideal romance" is characterized by a heroine who finds herself endangered, sometimes even assaulted, by the hero whom she will come to read, and therefore love, as a man who was always already tender and nurturant but whose ability to express these "feminine" traits was obscured by some damaging act in his past. Realizing that Reese's desiring fantasies, as she reads them acted out in this "dumb show," include elements of pursuit, danger, and the threat of assault and are therefore not really that different from her own, Allison's narrator laughs, hugs herself against the tree trunk and rocks her hips back and forth, imagining now that she is tied to the branches above and below me. Someone had beaten me with dry sticks and put their hands in my clothes. Someone, someone, I imagined. Someone had tied me high up in the tree, gagged me and left me to starve to death while the blackbirds pecked at my ears. I rocked and rocked, pushing my thighs into the rough bark. Below me, Reese pushed her hips into the leaves and made those grunting noises. Someone, someone she imagined, was doing terrible, exciting things to her.[12]

The recognition that there is not that much difference between herself and her sister mitigates the terror of her own desiring-fantasies. Still, she can only imagine what Reese is actually thinking when she performs her private rituals. She continues to feel the difference between herself and others in the belief that Reese probably did not act these fantasies out in ways that went beyond maintaining a safe distance between her fantasies and her autoeroticism. But then one day Allison's narrator rummages through the house, and in her sister's drawer she finds a cord tied with a series of complicated knots, an old pair of her mother's silk panties, one of her stepfather's handkerchiefs, and a smooth ivory handle that looked as if it had been once fixed to a mirror. She breathes deeply and grins. Putting the handle to her mouth she thinks: "Little sister . . . little sister . . . little sister, just like me! It was true then. All of us hid the same thing behind our eyes."[13] The narrator goes out into the yard and gets her chain, locks it around her hips and as it moves under her jeans she savors its cool sharp touch and her recognition: "I was locked away and safe. What I really was could not be touched. What I really wanted was not yet imagined. . . . Somewhere far away a child was screaming, but right then, it was not me."[14]

As I will discuss in chapter 5, the trauma that Allison says she very nearly did not survive, the pain that she cannot abolish, was not produced by her step-father's rape or beatings. Rather, it was her enforced alienation from feminist community that left her irremediably wounded. In "Private Rituals," we see "Bone" not merely surviving but triumphantly engaging her fantasies, once she discovers that Reese too played them out. This community of "one" contributes to her ability to redeem herself, knowing that she is not alone in her difference, knowing that someone else—even if it is only one person—can accompany her there into these terrifying places where she finds her greatest pleasures in the very heart of her guilt, shame, and rage. There is nothing more painful than to have one's testimony go unheard, to lose contact with one's witness, to take a journey into the deepest recesses of one's memories and re-member them believing that one is accompanied, and find oneself alone.

There *is* a difference, a very vital and *real* difference, between thinking and doing. There is not, however, in that difference, a radical split, an unbridgeable gulf, a dualism. Differences are not unrelated to each other; there are intersections. Parallel lines are illusionary. It is not enough, however, to say that romance stories and the fantasies of women who are engaged in an eroticism that consciously incorporates existing power structures and the desire to mete out or receive bodily excitations whose intensities are stronger than what has been deemed "normal" are more alike than different.[15] It is not my interest to "rescue" s/m from public censure by making the argument that it is much like other forms of women's fantasies. First, I think that the differences are in fact more pronounced than the similarities. Second, I do not think that s/m sexuality is in any need of a "rescue."

I am, however, intrigued by the ways in which censorship arises in similar forms to silence seemingly disparate groups. And I want to ponder this particular convergence through a daughter/father dialogue in which the daughter speaks both her father's language and her own, with, I think, some fascinating results. In a commentary on the essay, "A Child is Being Beaten," Anna Freud cites her father's comment: "In two of my four female cases an elaborate superstructure of day-dreams . . . had grown up over the masochistic beating fantasy. The function of this superstructure was to make possible a feeling of satisfied excitation, even though the masturbatory act was abstained from."[16] Anna Freud discusses this comment in relation to one of her own case studies, a girl of fifteen, who at the age of five or six had acquired a beating fantasy that conformed precisely to the first two phases of Freud's case: first, a boy was being beaten by an adult; second, many boys were being beaten by many adults. Anna Freud reminds us that according to her father's analysis, these first two phases substitute for an earlier phase in which the "boy" was the child herself and the grownup her own father. This repressed memory has yet another antecedent in which the child being beaten was actually a group of other children, all of whom represented rivals for the father's love. This primary fantasy is replaced, through oedipal repression and guilt, with the secondary phases. And hence we can understand the beating fantasy as a desire for and expression of the girl's wish that her father loves only her.

In Anna Freud's case study, the girl first goes through a phase in which she attempts to separate the beating fantasy from her autoeroticism—in effect attempting to produce a split between her mental and bodily activity—for though she is disturbed by the fantasy's content, she is even more distressed by her desire to masturbate. In an attempt to hold onto the pleasure, despite her feelings of guilt, the girl then began to add complicated scenarios to the daydream, adding persons and institutions and settings that elaborated the fantasy beyond recognition of its rudimentary form. Anna Freud is quick to point out that this process is a *common* mechanism in the production of fantasies, and is *not* to be understood as a process induced by guilt. Rather, it is a way of heightening tension, by delaying, suspending, the anticipated pleasure.[17]

But as the girl grows older, the "moral demands of the environment . . . now [become] incorporated" into her fantasy-life. And the beating fantasy, which she once experienced as a primary pleasure, began to have feelings of unpleasure that preceded and followed it. So the girl initiated a new kind of fantasy—one that she called her "nice stories," which seemed to depict nothing but kind, affectionate, and tender behaviors. And there was no longer any autoerotic activity that followed these "nice" daydreams. Anna Freud gives several examples of these "nice stories," which were instigated by a story set in the Middle Ages that the girl had read.

The core story consisted in a fantasy of a medieval knight who is feuding with other nobleman; in the course of the battle he takes a fifteen-year-old male youth prisoner. The girl then began to elaborate a series of major and minor episodes, each in itself constituting an enclosed narrative, but spliced together so randomly and incoherently that "the frame of her stories was in danger of being shattered by the abundance of scenes and situations accommodated within it."[18] But even as her narrative was shattered by the inclusion of so many episodes, her daydreams contained the same two key figures: an older person (the knight) who is powerful and dominant, and a younger person (the imprisoned youth) who is weak and submissive to the knight. Many variations occurred within this simple frame, but all of them included scenes of threatened torture or punishment: the knight threatens to put the youth on the rack; the knight nearly kills the youth through prolonged imprisonment; the knight surprises the youth in some moment of transgression, and threatens him with various punishments. But each time, the youth is spared at the last moment. The youth endures all sorts of deprivations, but these only serve to increase "his" pleasure when he is granted a reprieve, and then the process repeats itself.

Anna Freud says that the girl never noticed how repetitious these plots were, despite the fact that she was an intelligent and discerning reader. And yet each of these stories had the same basic structure. Radway, too, comments that the Smithton women did not notice that the romance novels they read were all basically the same story. And one cannot help but notice the similarities between Anna Freud's fifteen-year-old girl's "nice stories" and the plot of the romance novels that the Smithton women read. In both instances, there is antagonism between a strong and weak person, the latter being at the former's mercy in some way. Radway's heroes and Anna Freud's knight are both initially menacing figures who threaten to harm the weaker women, "which justifies the gravest apprehensions; a slowly mounting anxiety, often depicted by exquisitely appropriate means, until the tension becomes almost unendurable; and, finally, as the pleasurable climax, the solution of the conflict, the pardoning of the sinner, reconciliation, and, for a moment, complete harmony between the former antagonists."[19]

The significance of Anna Freud's case study for my purposes is twofold: first, and most obvious, there is a striking similarity between the plots of romance novels—which "normal" women continue to read and enjoy in great abundance—and the "nice stories" of the girl who creates these fantasies in order to escape from the guilt of her primary beating fantasies, only to find out that the "nice" stories are much like her original "bad" story, with a few important exceptions. The nice stories end with reconciliation and forgiveness; the bad story ends with the beating. As Anna Freud explains, the nice stories also contain the threat of torture, but the execution of it is forbidden.[20] She argues that the replacement of the bad story with the nice story is primarily a way to effect "the omission of an element that is indispensable in the beating fantasy, namely, the humiliation in being beaten."[21] What she does not point out explicitly however, is that in the nice story "humility" (the pardon, the forgiveness, and the reconciliation) replaces the humiliation of the beating fantasy. Now what is important to notice here is that in the nice story it is the *youth* (an obvious stand-in for the girl) who has committed a misdeed and hence must learn humility from the knight. In the romance novels, it is the hero, who, according to Radway's readings, is out of touch with his own (somehow mysteriously already there) desires to love and nurture the heroine, who must be trained into humility by the love of a woman who can teach him, through her unflagging patience and endurance, that he does in fact really love her. Though little sign of this tenderness is evidenced by the romance hero, the female lover, with her superior abilities to read through and past his resistances, is able, in the end, to accept that he *is the man* of whom she dreams, rather than that she dreams of a man *whom the hero is not*.

Anna Freud argues that the beating fantasy and the nice stories are strikingly similar in their construction, quite parallel in their content, and admit the possibility of a "direct reversal of one into the other." But the "essential difference between the two lies in the fact that the nice stories admit the occurrence of unexpected affectionate scenes [and in Radway's account of the romance, similar scenes defy probability] precisely at the point where the beating fantasy depicts the act of chastisement."[22] She argues, then, that one can see that what appears to be a substitution of a nice story for the beating fantasy (specifically "an advance" from one to another) "is nothing but a return to an *earlier* phase."[23] Being manifestly removed from the beating scene, the nice stories regain the latent meaning of the beating fantasy: the love situation hidden in it, which is to say, the *incestuous scene* that is hidden in it. The beating fantasies and the nice stories are thus inextricably linked to one another, though they are representations that become manifest through different psychic mechanisms: the beating fantasy from "a return of the repressed," the nice stories through "sublimation."[24]

The "return of the repressed" is of course a "bad" (read: "regressive") thing—whereas sublimation is what founds civilization. Sublimation, however, is also, according to Freud (Sigmund) a psychic mechanism that is most appropriate to men, who are the "founders" of civilization. Leo Bersani reads a very interesting moment in one of Freud's footnotes (the "lower body" repressed from the "upper body") toward the end of *Civilization and Its Discontents*. Bersani refers to this footnote as a moment of "textual embarrassment," when Freud argues that one of the first acts of civilization was man's conquest of fire, accomplished through collective urination, interpreted as a form of competition between men, experienced as sexual pleasure and hence symbolically homosexual. For Freud, women are anatomically incapable of such a "conquest"—hence their relegation to the hearth, the tending of the fire. This "fantastic sounding conjecture," attempts to accomplish the task of consigning "women" to an act that *precedes* civilization, rendering them incapable of sexual pleasure, and positioning them as the bearers or upholders of civilization while eliding their ability to participate in its making.

I cite this example precisely because it is so fantastic, but also because some feminists have been complicit in reifying the same distinction, albeit using other metaphors—of women as "naturally" predisposed to nurture and preserve civilization. Furthermore, Bersani's reading of Freud's embarrassing footnote follows upon his discussion of a "theoretical collapse" in Freud's insistence on a nonaggressive form of eroticism. Toward the end of chapter 4 in *Civilization*, despite Freud's protestations otherwise (particularly in regard to his insistence on two orders of sadism, the first a will to mastery and the second sexual), Bersani locates a collapse between these two orders and argues that Freud essentially admits that "destructiveness is constitutive of sexuality."[25] Bersani's theory then builds to a triple equation: sexuality = aggressiveness = civilization. Violence is not then something that comes to bear on civilization, distorting it, but rather what indeed constitutes it. In the footnote, then, it is not just that "women" become the keepers of the hearth; more radically, they become virtually consonant with that which they preserve—the fire—which men must subdue in order to create civilization. Of course we are familiar with such configurations in which men stand on the side of civilization and women on the side of nature. Early radical feminists were particularly fond of this distinction. Reading Freud, not as the gospel on sexuality but as the producer of texts that have invaded western culture's unconsciousness, is not likely to placate feminists who oppose any and all psychoanalytic readings.

Nonetheless, it is important to recognize that there has been a rather widespread supposition among feminists that women are "nonviolent." "Violence" is a term that is tossed about very loosely, and it often takes some startling turns. Pat Califia, for example, points out that in the late 1970s feminists who organized WAVPM (Women Against Violence and Pornography in the Media) considered images of women kissing and having oral sex with each other to be "violent," and women "wearing high heels or being tied up was described with as much horror as getting raped."[26]

Remembering that Freud originally posited three kinds of masochism: erotogenic, feminine, and moral, it seems that early feminists aligned themselves with the latter—moral masochism—martyrdom to an ideal that was in fact largely constructed by the very discourse against which they stood so strongly. Moreover, in my reading of this history, violence and power became nearly conflated in feminist rhetoric. Perhaps we don't have to have violence to achieve feminist goals, but we certainly cannot do so without power. What many antiporn anti-s/m feminists are recommending for a "cure" for women who enjoy these practices is, precisely, sublimation.

In order for women to perform sublimation effectively, they must elide the difference between the sexes. And, indeed, in order for the girl to "advance" from her beating fantasies to her nice stories, she must, in effect, accomplish the same task. Anna Freud ends the first section of her essay with this strikingly resonant reminder: "The sublimation of sensual love into tender friendship is of course greatly facilitated by the fact that already in the early stages of the beating fantasy the girl *abandoned the difference of the sexes and is invariably represented as a boy.*"[27]

From this vantage point, it is possible to theorize, despite its manifest counterintuitiveness, that the romance novel—the *feminine* genre par excellence—is a disguised (male) homoerotic exchange. And what of the girl(s) who refuse to relinquish their beating fantasies—the ones who continue to take pleasure in their "bad" stories and fail to sublimate their sensual love into tender affection? According to this psychoanalytic paradigm, they were always already "boys" anyway (hence the repeated accusations against women who enjoy an erotics of power that they are "male-identified"). And yet, at the same time, even within this psychoanalytic construct, are they not the girls who *refuse* the terms of this contract in which, as we can see, sexuality itself becomes the (performative) property of men? Are they not, in other words, the girls who *refuse* to be boys?

It is bewildering to find that feminist thinkers have criticized women for their fantasies whether they are nice stories or bad ones. Perhaps negative perceptions of women who read romance novels *and* women who engage with s/m fantasies and practices are based on the sense(ation) that the former *are indeed* merely "disguised" forms of the latter. Both groups are subjected to censure by the charge of "internalized misogyny," which is just another way of saying that these are women who have, in a sense, introjected masculine psychic formations. Such critics have then, most ironically (for they are usually the ones who vehemently eschew psychoanalysis) fully consumed the very discourse that they find most indigestible.

I would like to explore a different way of thinking about these similarities and differences. And though I cannot do so without utilizing psychoanalysis to some extent (for I find that if I don't use it, it uses me), I would like to do so in a way that perverts the impasse of the masculine monopoly on sexuality. In the second part of Anna Freud's essay she develops more fully what she only hints at in the first section: the significance of acquiring the ability to narrate in the movement from an instinctual, primary, sexual pleasure to its representation of tender affection in its sublimated form. She has already told us that as the girl in her case study began adding episodes to the core of her fantasy, the very frame of the fantasy began to shatter.

In section two, she tells us that the girl decided to put her fantasies into writing, so she wrote a short story about the knight. This story *begins* with the prisoner's torture (remember that in the "nice" fantasy, the prisoner is *not* tortured) and ends with his "*refusal to escape.*" The youth's decision to stay is motivated, Anna Freud surmises, by his "positive feelings for the knight."[28] Furthermore, the story is told entirely in the past tense (whereas the fantasies occurred in the present tense) and the story is told as if it were a dialogue between the knight and the prisoner's father (a figure who does not make any manifest appearance in the girl's fantasy but who is quite consciously evoked in Anna Freud's essay *about* this girl)!

Constructed in the form of a dialogue, the story that the girl writes becomes more "theatrical" in form. She now has a listener, a spectator, someone to whom she can narrate her story. Now there is also an important convergence with the plot of a romance novel. For, as Radway repeatedly emphasizes, in the Smithton women's "ideal romance" it is the *gradual* development of the love between the hero and the heroine that captures their attention and gives a novel a top rating. Just so, in the girl's written story, "the friendship between the strong and the weak characters . . . extends over the entire period of the action," whereas in the daydream, the bond between them had to be "established over and over again in every single scene."[29] In the written story, then, the repeated "high points" (mini-[many-] climaxes) are replaced by a linear narrative that flattens all the situations out by dividing them equally over the whole of a linear plot. This change in structure—from repetitive, fragmented, and often incoherent episodes to a linear, causal, narrative—also changes the girl's pleasure: "in the daydream, each new addition or repetition of a separate scene afforded a new opportunity for pleasurable instinctual gratification. In the written story, however, the direct pleasure gain is abandoned." And with this change came a diminishment, if not annihilation of pleasure: "the finished story does not elicit any . . . excitement. A reading of it does not lend itself to obtaining daydreamlike pleasures. In this respect it had no more effect on its author than the reading of any comparable story written by another person would have had."[30]

This latter finding makes sense, given that the written story could be said to *have been written by another person* than the girl who had obtained gratification from her fantasies. Anna Freud points out that the girl's written story and her daydream/fantasies must have been differently motivated, "otherwise the story of the knight would simply have become something unusable in its transformation from fantasy to written story."[31] When she asked the girl what motivated her to write the story down, she answered that the impulse came to her when she felt that the fantasy had become too obtrusive, and that by giving the knight and the youth "an independent existence" she would be rid of them. This answer makes sense in the common wisdom about writing—that one writes in order to exorcize one's fantasies, to store them safely in a place of their own, to be "done" with them. Writers know, however, that this is a myth about writing that is harbored primarily by people who do not write. And Anna Freud, an accomplished writer, was suspicious of the girl's testimony that she was in fact finished with the whole business of the "knight" after having written it down.

For she notices that much is left unexplained by the girl's story. Primarily, that the very incidents that had purportedly most troubled her were *not included* in the written version. Whereas other things, that had not been manifest in the nice story daydreams *were* included in the written version—in particular, the torture scenes, which are not only included but "dwelt on extensively."[32] Also, the written version contains the father figure, who was explicitly excluded from the fantasy. Anna Freud turns to Bernfeld's theories (1924) for an explanation and deduces that the motivation to turn such fantasies into written stories originates in the ego. Applying this theory, she makes the following conclusions about the girl's impulse to write:

> the private fantasy is turned into a communication *addressed to others*. In the course of this transformation regard for the personal needs of the daydreamer *is replaced by regard for the prospective reader*. The pleasure derived directly from the content of the story can be dispensed with, because the process of writing by satisfying the ambitious striving indirectly produces pleasure in the author.
>
> The renunciation of the direct pleasure gain, however, also obviates the need to accord special treatment to certain parts of the story—the climax of the daydreams—which were especially suited to the purpose of obtaining pleasure. Likewise, the written story (as the inclusion of the torture scene demonstrates) can discard the restrictions imposed on the daydream in which the *realization of situations stemming from the beating fantasy had been proscribed.*[33]

Despite this fascinating rereading of Freud, Anna Freud does not escape (in her writing) from the orthodoxies of the laws of her father. For although she points out that the girl has learned to sublimate her direct pleasures in the service of others, and thus become guided solely by "regard for their suitability for representation,"[34] she nonetheless concludes that the girl's *indirect* pleasure gain will far outweigh her loss of access to direct pleasure. She will learn that "making an impression on others" is more productive and a significant developmental step. Anna Freud thus sends her girl, whom she calls "autistic," off onto the psychoanalytic rode toward "normality," where she will leave her life of pleasurable fantasies and enter onto the royal road of reality. She will, thus, forever experience (or perhaps fail to experience) a *disjuncture* between the "real" of her public/social life and the structure of her desiring-fantasies. And this, according to Anna Freud and some feminists, is how it should or must be.

Now I am not implying that one can or should ignore "reality." But there is nothing in this girl's case study to indicate that her fantasies were interrupting her ability to function in the social world. She was not even acting them out privately. And they were not intruding into her daily activities (she had not, for example, begun treating everyone who came into her path as if she were the "knight" in her fantasies). What was it then that necessitated the proscription of these fantasies? I would suggest that the "problem" of the beating fantasy for the *girl* is that it enabled her to complicate the rigid binary of sexual difference in her psychic identification with the male "youth." Furthermore, it is not merely that she became a "boy" in her fantasy life, for that would only be a reversal or substitution of roles, but that this fantasy also allowed her to be a participant in a male homoerotic exchange. Moreover, in this exchange, she occupied the position of a boy who needed to be trained into "masculinity" by being humiliated and tortured by an older man—the "knight." And to understand this fantasy as even more threatening of the heteropatriarchal social order, that training occurred in the fantasy through a "feminizing" of the youth—by forcing him into submission, the conventional female role in culture. So not only was the girl aggressively appropriating a "male" psychic identity, she was also identifying with it *as a girl* and fantasizing a scenario in which the path toward "manhood" was achieved through a feminization that was not to be eradicated (as in the Freudian paradigm of the boy's journey toward manhood through the abandonment of all things "feminine") but, on the contrary, was the very *condition* for the achievement of self/manhood.

Teresa de Lauretis points out that Anna Freud was herself one of the cases that her father was analyzing when he wrote "A Child is Being Beaten." Lauretis reads Anna Freud's essay as a "barely disguised psychoanalytic confession" and argues that

> Anna Freud handled her not-so-successfully repressed Oedipal wish and the guilt associated with masturbatory fantasies by sublimating instinctual demands with the socially gainful, if masculine, activities of writer, training analyst, and heir to the Freudian institution. Thus her public life and work supported not only Freud's own lack of insight into lesbianism . . . but also the dismissive attitude toward lesbianism . . . characteristic of psychoanalysis ever after."[35]

While I agree with Lauretis for the most part, and find her chapter on "Psychoanalysis and Lesbian Sexuality" sound, illuminating, and highly provocative, in my reading of Anna Freud's essay there is room for a bit more optimism. For, albeit inadvertently, Anna Freud has given us a version of her father's teleology of sexual difference that *interrupts* the narrative, fragmenting its whole by locating a hole in the fantasy through which the girl, like Alice entering wonderland, can slip through the prison of sexual difference. This interrupted narrative is sutured only by the arbitrary intervention of a social prohibition against the fantasy. The girl receives from her analyst, Freud's daughter, the simple prescription to become a woman, *merely* because she already "is" one.

The psychoanalytic paradigm that leads to the constitution of sexual difference enjoins the girl to *become* what she already is; whereas the boy must become what he is not. Hence "woman" becomes the always already ontological category that refers to something presumably inherent *within* the female body. In linguistic terms, "woman" is the constative utterance— "she" *refers* to a model that precedes her. The boy, on the other hand, by becoming what he is *not*, takes up the *performative* role—what he utters is a "doing," rather than the "being" of the woman. And of course one of the primary things he must utter in order for this difference to be maintained *is the being of woman.*

What is interesting, for me, in looking again at this banality of sexual difference, is the way in which it is constituted through the sexual fantasy of dominance and submission. In chapter 3 of this book, I will discuss at length the ways in which masochism is proscribed for women even as it is understood, indeed precisely because it is understood, as the ontological condition of femininity. Despite the numerous testimonials of women who describe their masochistic experience as performative, the presumption remains, among many theorists, that masochism can only be performed by men. In the rare instances when it is acknowledged that women not only entertain masochistic fantasies but also desire to and do act them out, the assumption is often made that they are merely repeating that which is already given to them, or that they are deluded in and by their desires and should strive to eradicate them and "advance" to their next (destined) phase.

As the s/m subculture has become more public, and the media has made some of its practices more available to mainstream audiences, some of the taboos about speaking these desires appear to have lifted. However, the dominatrixes who appear on American television talk shows are generally paraded about to show off their freakishness to prurient and repulsed spectators, who desire their presence to stand in for their own disavowed desires. Furthermore, it is nearly always the female "top" who is invited to show and tell in the media—the dominatrix who caters to the desires of heterosexual men. We have yet to see what women who are avowed masochists might have to say in a mainstream public medium, and it is highly unlikely that anything they could or would say would not be completely overshadowed by the presumption that masochistic women are the most pitiable and/or despicable group amongst a multiplicity of sexual positionings—precisely because they would be exhibiting the very "shameful" thing that they already are!

Recently, however, in the "Women's Issue" of *The New Yorker*, Daphne Merkin took the unlikely step of revealing her "Unlikely Obsession." Always striving to reach the cutting edge of the East Coast "intelligentsia," *The New Yorker* made the bold move of including this "secret fantasy" in their magazine. Accompanied by a drawing of the upper body of a blond-haired, blue-eyed, young middle-aged woman with her hands enveloped in long red gloves covering her eyes, the image predisposes us to anticipate the outcome of this narrative; and indeed it over reads the narrative, even if it does not override it, by saying what *The New Yorker* might have us imagine, even if it is too chic to say so in words. The image of the gloves merges so completely with the woman's "flesh" that it appears as if she has dipped her arms in blood up to her elbow. There is a trace of the "blood-stained" hands on her chest, and her lipstick is smeared the same blood-red, as if she had been drinking the blood. So much for *The New Yorker's* "radical" look at an unspeakable fantasy.

The narrative itself is told by an upper-class, highly educated white woman, all qualities that purport to make this story even more scandalous while, at once, legitimating it. Merkin begins by confessing that on her bookshelves, lined with the great classics of Western literature, she also maintains a minilibrary of s/m texts—from "The Story of O," to Jessica Benjamin's *Bonds of Love*, through Stoller and Reik, and on to the seamier side with novels such as Jenny Diski's *Nothing Natural* and "some cheesier stuff" such as "Half Dressed, She Obeyed," and "The Training of Mrs. Pritchard." The authors are unremarked in this latter category.

Her favorite novel is Robert Coover's *The Spanking of the Maid*, which Merkin loves best because it "speaks both to the literary snob in me and to my baser—my debasement-*seeking*—sexual self."[36] Although Merkin constantly reminds us of her upper-class status, a repetition so frequent that it becomes an obvious reflex for counteracting the anticipation of disapproving readers, she evidences no consciousness whatsoever of *class or racial* formations in her favorite fantasy, in which she identifies with both the maid (the one who is spanked by an upper-class white man and who, given the statistical realities, is highly likely to be imagined as a woman of color) *and* the man who spanks her. One wonders what the source of her "self-debasement" is in this fantasy; for while she assumes that it is simply the humiliation of putting herself in the vulnerable position of being spanked, surely the source of her "shame" might be attributed to her identification with a lower-class person and with the upper-class man who beats her. Merkin is fairly sophisticated at describing how this fantasy appeals to her on a visceral level. She finds its repetitiveness "mesmerizing" and is especially intrigued with the way in which it "veils its randy core with tireless wordplay and Talmudic inventories" of the various instruments he uses to spank the maid and the ways in which he positions her for the beating. But on the level of psychic identifications, Merkin altogether misses the point of her class, gender, and, possibly, racial cross-identifications and the ways in which they charge the scene for her erotically.

I do not mention this as a gesture toward critiquing her fantasies per se. All our sexualities are constructed in a classist, racist, heterosexist, and gendered culture, and suppressing or repressing these fantasy scenarios is not going to accomplish changing that social reality. I am also not a sexual libertarian (or any other kind), and I do think that being *conscious* about these issues as they appear in our desires is important to discuss, theorize, and suspect. It will certainly not automatically change them, but it makes it less likely that they will spill over into our social interactions or become psychically rigid. The fact that the issue of class, especially, is everywhere evoked and nowhere mentioned in Merkin's narrative speaks directly to the problem. Class, in her fantasy and in her reality, becomes only a "reality" category that she uses to counterbalance the fear of disapproval concerning her "baser" self, which is obviously a term in itself overwritten with class and race affiliations. Furthermore, though Merkin pretends to defend her spanking fantasy, she clearly considers it to be already shameful and particularly vital for that very reason: "the more strong because I felt it to be so at odds with the intellectually weighty, morally upright part of me."[37]

Interestingly, Merkin's path follows somewhat along the lines of Anna Freud's girl. She too finds "relief" (but also shame) in writing it down and thinks of it in terms of a confession, and therefore a kind of absolution. Sliding back and forth between rather astute analysis of the pleasures involved in the fantasy (and its actualization—for once she realizes the fantasy she finds it to be just as satisfying as she had expected), Merkin claims that the fantasy, as well as the practice, "not only arouses me but actually soothes me—enables me to jump over my own shadow, across the inhibitions that impede me, and to land on the other side of sexual pleasure, at a place where the body takes over and the mind leaves off."[38] Although her mind/body split is problematic, this description of her experience accords with many other testimonials by s/m advocates who are quite conscious and articulate about their desires. But then Merkin slides into the dominant culture's views again, wondering "how a putatively independent-minded woman like (herself) had managed to cultivate an impulse toward sexual humiliation alongside an impulse toward normative life?"[39]

Nevertheless, Merkin is aware of the fact that people experience physical sensations very differently and that a spanking may be for her no more than "overly vigorous caresses."[40] She argues that a certain level and kind of "violence" with a person whom she trusts, "lubricates [her] mind—strangely—releases [her], if only for a moment, from [her] vigilant distrust of men," and that "equality" or "parity" between people may be an important social ideal but is not necessarily "the surest route to sexual excitement."[41]

Nonetheless, Merkin falls into the "slippery slope" fallacy as she begins to contemplate acting out her fantasy, wondering if a simple spanking would inevitably lead to whips, chains, and pulleys, and from there to an inability to distinguish between "mutually agreed-upon love play, however aggressive, and domestic abuse."[42] By this time the specter of Hedda Nussbaum has begun to haunt her, and Merkin has gone quite over the edge, not the one that will release and soothe her but the one that the dominant culture continually evokes in order to terrify women into a sexual submission that has nothing whatsoever to do with their desires. A relationship with a man who desired to control her—"to offer and then withdraw affection on an erratic and hurtful schedule of his own devising"—leads her to conclude that this behavior coincides with her wish to be "mastered."[43] Such is the kind of sloppy, analogical thinking that leads to books such as *Sadomasochism in Everyday Life*,[44] in which s/m sexuality becomes *nothing in itself* because it is everywhere and everything.

From this point on, all the clichéd thinking about s/m sexuality rains down on Merkin, until she is awash with contradictions that she simply cannot bear and becomes determined to resolve them. She begins to think that because one man in her life could not seem to find the way to spank her as she wanted (it was always too hard or not hard enough), her "real" desire must have been to have her existence numbed, even to be spanked *to death*, rather than drawing the much simpler conclusion that she was with a "bad top," just as one might realize that her partner was simply incapable of giving her the emotional nurturance that she needed, rather than thinking that one desired to be deprived of affection until one died from its lack! Finally she realizes how "far [she] was from healthy intimacy, from the *real* give-and-take that makes a relationship viable."[45] She gives up hope in her "magic trick, an impossible reversal," begins to "see an opening in the maze," and rises to the occasion of "erotic affection without first wrapping [her] arms around a punitive fantasy."[46]

Like Anna Freud's girl, Merkin begins to find her way toward "true womanhood," and she leaves us on this journey the bread crumbs of her travails down the treacherous path of her infantile fantasies. *The New Yorker* has succumbed to the overwhelming evidence that women do indeed have masochistic fantasies and that some of them actually *perform* them quite consciously and theorize about them astutely. Their response has been to give us a narrative to follow that teaches us how to be "real" women, a lesson that must be constantly repeated given our unruly "natures." Merkin tries to coach us back into a narrative of our shame. S/m constitutes one of the greatest threats to this narrative, particularly because it addresses the "shame" narrative so confrontationally, and I suspect that we will hear many more of these repetitions as our voices get louder.

I would like to make one last point about Anna Freud's fifteen-year-old girl. As threatening as women's masochistic fantasies are in all of their permutations, I think that Anna Freud's case study points to something that I dare say is a kind of bottom ground. The second phase of Freud's beating fantasy—when the girl fantasizes that she is no longer the spectator but the one who is being beaten—"my father is beating me,"—is to remain *unconscious* (indeed Freud claims that there is no "evidence" to support it in testimony but that it must be inferred as the middle of the other two phases). The reason that it must remain unconscious is because it is an incest fantasy (the beating substituting for the girl's desire for the father's love). As I have already mentioned, and will discuss at greater length later, incest is deemed "impossible" in the cultural consciousness precisely because it is the right and the prerogative of men—their "right" to practice/perform it, and their right to keep it silent/hidden by proclaiming it the founding taboo of the culture (and hence the most potent of transgressions). Recently, the "daddy" phenomenon in lesbian s/m desires has been the site of much consternation. Califia's anthology, *Doing It For Daddy*, is the best-known example and the only collection. But "daddy" fantasies are appearing with greater regularity in lesbian pro-sex magazines. Women are claiming their rights to rewrite incest fantasies. Tapping into this founding taboo is, perhaps, the ultimate transgression. Lesbian sado-masochists are representing—and playing out among themselves—the very practice that makes "civilization" (as we are *supposed* to know it) possible.

This is a book about women—and some men—who have refused to travel that road. Women and men who have chosen their pleasures, with all the risks and perils their choices entail. It is a book about what places they have occupied in their own and others' fantasies and what it has meant to have attempted to actualize those fantasies in a social order that explicitly prohibits them—indeed often forecloses them.

2 · To Each Her Other: Performing *Lesbian* S/M

Loving in the war years
    calls for this kind of risking
    without a home to call our own
    I've got to take you as you come
    to me, each time like a stranger
    all over again. Not knowing
    what deaths you saw today
    I've got to take you
    as you come, battle bruised
    refusing our enemy, fear.

    We're all we've got. You and I

    maintaining
    this war time morality
    where being queer
    and female is as rude
    as we can get.

               —Cherríe Moraga

A cartoon in the January 1991 edition of *Bad Attitude* depicts a well-dressed, white heterosexual couple strolling arm in arm past a white lesbian couple holding hands. The heterosexual couple turn their noses up and admonish the lesbians: "How dare you flaunt your sexuality!" In the second frame the lesbian couple is attending a women's festival. Transformed for the occasion, they both wear birkenstocks; one woman is naked except for a necklace of flowers around her neck, the other is topless, skirted, sporting a crystal around her neck. The radical dykes now address an interracial s/m couple (the top is a bare-chested woman of color who is leading her white bottom with a leash) and repeat the words of the hetero pair in the first frame: "How dare you flaunt your sexuality!"[1] The cartoon accompanies the editor, Jasmine Sterling's, commentary on the anti-s/m policies of the Michigan Womyn's Festival: "for the past few years Michigan has been treating SM women like they are dangerous criminals," she writes.[2]

This cartoon appears to be a neat, encapsulated, imagistic history of a linear movement from lesbian feminist politics of the seventies through the sex wars of the mid-eighties to radical pro-sex feminism of the late eighties and nineties. The second "stage" is an inference, a missing frame, the lacunae in the cartoon. The trajectory ends with the whips, chains, and leather of the s/m couple. This history is a popular story, a mass-marketed fantasy that is not as linear as the cartoon implies; but the effects of this fantasy formation have created tremendous dissension within feminism. The fantasy is also a narrative about redemption and/or damnation with an onto-theological tone that hints at the identitarian logic from which it emanates. In part, this narrative tells the story of a particular era in feminism that sought to eradicate all signs and significations of "masculinity" from the feminist community. If the telos of the narrative promised salvation, the means to that end was largely through the psychic and social erasure of masculinity. While not necessarily separatist per se, a significant constituency within the early contemporary Anglo-American feminist movement engaged in this struggle to elevate "femininity" and divorce women from masculinity, tacitly accepting and thus reifying a dualistic gender system. Not everyone, of course, bought into this social movement. Nonetheless, it was a widespread mythology.

Nearly a decade prior to the historical myth this cartoon mocks, Michel Foucault was asked to comment on a twofold distinction between gay men and lesbians; first, in regard to "the very different physical things that happen in the one encounter and the other" and second, on the basis of emotional differences. When the interviewer explained that American radical feminists think that lesbians "want from other women what one finds in stable heterosexual relationships: support, affection, long-term commitment, and so on." Foucault responded: "All I can do is explode with laughter."[3] Not interested in pursuing the matter further, Foucault would say only that this difference seemed peculiar to American intellectual circles. His laughter suggests that the construction of lesbian desire as a longing for permanence, commitment, and endurance was geographically and historically specific, and perhaps even generally illusionary.

Such values did, for a time, serve a particular American feminism's foundational fantasy of "role-less equality." And this feminism was able, for a while, to keep this myth relatively coherent and contained until women began to challenge it from racial, ethnic, generational, and sexual locations that were in discord with and excluded from the foundation of this image. The group on which I will be focusing in particular constitutes an expanding subculture that has established some visibility in reference to its sexual practices.[4] More important, however, this group has accomplished the always tenuous but nonetheless readable task of making political and theoretical alignments along a continuum of lesbigay, transgendered, transsexed, and even some heterosexual epistemologies. Although members of "leather" or s/m communities do sometimes claim identities as such, they do not generally claim a stable identity as a homogeneous group. They have, however, been interpellated as a communal group, largely through the rhetoric and images produced by magazines, newsletters, and publications in the mainstream media, effectively making this community into an oppositional construct that serves to both challenge and shore up the crumbling identity of more mainstream sexual identities, both heterosexual and lesbian or gay. Although s/m cultures carry more than a trace of the egalitarian and romantic myths that they are presumed to oppose, often by upholding and extending such values by rendering them in extremis, lesbian s/m communities have been posited as absolute alterity by some feminists and have certainly been used as the epitome of the "outside" by the dominant culture. The resistance and refusal to recognize similarities between these communities produced an historical moment of impasse, in which what came to be known as "vanilla" sex was established in opposition to a range of other alternative sexualities—including commercial sex workers, sadomasochism, transvestism, transsexualism, transgenderism, pedophilia, bisexualism, and "homosexuality" in general. This is an historical process that has gained momentum in the last few years as *all* sexual alternatives have come under fire from the New Right. Although the dominant culture condenses all these varieties of sexual expression together into one inchoate mass, each has its own historical differences; at the same time this assault has produced a counterdiscourse that has enabled a certain (often uneasy) coalition among these disparate groups.

What I am tracking in this chapter is the opposition between the crossover term *vanilla*,[5] used particularly to name a lesbian and gay sexual practice and sensibility that has come to signify a difference between lesbian-feminist (and to some extent gay, though my interest here is primarily the way in which the term has circulated within feminism), and lesbian s/m sexualities. The s/m dyke and the "vanilla" lesbian have come to confront each other from what appear to be different sides of an unbridgeable gulf. Locked in a hostile debate that swells and subsides every few years, the two groups seem to have little potential for seeing eye to eye. Perhaps, however, the stalemate between them is not due to their irreconcilable *differences*; rather, it may be due to the possibility that they are not one another's opposites but one another's doubles. One can, of course, never see one's own double, if by double we understand the internalized other that is necessarily misrecognized in order to sustain the fictive coherence of one's "self." I want to map a vanishing point where two claims to reality contest a sign that is presumed to have a limited occupancy, and to suggest that it is identitarian logic that produces this doubling effect, and with it a violence more virulent than any fantasy of the "violence" of lesbian s/m sexual practices.

The anti/pro s/m debates have not, of course, been confined to women's music festivals or to the struggle between leather dykes and lesbian feminists. The sex battles between the dominant culture and its appropriation of feminist principles and an entire community of people who are marked as practitioners of deviant sexualities have been well documented over a decade of struggle.[6] My project is not to rehearse that history but, rather, to focus on a structural mechanism that has informed the possibility of that history having taken place and its continuing effects. Beginnings are always arbitrary. I am selecting one particular exemplary moment that stands out in recent history to begin this analysis—the 1980 passage of the National Organization for Women's (NOW) resolution that at the same time qualified what could be constituted as feminist supportable expressions of sexuality and linked sadomasochism with gay and lesbian sex. Delineating, and delimiting, lesbian and nonlesbian rights issues as their official position, the organizers of NOW wrote:

> *Whereas,* NOW defines Lesbian rights issues to be those in which the issue is discrimination based on affectional/sexual preference/orientation . . . *Whereas* NOW does not support the inclusion of pederasty, pornography, sadomasochism and public sex as Lesbian rights issues, since to do so would violate the feminist principles upon which this organization was founded . . . *Be it resolved* that NOW will work in cooperation with groups and organizations which advocate Lesbian rights as defined above."[7]

The only referent "above" with positive content consists of this: "Lesbian rights issues [are] those in which the issue is discrimination based on affectional/sexual preference/orientation."[8] The remainder, and the bulk, of this resolution is comprised of series of disclaimers, disavowals, displacements.

The historical outcome of this has been that the groups and organizations with which NOW affiliated unwittingly have come to mean the New Right and the various Christian coalitions.[9] The sexual practices NOW rejected, which it claimed had been mistakenly correlated with lesbian/gay rights, were reinstated by its resolution, through negation. As a collective of protesters put it: "by the very fact of its using a gay rights resolution as a platform for condemning 'undesirable' sexual activity, NOW plays into the erroneous but common belief that homosexuals have a special affinity for such behavior." It must be remembered that this was NOW's *gay and lesbian rights platform.* Thus NOW simultaneously sought to erase any connection between these other "perversions" and lesbian and gay sexualities while it inevitably *fused* them. The organization silently evoked a lesbian identity and practice which was presumably consonant with an unspoken, indeed unnecessary to articulate, feminist identity. Again, the same protest letter spelled that out clearly: "in its appeal to `feminist principles,' the resolution enshrines the political views of one faction of the women's movement as *the* feminist position. It implies the existence of a non-existent consensus."[10]

What is particularly noxious about this platform is the deeroticizing move that it attempts to make quietly. In the first paragraph, NOW states that it is committed to "equality, freedom, justice, and dignity for all women," which is "*singularly affirmed* in NOW's advocacy of Lesbian rights." Notice that the word *gay* drops out here. It then becomes "The Lesbian," as NOW chooses to identify her, an identity that has nothing to say about lesbian sexual practices but only characterizes lesbianism as "affectional" or as a "preference" or an "orientation" that becomes the singular location where feminism asserts its freedom, justice, and dignity. The word *sexual* does appear in the resolution, but it is linked to and follows *affectional* and it modifies *preference* or *orientation*. Thus lesbians, according to NOW, had the right to a "lifestyle" (orientation) and/or to a woman as object-choice (preference). In other words, they could *be* lesbians, but they couldn't *do anything*. Also, by not-so-subtle implication, the "dignity" of this feminist movement erected itself on the static, deeroticized identity of the lesbian. As such, an "identity" for lesbians was both presumed and constructed in this platform as the term that required marking. And the logic of identity formations was revealed— they are constructed through a series of exclusions that are necessary to create and maintain the fiction of a positive identity for the rhetor.

According to Gloria Brame et.al. in *Different Loving,* the NOW resolution was one of three events, all occurring in 1980, which sparked (and participated in) the backlash against s/m. It was the same year that the film *Cruising* "portrayed the leather scene as inherently sordid and violent" and that *Gay Power, Gay Politics* was aired by CBS, a documentary that "erroneously stated that S/M is a mostly gay male practice, and that 10 percent of all gay deaths in San Francisco were S/M-related."[11] Nan Hunter provides a different context from Brame's, pointing out that 1980 was the year that *Take Back the Night*, a collection of antipornography articles, was published; Samois picketed a forum on (against) s/m at the University of California, Berkeley; Deirdre English's critique of antiporn feminism was published in *Mother*

Jones, as was Pat Califia's, "Among Us, Against Us—The New Puritanism" in *The Advocate;* Califia's book *Sapphistry: The Book of Lesbian Sexuality* was published by Naiad; and Ronald Reagan was elected president.[12]

This schematic outline is a beginning, of sorts, for the "culture wars" that are raging still among us and within us. Although the popular notion is that the "sex wars" are over, or at least have significantly subsided, (often written as "the sex wars *of the 1980s*"), the "culture wars" are their continuation, their byproduct, or their return (after a brief repression). One only need look at the list of materials that have been confiscated at the Canadian border under the "Butler decision," to see that "the culture wars" and "the sex wars" constitute a semantic substitution (and, in this instance, a geographical shift). The confiscated material has included: Jane Rule's *Contract with the World,* Marguerite Duras' *The Man Sitting in the Corner,* Dorothy Allison's *Trash,* David Wojnarowicz's *Memories that Smell Like Gasoline,* Joseph Beam's *In the Life: A Black Gay Anthology,* Kathy Acker's *Empire of the Senseless,* Richard D. Mohr's *Gay Ideas: Outing and Other Controversies,* Pat Califia's *Macho Sluts,* and bell hooks's *Black Looks: Race and Representation.* It is to state the obvious that the feminist contribution to the sex wars has been seized and distorted by the New Right. What has remained high on this list are depictions of gay and lesbian sadomasochistic sexuality, as well as other relatively common sexual practices—such as anal sex—that are nonetheless merged with the category "s/m."

Writing with the intention of making a case for liberalism, Wendy Steiner's latest book also offers a meticulously detailed account of the culture wars and their relationship to the feminist sex wars.[13] As I read her book, I hear the same echoing litany of the NOW resolution: sadomasochism, pederasty, pornography, public sex. Compare the NOW resolution to Jesse Helms's proposal to forbid National Endowment for the Arts (NEA) support for "obscene or indecent materials, including but not limited to depictions of sadomasochism, homoeroticism, the exploitation of children, or individuals engaged in sex acts [has the *representation* of "sex acts" taken the place of "public sex" in the NOW resolution?]; or material which denigrates the objects or beliefs of the adherents of a particular religion or non-religion; or material which denigrates, debases, or reviles a person, group, or class of citizens on the basis of race, creed, sex, handicap, age, or national origin."[14] The second clause in the Helms amendment is also reminiscent of, if not almost parallel to, the rhetoric of radical feminism's stance, which advocated the extinction of biases based on race, gender, ethnicity, religion, age, physical abilities, etc. The joining of radical feminism and the New Right is not only one of the most bizarre alliances in history, it is also one of the most brilliant appropriations. Understanding how this has occurred is crucial to our ability to resist it. Although the Senate defeated the Helms amendment, a one-year prohibition was approved. Significantly, the *second* clause in Helms's amendment was eliminated (that section that reminds us of radical feminism's misguided but nonetheless well-intentioned effort to guarantee equality [liberalism] to all people regardless of race, creed, ethnicity, age, religion, sexual orientation, etc). Most feminists supported that agenda, until it started to become apparent that a certain tyranny was inherent in its principles.[15] But in the one-year arrangement, what was retained from the Helms amendment were prohibitions on sadomasochism, homoeroticism, the sexual exploitation of children, and the representation of individuals engaged in sex acts.

The boundaries of these culture wars appear to be limitless, but there is *a* sexual practice and *a* sexual identity that constitutes the core from which this endless proliferation of prohibitions is emanating. Sadomasochism and homosexuality are that core (the "sexual exploitation of children" seems to be the third term that is constant, but, in my reading, this is merely a euphemism for "pederasty," which is often held to be a subset of homosexuality by the dominant culture, despite the fact that the creation and consumption of child pornography are primarily activities of heterosexual men). If *they* could be eliminated, it is as if all the others would cease to be sites of contestation. Within that core, it is my supposition that there is yet another "center," one that is relatively secreted, seen as one term in a litany. I propose to look at the ways in which *lesbian sadomasochism* both fuses those two sites and differentiates them.

As I pointed out before, the NOW resolution dropped the word "gay" from its terminology as it began to prescribe a feminist identity by negation. This subtle erasure could be read as signification of my earlier remark—that liberal feminism was engaged in a project to eliminate all signs of masculinity from their agenda. "Lesbian" alone thus became the placeholder of that lack. Liberal feminists who constituted organizations like NOW were not interested, particularly, in gay rights *or* in gay identities, if they were not implicitly or explicitly hostile to them. The word *gay* does reappear, significantly, in the clause that first lists the offending acts, only then to say that "some gay organizations" have "mistakenly correlated" those acts with lesbian/gay rights. Implied in this exclusion and momentary reappearance is that any and all "masculine" identities or psychic identifications were *already* excluded from the platform prior to the execution of its rhetoric, even as the resolution performatively enacted that presupposition. The terms that did then become articulated as prescriptions—sadomasochism, pederasty, public sex, and pornography—were implicitly proscribed for lesbians *because* they were terms already associated with masculinity—and particularly with gay masculinity. To put it succinctly, the NOW gay and lesbian rights resolution essentially stated that lesbians were allowed to be part of the feminist movement as long as they were "women," which is to say, as long as they were *heterosexual* women. The resolution then did not merely *limit* what constituted lesbianism; it effectively (re)*eliminated* lesbians from the feminist movement, in the very *name* of constituting their inclusion.

Although the NOW resolution was merely one moment in the construction of a feminist identity, it was exemplary of the way in which identity formations have been constitutive of liberal feminist politics. By excluding certain sexual practices, and attempting to divorce them from lesbian identities, NOW was in effect producing its own construction of a *feminist subject*, excluding *all* kinds of sexual practices that then by (its) definition were deviant.

Producing "a" Subject

The assumption that underlies the process I have described above is that "subjectivity" exists prior to its enunciations, rather than emerging in and through linguistic articulations. The NOW organizers were basing their platform on an idea of "women" that was, in fact, produced by the dominant culture, which they presumably opposed. Unintentionally, they thus played right into the hands of the very cultural constructions that relegated "women" to the ground of representation. Their *own* identities, in other words, were being self-produced as "subjects" constituted through *negating* what is always already *negated*. That is, "the" feminist subject that NOW purported to advocate, defend, and preserve in their lesbian and gay rights platform, is a subject that is not one. It is not just that it is not "a" feminist subject, it has no positivity *as* a subject whatsoever. Ironically, of course, the more one attempts to conceive such a "positivity," the more one comes up against the impossibility of doing so, for the "subject's" very existence is predicated as an absence—it *is* only everything that it is *not*. It produces itself through a series of displacements onto another "subject" whose existence it purports to presume, while in the very gesture of presuming it, it is constructing it. "Lesbian" was thus reiterated as the "lack" in the very moment of its purported inclusion.

Understanding this logic of identity formations, we can return to the frames of the cartoon with which I opened this chapter. It is aptly entitled "Stonewall Riots." And of course it is meant as a joke. But the "joke" of this cartoon is not so much that "Stonewall" has become a "Riot" (a joke) through dissensions within the ranks of the community (and thus we would read the cartoon as a plea for understanding the absurdity of the fracturing of groups *within* a community); rather, it is that we can read it as a series of displacements in which *some* figure must occupy the constitutive outside (what Lacan calls the "intimate exterior" or *extimate*) in order to sustain the fictive identity of another. The mirroring of the couples in this cartoon is a powerful image that reads in excess of the linear narrative and interrupts its coherence. Like Banquo's ghosts, the procession is endless and what one sees in the mirror is never one's own image directly but, rather, the refractions of a psyche that can never be self-identical.

Identity and Aggression

We know, from Freud, that the structure of jokes always contains an element of aggression. Gayle Rubin's eloquent article, which occupies a central position in the San Francisco lesbian s/m support group SAMOIS's book, *Coming to Power*, shows us how that aggression is constitutive of identity constructions. I want to place emphasis on her words "constructing a new demonstration of s/m," to underscore that the consequences of such a construction will inevitably not yield a new conception of s/m but, as Rubin presciently points out, will signal the approach of a move to "clean it up." I want to push harder at this point to emphasize that such constructions are not simply historical heralds of what is to come but are also the very act of the "cleaning up" in and of themselves. That is to say, these historical moments are not the origins of a narrative; they *are* that narrative. They are *performative*.

After describing a variety of media misrepresentations of the s/m community's theories and practices, Rubin writes:

> All of this slanted media coverage is constructing a new demonstration of S/M and probably heralds a campaign to clean it up. It is very similar to what happened to homosexuals in the 1950's. There were already plenty of antigay ideas, structures, and practices. But during a decade of headlines, arrests, investigations, and legislation, those pre-existing elements of homophobia were reconstituted into a new and more virulent ideology that homosexuality was an active menace which needed to be actively combated. Currently, there are already plenty of anti-S/M ideas, structures, and practices. But these are being drawn into the creation of a new ideological construct that will call for a more active extermination campaign against S/M.[16]

The analogy that Rubin makes here has indeed come to pass. But it is also vital that we read the present moment retrospectively—*in that moment.* For what Rubin predicted was already happening in the moment that she articulated its future. Identifying that moment when one sees something that is about to occur works in much the same way as identities—they are always belated. Indeed this is the very problem of a political movement that constitutes itself around identity formations. For identitarian logic holds us locked into a passive, reactive position, one in which we can always only read the present and the future as it has passed—*as the past.* Because identities and identitarian logic are belated, they are historically static, which does not mean that identities cannot and do not *change* over the course of history (as they very clearly have and do). Rather, since they are retrospective, they are always destined to be constructions that are made up from the remnants of the past. Like quilts, identities get fabricated from what is left over. That nebulous body that we still refer to as "the Left," depending as it does so heavily on coalitions that are identity-based, is always in a defensive posture, reacting to whatever the "Right" invents as its latest onslaught. I am much more concerned with the ways in which identitarian logic renders political action passive than I am with its inherent instabilities and incoherencies. Indeed it is the latter that is its redeeming feature, not its problem, as some feminists would have it.[17] I am, therefore, focusing on the ways in which political oppositions emanate from *inside* a community, for I think that it is from that angle that we can understand what limits our ability to act effectively—to gain the offense—rather than to find ourselves (always already belatedly) *finding ourselves.*

Antidotes?

A number of other feminists have voiced the same concern, but none perhaps so forcefully and radically as Wendy Brown and Joan Cocks, who have suggested that the North Atlantic Women's Movement has become toxic with Nietzschean *ressentiment.* Cocks finds Nietzsche's theory an "antidote to the sanctimonious inclinations" of this movement (however "ugly" Nietzsche's theory is "as a politics of its own"). Cocks, in my opinion, overstates her case that the feminist movement in its "sanctification of powerlessness, celebration of weakness, championing of victim status," etc., has become a "witch hunt against strength, talent, charm . . . [and] a tyrannical suppression of all in life that is forceful and fierce";[18] nonetheless, her argument that Nietzsche's man of *ressentiment* produces his own identity by first conceiving the "Evil One"—the "basic concept, from which he then evolves, as an afterthought and pendant, a `good one' himself."[19] is apropos of the problem of *all* identity formations. Cocks's opposition between Nietzsche's noble slave, who hates the power of the master, and "victim" ideology, which transforms hatred and revolt into envious demands, is curiously and provocatively broken *as an opposition* in the space *in between* "a stylistic embrace and a substantive repudiation of sensuous and sensual life."[20]

One thinks here of Andrea Dworkin's novel, *Mercy*, which in its efforts to illustrate graphically the abuses and victimizations of women also becomes, in moments, a near reenactment of pornographic scenarios, potentially arousing its readers. Citing Catherine MacKinnon's portrait of sexual desire as in itself "a social construct of male power," Cocks points out that it is the lesbian counterculture and the academics that have posed the strongest challenge to this theory, "while the portrait itself has increasing purchase in the dominant culture and the legal-political arena."[21] Cocks proposes a paradoxical return to a "reconceptualization of power *à la* Augustine"—for whom "hierarchy, domination, and self-abnegation are not only part of the order of things but a necessary and good part"—[22] as a "step forward, not for the strong, as Nietzsche proposes, but for the weak."[23]

Brown also suggests that "much North Atlantic feminism partakes deeply of both the epistemological spirit and political structure of *ressentiment* and that this constitutes a good deal of our nervousness about moving toward an analysis as thoroughly Nietzschean in its wariness about truth as postmodern political theory must be."[24] Attempting to account for the feminist panic in the face of postmodernism's disintegration of the subject, historical continuity, and epistemological certainties, Brown proposes that the strategy of *ressentiment*, which gains its force by negating its involvement with power, denying that "it contains a will to power or seeks to (pre)dominate," leads to an account in which "powerlessness is truthful (moral) while power inherently distorts."[25] One can certainly see in this model the terms of the battle that have characterized the sex wars. Brown also links this to the formation of and fierce insistence upon identities, which are anxiously produced and tenaciously held in the atmosphere of postmodernism: "Drawing upon the historically eclipsed meaning of disrupted and fragmented narratives of ethnicity, race, gender, sexuality, region, continent, or nation, identity politics permits a sense of situation— and often a sense of filiation or community—without requiring profound comprehension of the world in which one is situated. Identity politics permit positioning without mapping."[26]

What I find particularly pertinent about Cocks's and Brown's essays in conjunction with my thinking about radical feminism's assault on lesbian s/m is that lesbian sadomasochists are a group within the lesbian subculture who not only play openly with power but who also assert their absolute right to do so. Occasionally some lesbian s/m rhetoric succumbs to the attack and apologetically appeals for understanding and tolerance, but for the most part lesbian s/m culture assiduously avoids any such liberal rhetoric. It is not only, then, that s/m lesbians *play* with power and hierarchy configurations *within* their sexual practices, but that they also pose a challenge to mainstream feminism's ethical ground. If, as Brown argues, feminist panic is about a "lack of confidence in our ability to prosper in such a domain," in which "truth is always grasped as coterminous with power, as `already power,' as the voice of power,"[27] then lesbian s/m represents a threat not only because of the fear that its practices might somehow seep into the fantasies of women who do not prefer it (the "contagion/possession" panic that I will discuss below) but also, and perhaps much more important, lesbian s/m represents a strategy of resistance that is at odds not just with the "morality" of mainstream feminism but in discordance with the notion of a separation of morality and power altogether. S/m sexual *practices*, then, can be construed as representations that reproduce the very thing that they signify. Hence the war on sex and the war on art come together in this particular highly contested site.

Totalizing Tendencies

The fact that vocal opposition to lesbian s/m has come from within lesbian-feminist communities signals the contest for habitation of a sign whose borders can presumably be controlled. One would think, as Rubin points out with depressing irony, that women didn't join the feminist movement in order to have their sexual practices policed by feminists themselves.[28] However, the history of the feminist movement and the construction of lesbian identity within it helps to clarify, though not justify, some feminist reactions to lesbian sadomasochism. I am, therefore, going to take a brief, schematic, historical detour, not in order to fill in the contours or trace the origins of some of the issues that are pressing us with considerable force but in order to "retrieve the moment"—this moment, not that one.

Neither sex nor violence, the operative terms in the s/m debates, were a part of the purist vision of a certain sector of feminism as it was theorized in the 1970s and 1980s. Pervasive in the literature of lesbian feminists of the 1970s are accounts of persecutions grounded in the reduction of lesbianism to sexuality. Margaret Cruikshank's *The Lesbian Path* is a typical example of testimonials that emphasize the pain experienced by lesbians who came out in the 1960s and 1970s to find themselves perceived by parents, friends, and lovers as sexual perverts. Sexual promiscuity was the charge that was often the most damaging for these lesbians: the college student who wants to shake her economics professor and make him understand that "being gay . . . means more than just sex"; the mother who accuses her lesbian daughter of nymphomania and designs to entertain a "lesbian harem in her bedroom all summer"; the schoolgirl whose parents inferred sexual desire when their daughter gave a flower to her best friend in the third grade.[29] These lesbians defended themselves by insisting on the naturalness and purity of their love and by disassociating their lesbian "identities" from sexual passion. These are stories that support and are supported by lesbian theories like those of Charlotte Wolff, who argued that for "most [lesbians], emotional intimacy means all and everything. With an emotional disposition inclined to intensity and drama, homosexual women resemble hunters in constant pursuit of `magical' love."[30]

Such opinions were also prolifically voiced by feminist artists who emphasized "Woman-centeredness," which became a key trope in some feminist thought. Woman-centeredness was *not* "portrayed through S&M, violent, pornographic, or victim images," as one feminist artist put it.[31] Preferred were representations like Nancy Fried's bread-dough porcelain plaques, which depicted women "usually undressed, relaxing at home— lying around, getting something out of the refrigerator, taking a bath, or perhaps snuggling up in each other's arms in front of the TV."[32] Kate Millett's series, *The Lesbian Body*, included a drawing depicting a "relaxed, chummy conversation between two breasts about life and love with political overtones,"[33] representing an eroticism between women that some women did, and do, indeed prefer. Nonetheless, alternative representations of lesbian sexuality were suppressed in a feminist movement that was never monolithic but, in some circles, was definitely dominant. Some members of this group even proclaimed sole occupation of the "real," not many as blatantly as Mariana Valverde, who in response to criticism of her anti-s/m commentary replied: "to tilt at the windmills of puritanism and then claim victory over *the real feminist movement* is to be completely ignorant of the whereabouts of feminism these days";[34] but the assumption that some feminists had a privileged relationship to this "real" was, and to an extent continues to be, pervasive. What is significant to realize in this history is that "lesbianism" was constituted as a sign that was, at once, sex-based and at the same time deeroticized. That is to say, whether lesbians were downplaying or emphasizing sexual practices, the sign *lesbian* was caught up in a signifying practice that, rather than expanding the parameters of the sign, was delimiting it to what *kind* of sexual practices it could signify.

Of course there were always feminists who found little pleasure in Kate Millett's "lesbian body" and much preferred Monique Wittig's:

> I rise up, I maintain m/yself at your eye-level, then you m/y most infamous one chase m/e brutally while I fall speechless, you hunt m/e down m/y most fierce one, you constrain m/e to cry out, you put words in m/y mouth, you whisper them in m/y ear and I say, no mistress, no for pity's sake[35]

But voices like Pat Califia's were relegated to the "secret side" of lesbian sexuality, with all the titillation, opprobrium, and space for phantasmatic projections that "secret" evokes:

> as I understand it, after the wimmin's revolution, sex will consist of wimmin holding hands, taking their shirts off and dancing in a circle. Then we will all fall asleep at exactly the same moment. If we didn't all fall asleep, something else might happen—something male-identified, objectifying, pornographic, noisy and undignified. Something like an orgasm.[36]

With at least a decade of such a history behind us, and with a heightening of these debates with us and before us, it is crucial that we historicize these issues in order to theorize our way past the impasse that seems to be becoming increasingly fortified. The charge of "puritanism" is woefully insufficient to explain why so many lesbians and feminists became caught up in the project to desexualize lesbianism. Their response was primarily defensive, and the effects of such reactions have much to teach us about the consequences of retrenchment when we are faced with the renewed vigor of erotophobic forces today.

First, lesbians were, and still are, reacting defensively to the sexologists's construction of inverts. Lillian Faderman points out that many early twentieth-century women, faced with the discovery of the sexologists's medicalization of lesbianism, rationalized their love as spiritual to set themselves apart from "true lesbianism"—"those [women] who do it a lot are the real ones."[37] The other operative term in the s/m debates, violence, is in some ways more readily understood as anathema to lesbian feminists. Nineteenth-century sexologists often evoked the connection between violence and sexual degeneracy. Faderman points out that as American literature began to reflect the sexologists's theories, many of the first stories of lesbian love were concerned with violence: Constance Fenimore Woolson's story "Felipa" (1876) depicts a lesbian who wounds her lover's fiancé with a knife; Mary Wilkins Freeman's "The Long Arm" (1895), in which an aggressive "masculine" businesswoman kills the male rival to her female lover; Mary Hatch's novel, *The Strange Disappearance of Eugene Comstock* (1895) features a cross-dresser, Rosa, who is a murderer; and Dr. John Carhart's *Norma Trist; or Pure Carbon: A Story of the Inversion of the Sexes*, whose protagonist kills her woman lover when she finds out that she plans to run off with a male sea-captain. As Faderman elaborates, these stories of lesbian desire had much to do with the real-life case of Alice Mitchell and Freda Ward, a sensationalized event that bolstered the argument that sexual inversion led to violence when Alice killed Freda after suspecting that she was about to marry a man.[38]

The Legacy of Sexology and Psychoanalysis

When Havelock Ellis introduced the female invert into literature, many of his case studies included some act of violence perpetuated by inverts. The Alice Ward/Freda Mitchell case was perhaps the most notorious, but Ellis also suggested that inverts' passions, in general, often led to violence. The equation between lesbianism and criminality was also made by August Forel, who wrote that "nearly all inverts are in a more or less marked degree psychopaths or neurotics," and Albert Moll, who includes a gloss on "murder" under his chapter on "Love Life" and cautions "passion may cause a Uranist to forget the fundamental rules of honesty and even to commit a crime."[39] Furthermore, sexual degeneracy was mapped onto the ideology of racial differences. As Ann McClintock points out: "The first contradiction—between 'natural' heterosexuality and the 'unnatural' perversions—was primarily managed by projecting the 'perversions' onto the invented zone of race. Sexologists such as Krafft-Ebing demonized s/m as the psychopathology of the atavistic individual, as a blood flaw and stigma of the flesh . . . as a regression in time to the 'prehistory' of racial 'degeneration,' existing ominously in the heart of the imperial metropolis—the degeneration of the race writ as an individual pathology of the soul."[40]

Meanwhile, femininity and masochism were being soldered by Freud, who outlined three types of masochism: moral (martyrdom), feminine, and erotogenic. While in Freud's theory males and females could both occupy any one of these three masochistic scenarios, Freud did claim that masochism was essentially feminine, which did *not*, in his theory, mean that men could not be "feminine masochists." Ironically, however, it did come to mean that *women* were presumed to be inherently masochistic, and thus women were symbolically barred from assuming erotogenic masochism actively. As Freud was appropriated by American psychiatrists in the twentieth century, lesbians found themselves subjected to the "cure," and the medical literature of the 1940s and 1950s was rife with accounts of homosexuals as psychopaths and murderers.[41]

Such theories influenced pulp novels of the 1950s and 1960s—the "dime-store" variations that made lesbian stories first available to a wider reading audience. Yet they could have been, and undoubtedly were, read by some as titillating parodies of the "pathological lesbian." They also, however, could easily have been interpreted as warnings against the evils of homosexuality, for often they suggested that homosexuality led to criminal behavior. Ann Bannon's "Beebo Brinker" series frequently represented lesbians as violent toward themselves and each other; scenes of butches beating up femmes were often followed by steamy love scenes; occasionally characters like Beebo performed acts that seemed more appropriate to contemporary psycho-serial killers. For example, in one of the Brinker novels, Beebo slaughters her pet dog by ripping open its belly with a knife that she frequently wields threateningly against her lover.[42] In opposition to these characters, the "ideal" lesbian lover became a character whose sexuality was either very subdued or nonexistent. In one of Valerie Taylor's novels, for example, the main character is a Holocaust survivor whose entire family was murdered by the Nazis. When she arrives in the United States to live with an American family, she is initiated into lesbian sex by the family's daughter and her girlfriends, who physically abuse her until she is rescued by her music teacher, an older lesbian who develops a Platonic love relationship with her.[43]

Because the pulp representations of violence are nearly always accompanied or followed by sex scenes, they could easily be suggestive of sadomasochistic sexuality, as it is *misunderstood* by the masses. Feminist theory and its relationship to sexual practices cannot be divorced from this history. Contextualizing and historicizing feminism's anti-sex, anti-s/m standpoint does not, however, justify it, nor should it detract from the necessity of analyzing a kind of rhetorical violence that has been its product.

Feminist Theory, Lesbian Practice?

In the introduction to *Coming to Power*, the editors puzzle over the extremity of the assaults by feminists on s/m. As the feminist movement became increasingly polarized around these debates, members of Samois suggested that "this turbulence is symbolic of a much deeper, more invisible and less-than-direct ideological power struggle."[44] Since the Samois editors do not articulate details of the "symbolic" struggle, one can only speculate about what it left implicit.

Exactly *what* constitutes the threat is impossible to explain, for surely there are a multiplicity of complex stakes that this struggle represents. I do think, however, that the issue has less to do with "violence" and sexual practices and more to do with the way in which "the Lesbian" became, ironically, positioned as the sign of purity within a liberal feminist agenda. Lesbian feminists make little effort to conceal that s/m threatens their definitions of lesbianism. But rarely do they make explicit that lesbian identity, as such, is the issue. Having constructed and then naturalized a lesbian identity, in an astonishingly short period of time, lesbian feminism has jealously guarded that construct. And recently the mainstream media has promulgated that issue in the name of supporting a certain kind of lesbian "visibility."

This is a violence, a rhetorical violence with very real material effects, inherent in the process of any identity constructions, as the NOW resolution exemplifies. This rhetorical struggle among feminists has done more damage to the feminist movement than anyone imagined. Rubin attributes the controversy about s/m within feminism to, in part, a confusion between sexual orientation and political beliefs. She traces this problem back to the feminist slogan, "Feminism is the theory, Lesbianism is the practice."[45] Legend has it that Ti-Grace Atkinson said this at a conference in the early 1970s. Katie King has argued that these words were misheard. According to King, what was actually said was: "Feminism is *a* theory, Lesbianism is *a* practice."[46] King points out that this slogan was invoked variously to *privilege* lesbianism as something like the quintessential expression of feminism *and* to point to an inherent disjunction between feminism and lesbianism. The article *a* signifies the latter, the article *the* signifies the former. King's historical recovery challenges us to reconsider the history of feminism and lesbianism in the last few decades. The shift from *the* to *a* represents some recognition that both feminism and lesbianism do not constitute unified, monumental categories with different referents. Nevertheless, the essential split, between theory and practice, remains intact in both the original version and the recovered one. It doesn't change the *effects* of this legend, which have had widespread implications in feminist theory. The slogan generated tremendous dissension among feminists, for it implied that only lesbians could have both theory and practice, and hence a "holistic" agenda. At the same time, this was something like a Cartesian moment in feminist history: the "mind" of feminism and the "body" of lesbianism split.

The division between theory and practice has recurred in another guise in the more recent constructionist/essentialist debates. "Theory" has been overwhelmingly on the side of constructionism, indeed nearly synonymous with it, whereas "practice" has been a more slippery term that tends to slide back and forth across the constructionism/essentialism divide. Nonetheless, the triple equation of essentialism/practice/lesbianism has left a residue that continues to produce tension and dissonance between and among feminist communities. The notion of a "strategic essentialism" has been an effort to reconcile the division. Gayatri Spivak led the way by conceptualizing essentialism as a political maneuver rather than an evocation of something inherent to the category *women*; and other theorists have attempted to merge the split into a coherent program, so that one could be a constructionist in theory and an essentialist in practice. Naomi Schor and Diana Fuss, to mention just two prominent theorists, have attempted to reconsider the essentialist position: Schor pointing out that essentialism has been essentialized; Fuss proposing that even if essentialism is a phallocentric ruse, it may be a risk worth taking, depending upon who practices it and the positionality of the speaking subject.[47] As valuable as such reconsiderations have been however, the division between theory and practice seems to remain at a standstill, for it is still presumed that "practice" might necessitate some actions that are disconsonant with one's theoretical standpoint.

The essentialism/constructionism issue is, of course, all about "identity." One way of tracing this history might produce a map that would look like this:

Feminism = Theory   Lesbianism = Practice
Constructionism   Essentialism
Discursivity = the "Body"   Materiality = the "Flesh"

What is interesting about this map, however, is that lesbianism, as it was incorporated into some versions of feminism, has rarely been conceptualized as a practice. Rather, it is lesbianism as an *identity* formation that has been crucial to the feminist movement. The constructionist/essentialist debates testify to feminism's inability to function without some recourse to the "real." Feminism has needed and continues to need a referent. While the female body has been acknowledged as a series of historical/discursive formations constructed to shore up the fiction of a coherent category of women, the lesbian body has been located precariously both inside and outside the discursivity of the female body. As "outside" the body of feminist theory, the lesbian body has been charged with the task of retaining some recourse to the flesh, the real, the referent. As "inside" that body, the lesbian has been incorporated so that she assimilates into the model and loses her difference, effectively becoming heterosexualized. To look at the story from one perspective, feminist identities are theoretical; lesbian identities are *real.* Once the "lavender menace" was permitted to enter the feminist movement, lesbians moved rapidly from the status of threatening intruders to idealized figures. Radical feminism permitted their company on the condition that they conform to certain identity formations that did not demand analysis and were riddled with associations of the natural and original.[48] Lesbians thus became charged with a divine mission—an impossible one—to represent the unrepresentable. In the name of "visibility" lesbians were canalized into a singular category.

"realesbians" to "Real" Lesbians

In complicity with this construction, lesbians themselves began to perpetuate the most naive illusion—the *realesbian,* a contradictory entity both born and made. For example, the Gay Revolution Party's (GRP) Women's Caucus complained of the danger of "political lesbians," whom they defined as women who were committed to other women socially but not necessarily sexually. These political lesbians sometimes sought out "realesbians" to initiate them sexually. The GRP maintained the integrity of realesbians as an inviolate category, yet urged straight feminists to confront their passivity and *become* lesbians. To do any less was not to join in the struggle.[49]

While historically it may have been true that some heterosexual feminists merely wanted to have some lesbian sexual experience in order to claim access to the "practice" side of the slogan, desire is much too complicated to explain as merely a strategic gesture. Though one can readily understand the suspicion among lesbians that they are being sexually used in order to fulfill a fantasy of conquest or control (a kind of "mastery" that is radically dissimilar to the top's desire in an s/m exchange), nonetheless, the conception of the "realesbian" proposed sexuality between women as the essence of liberation. And in so doing, lesbians contributed to essentializing themselves while allowing heterosexual women the potential for sexual fluidity.

Judith Butler asks: "To what extent do identitarian logical systems always require the construction of socially impossible identities to occupy an unnamed, excluded, but presuppositional relation subsequently concealed by the logic itself?" [50] While it is certainly accurate to say that identitarian logical systems *produce* such impossible identities, it is also the case that some of these identities are historically ready-made. Feminist identitarian logic had such a construction easily available to it from the historical construction of the lesbian as a socially impossible identity, made by a combination of sexological theories and psychoanalysis.[51]

We might think of the lesbian identity within feminism as having assumed the paradoxical situation of the Lacanian Real. While the lesbian identity, like all identities, doesn't "really" exist, it does have a set of properties that produce a series of effects that can be reconstructively imagined. Žižek offers this "joke" structure to exemplify the Lacanian Real: " 'Is this the place where the Duke of Wellington spoke his famous words? Yes, this is the place, but he never spoke those words.'" [52] Another way to think about this "Real" is in terms of the Freudian fetish: "I know very well but all the same." [53]

Identity formations are fetishistic, which also means that they have a very powerful erotic appeal. But like Lacan's Real, they are nothing *in* themselves; they are *impossible*, but it is precisely in this that lies the potency of their effects. The legendary slogan, "feminism is the (a?) theory, lesbianism is the (a?) practice" might be understood according to this formula. Whoever said it, where it was said, exactly how it was articulated, or indeed whether or not it was actually ever said at all, does not erase the material effects that it has produced. The split between theory and practice and the alignment of feminism with the former and lesbianism with the latter has produced a notion of "the lesbian" as a fetish. Ironically, women are not supposed to be capable of fetishism according to psychoanalysis; perhaps it is time to think of women as more adept fetishists than Freud ever dreamed.

Diffusion/Contamination

Objections to s/m have taken many forms. One of the most prevalent has been the theory of diffusion or contamination. While opponents of s/m at large tend to focus on the "sadist," it is interesting that the figure of the masochist is the one that has garnered most of the attention between and among feminists. One would think that feminists would find the sadist *more* offensive, given that she is the one who purportedly enacts the "violence." The focus on the masochist, I think, can be explained in three (at least) ways. First, the concern about women enacting their masochism is clearly an acceptance of the psychoanalytic precept that masochism is inherently feminine. Once again, then, the very feminists who most eschew psychoanalytic paradigms seem to be the ones who have most thoroughly ingested them. Second, because the masochist is the figure of radical impossibility (as I will discuss at length in chapter 3), there has been a conflation of "performative" masochism with the masochist of clinical fame.[54] Insistence that the lesbian masochist is the *same* as the inherently masochistic woman of Freudian lore is much like arguing that lesbians are inverts.

The "logic" of feminism's denunciation of lesbian sadomasochism is a tautology that reads something like this: lesbians should strive to purge themselves of their masochistic desires, for as we all know, no women are really masochists, and if they are, they should be protected from themselves. Such is precisely the "logic" that informs the prohibitions on children's sexuality—i.e., that elaborate mechanisms must be constructed to ensure that it is not acted upon, because children do not *have* any sexual desires—that Foucault discusses in his *History of Sexuality.*[55] Third, representations created *by* women *for* women who enjoy being sexually submissive are relatively scarce. This is a problem of representation that is being remedied as women write about their sexual desires in stories and essays such as those contained in *The Second Coming,* particularly in part 5, "Black Hanky Fiction (The Heavy Stuff)."[56] It is the figure of the lesbian sadomasochist who has forced feminists to look directly at lesbian sexual practices and at the ways in which they have informed but not constituted lesbian identities and thus disrupted the notion of a unified lesbian identity that serves the purposes of a feminist theory.

(A)historical Violence

Violence, no less than gender, is not ahistorical, monolithic, absolute. At the height of the sex wars in the 1980s the battle lines of s/m politics were clearly drawn. Pro-s/m feminists and lesbians claimed that s/m sexual practices were safe, consensual and nonviolent. Anti-s/m lesbians and feminists argued that sadomasochists internalized the violent dominant/submission patterns of heterosexist patriarchy and were thus unwitting victims who perpetuated the oppressive model. Notice that in this rhetoric lesbian sadomasochists are figured as both victims and oppressors, in much the same way that lesbian "monsters" of the 1930s were contradictorily figured as *both* immoral *and* sick.[57]

Also notice that this debate was set up as a consciousness vs. unconsciousness issue, with sadomasochists on the side of consciousness. Sarah Kofman has provocatively implied that the woman who performs with *consciousness* is effectively criminalized in Freud's inquiry into the feminine enigma. The problem, she says, is to determine whether Freud proceeds in his analysis as if he were dealing with a criminal or with an hysteric: "Does he admit that woman is the only one who knows her own secret, knows the solution to the riddle and is determined not to share it, since she is self-sufficient, or thinks she is, and has no need for complicity? . . . Or does Freud proceed, on the contrary, as if woman were completely ignorant of her own secret . . . that she cannot get along without man if she is to be 'cured.' "[58] Obviously Freud selected the latter path. But what is interesting for this discussion is the association of the woman with consciousness—the one who knows her own secret and refuses to divulge it—with the *criminal.* Is it not arresting that lesbian sadomasochism, which is surely the most consciously *performed* of any expression of lesbian sex, has been criminalized by some feminist rhetoric? And, at the same time, anti-s/m feminists hystericize the lesbian sadomasochist by claiming that she doesn't know her own mind, suffers from repression, needs to be cured.

Bracketing for a moment the peculiarity of such a position emanating from a theory that discounts the role of the unconscious on most other occasions, and indeed *champions* consciousness as necessary for women's liberation, let us turn for a moment to this notion of "free choice" that is crucial in these debates. The idea of freedom of choice is bound up with liberal notions of individualism. The individual—the one who is "in-divisible"—is difficult to reconcile with the member of a community. As Sandra Bartky points out, the feminist who insists that women can simply alter the structures of their desires and freely choose their sexual preferences comes close to a behavioristic model and risks reinstating a bourgeois individualistic notion of free choice against a model of determinism.[59]

While lesbian sexual practices have been marginalized in academic feminist and lesbian discourse, they have been central to the wider feminist movement. I think that the s/m debates are signs of a much larger dilemma within feminist theory than has been recognized. In fact, I believe that these debates are fundamental to any discussion of the relationship between feminist theory and theories of sexuality. Lesbian s/m strikes a chord that resonates deeply within the feminist movement. The pros and cons of s/m practice seem to have abated since the height of the sex wars in the mid-1980s. However, as recently as 1993 a second collection of essays, aimed particularly at s/m lesbianism, was published; the most widely recognized magazine devoted to s/m lesbians went out of business, the "Butler" decision in Canada, modeled on the MacKinnon/Dworkin antipornography legislation, has successfully censored lesbian erotica; and the NEA/NEH wars have prominently featured sadomasochism.[60] These are only a few of the recent incidents that implicate s/m as a lightning rod of sexual censorship. Why should a particular sexual activity, practiced by a minority population within a minority, have generated such controversy? S/m was the line that many lesbian feminists simply could not seem to cross over at the height of the sex wars—in fact, it was, for some *the* limit—the border over which one could not pass and remain a feminist. As one contributor to

Against Sadomasochism succinctly put it: "The part of it that concerns me is when it is presented as a feminist issue or when it's held out as being part of the . . . lesbian-feminist movement, that's when I draw the line." [61]

The line that is drawn, however, keeps shifting, for no one is able to circumscribe s/m sexuality. The boundaries erected continually disintegrate, not only between "normal" and "perverse" lesbian sexual practices but also between and among an entire technology/industry of sexual practices and their relationship to sexual identities. While the hetero/homo binary is crumbling despite the frantic efforts of the sexual legislators to fortify it, within that nebulous domain of sexual "perversities" there is virtually no status/stasis of the human body. As it has become more widely accepted that sexualities are both historically produced and psychically/physically malleable, and thus particularly resistant to any effort to categorize or contain, opposing camps are even more desperate to maintain and patrol the borders. As soon as actual sexual practices begin to be discussed, which is rare, the ground begins slipping and sliding away. Boundaries dissolve immediately when feminists attempt to secure differences between being penetrated with a finger, a fist, or a dildo; being held firmly, held down, tied up, handcuffed, or chained; being persuaded, seduced, or coerced. When Mariana Valverde asserted her opprobrium for fetishism and fistfucking, she inadvertently put her fingers right on the spot of contestation: "The next time someone leads me from 'feminism' through 'fetish' to 'fistfucking,' I'll know that somewhere along the way *I* got lost."[62]

Tacie Dejanikus indicated how the "I" gets constructed through memories that are then reconstructed as analogies in the present tense, which disregard the complexities of differences within subjectivity, displacing them outward onto the unsuspecting and producing improbable correlations. She remembers swallowing sperm when she did not want to and faking orgasms, and equates this "ritual enslavement" with "masochistic-role-playing." This experience leads her to correlate and appropriate further the experience of a black man who recalled letting whites onto the elevator first, then stopping this practice when he came to the realization that he had internalized the dominant culture's racism.[63] Significantly, Dejanikus's commentary appears in an essay entitled, "Our Legacy." Exactly *which legacy* does she refer to here? The ways in which internalized racism and internalized misogyny are historically and psychically intertwined is a crucial matter to consider. But certainly they are not simple analogues. To equate the consciousness of a black man who defers to whites with the consciousness of a woman who engages in sexual practices then retrospectively feels that she was coerced grossly ignores the very different psychic identifi-

cations and disidentifications of both parties as well as the material differences of their histories. Such analogies do justice to neither party. This kind
of slippage, as Judith Butler points out, "is not only a mistake in judgment,
but the exploitation of the sign of racial violence for the purposes of enhanc-
ing, through a metonymical slippage, the putatively injurious power of
pornography."[64] When a critic such as Andrena Zawinski fails to see the
"difference between the sadist and the rapist," and asks, "why does [the s/m
contention that the bottom is controlling and consenting to the scene]
remind me of the dangerous cliche of 'women who ask for it'?"[65] does she
really assume that there is no difference between a woman who boldly
announces her desire, as in this exchange: "Mandy . . . would you take me
to the sleeping cabin and spank me? . . . As we walk to the cabin will you
tell me what I have to do when we get there?"[66] and a rapist who tries to
claim that the woman he raped was "asking for it"? According to this reasoning, the enunciation of the speaker is irrelevant. How then could she
possibly negotiate the difference between this scenario and one in which the
woman clearly says "no"? For Zawinski, what counts is the elusive referent
for the "it," that she is "asking for," which is presumably sex (it)self. These
examples are more than peculiar instances of bad reasoning; rather, they are
indicative of contradictions that emerged from a feminist movement that
was foundationally dependent on a homogeneous category of women.

Linda Wayne has taken on what is perhaps the most difficult thing for
anti-s/m lesbian feminists to accept—the use of symbols associated with
historical atrocities, particularly fascist imagery. She argues that these
images operate "through [their] pure presence as . . . effigies, or as recognizable piece(s) of the past that convey latent ideological messages of the
present, [their] *meaning[s]* are given to us as visually self-evident." While
this is an argument about proximity and resemblance working to erase differences through the dominance of the visual, which I will take up in later
chapters, Wayne makes a very important, nuanced point in her essay that
does not merely call for the recognition of differences or the reclamation of
symbols that carry the weight of the past so powerfully that they cannot be
undone. She also points out that "it is crucial to reiterate that it is not
merely a dominant *assimilation* (my emphasis) of subgroup representation,
but a collapsing of *living* symbols of subgroup empowerment into a *dehis-
toricized* figuration of evil."[67] Her point is subtle but highly significant.
While I have myself, like many other pro-s/m lesbians, found it extremely
difficult to accept the wearing of such symbols, Wayne is, I think, right to
point out that to view them as static representations, iconographically and
inextricably linked to acts that they once signified, contributes to their

power to represent these acts as if they are *outside history.* That is not to say that what they have represented is not historical, but it does seem to suggest that this history has obtained a certain static, immutable quality, a timelessness. In a culture that so highly values immortality, this renders them even more potent as reminders of what was, rather than as symbols of what continues to be or what may become.

> The finding of an object is in fact a refinding of it.
>
> —Freud

Lesbian s/m appears to be fundamentally opposed to a principal tenet of mainstream feminism. Whereas the latter focuses on "finding ourselves," the former often assumes the rhetoric of "losing ourselves." Sadomasochists frequently refer to the experience of becoming "nothing," whereas lesbian feminists speak of creating and asserting their self-identities. Feminists invested in the construction of a coherent self are understandably horrified by passages such as this one from an s/m story: "she began to erase herself . . . she began to crumble herself at the edges, fade into the air, render herself will-less and invisible."[68] It is not only a particular identity, but identity *as such* that is violated by these descriptions of the masochistic experience.

Anti s/m arguments, however, do not focus on identity as such; rather, the battle is for possession of a particular identity formation. It is in this sense that the arguments are displacements of the vanishing point where the two claims to reality meet. For neither side can claim a coherent identity without recourse to the other. Hence we can see why the illusion of a radically different and coherent s/m subculture is necessary to the mainstream feminist movement and begin to understand why these controversies surface again and again. The opposing sides are caught up in an endless cycle of naming and renaming that does not recognize the inherent contradiction of "epistemological resolution." It seems absurd (if not obscene) to have to say that "ways of knowing" *differ,* for surely all feminists already know this. But if "the lesbian body" in feminism was the site where a referent could be fixed, lesbian s/m has played a large part in launching lesbian identities out of their safe harbor and into the sea of the arbitrary play of signifiers.

Masochism continues to be the term that signals a red flag within feminism, not only because of its historical associations with a "feminine ontology," but also because it is the masochistic sexual desire that most profoundly signifies a destabilization of "self" that feminism so jealously guards. Roy Baumeister, in his article, "Masochism as Escape From Self," offers the following example of a heterosexual male's experience with a dominatrix to support his claim that masochism is an escape from identity: "Being dressed up in brassiere and panties, handcuffed to a bed, and spanked, afterwards licking a prostitute's feet or genitals, is simply incompatible with one's identity as a male U.S. Senator."[69] Baumeister argues that the masochist desires to escape from the high-level, abstract self-awareness that is fostered in highly individualistic culture. Pain, bondage, blindfolding, and humiliation free the submissive from initiative and choice, allowing him to retreat momentarily from identity to the body and create a new fantasy identity that is often in diametric opposition to the "self" he presents in the everyday world.

This empirical/sociological study has its obvious limitations. Though it might sound a bit like Leo Bersani's theory of sexuality as a "self-shattering pleasure" (which I will be discussing at length in chapter 3), Baumeister's example sounds more like trading in one set of clothing and activities for another and with them one "real" identity for a fantasy one. It is just this kind of facile understanding of s/m in the literature of many empirical studies that leads feminists to scorn its practices and denounce its elitism and appropriation of the services of sex workers. Some lesbian sadomasochistic literature makes similar banal assumptions; but the concept of "losing one(self)" is not about trading it in for another one; rather, it is about a profound alteration in consciousness that can understandably be perceived as quite terrifying. Nevertheless, it is a leap into a corporeality that can facilitate a process of coming to realize that the "self" is not only a construct, a prosthetic device, but often a burdensome one.

One Is Not Born a Lesbian

Identitarian logic appeared to have suffered a major blow in 1981 when Monique Wittig proclaimed that lesbians were not women. Her declaration was received by some women as a crucial shift that permitted lesbians to begin defining themselves outside the discourse on gender.[70] Of course lesbians had only been "women" for a couple of decades; it was feminism that gave lesbians an identity—as "women-identified-women." Wittig's position potentially reclaimed the power of lesbians by situating them like the sexologists' "intermediate sex," not-women, not-men. By removing lesbians from the category of women, Wittig did seem to eliminate object-choice as a criteria for defining the category of lesbians. For, if lesbians are not women, lesbians obviously cannot be defined as women-loving-women. Object-choice, however, tenaciously clings to gender constructions, even intermediate ones. Indeed it is perhaps in the resistance to unbinding object-choice from gender that gender constantly gets made and remade. Following Wittig, we seem to be trapped in a tautology: lesbians are lesbians who are erotically cathected with lesbians.

Who is allowed "membership" in a lesbian community and how that is determined remains an extremely divisive issue. S/m support groups have policies that range from the Seattle group, "The Outer Limits,"—a rather ironic title since its membership "is open only to female-born lesbians,"[71]— to "The Outcasts" in San Francisco, whose policy of inclusion is as wide as possible. Gayle Rubin points out that in 1984, when a group formed to initiate a replacement for the defunct Samois, the same conflict that had led to the demise of Samois arose once again: "how to *define* lesbian and who could belong to a lesbian group." Rubin further elaborates:

> Some separatists quickly stated that they wanted the new group to exclude bisexual and transsexual women: it would be lesbian-only and restricted to so-called "born" (presumably genetic) women. In addition, they wanted only those lesbians who had sex only with other lesbians who had sex only with other lesbians who had sex only with other lesbians, presumably into the tenth generation of fuck partners. This last criterion was a novel one.[72]

Although there are real fears and fantasies that underwrite this kind of exclusion, it nonetheless makes manifestly clear that identity politics can lead to infinitely regressive determinations, until theoretically *no one* could qualify for the position. Although identity politics have in some ways been influential in the formation of communities, Rubin's example shows that identity formations are finally individualistic.

The title of Wittig's article, "One is Not Born a Woman,"is, of course, a direct allusion to Simone de Beauvoir's paradigm-shifting thesis. In Wittig's thesis lesbians are not sexed subjects but rather the subjects of a certain sexuality. Wittig does not say what this sexuality looks like, which might suggest that lesbians are not able to be captured within the visual field, where identities get constituted.

Nevertheless, while Wittig would certainly not argue that one is born a lesbian, she retains an ontological undercurrent in her thesis. Her essay teases us with the suggestion that "one is not born a lesbian," but Wittig is only able to define a lesbian by what she is not—in this case, not a woman. Not being women allows lesbians to inhabit a much wider playing space than the confines of gender permit, but certainly Wittig would not argue that not being women is *sufficient* to an understanding of lesbianism. Even theorists as sophisticated as Wittig do not seem to be able to unmoor lesbians from some presumptive recourse to the real. Judith Butler argues that Wittig's political project is sometimes situated "within the traditional discourse of ontotheology" since it is dependent on a notion of equal access to language—"women *speak* their way out of their gender."[73] Thus by retaining a coherent "I," Butler argues that Wittig also presupposes a unity of being. What Butler calls Wittig's "foundationalist fiction" might also be thought of as a strategic essentialism, which she needs to retain in order to launch her social critique. While Butler is sympathetic to that necessity, she asks: "what contingent social relations does that presumption of being, authority, and universal subjecthood serve?"[74] This is indeed a critical question and not one, I think, that can be addressed adequately without historicizing Wittig's position.

In Wittig's theory it is clear that the coherent "I" she desires to retain is a subjectivity that she wants to name "lesbian." Although Wittig's subtle theorizing would seem to have little in common with lesbians who define their sexuality in the language of discovery or reclamation, this theoretical discourse may yet have something in common with lesbian testimonials—"coming out" narratives—for the desire to situate lesbianism as a starting point to which one returns is a rhetorical maneuver common to both. So while theoretically I would agree with Butler that the presupposition of a unity of being serves no apparent "contingent social relations," it does perhaps serve a constituency that has built an historical political movement around the ability to "come out" *as* a lesbian. It may, in fact, not have been as politically efficacious as it might have appeared. But that is the project for the present and the future, and it is difficult to project how abandoning that strategy will serve us when the retrospective view becomes available.

Part of the anti-identitarian project has become thinking sexualities apart from gender (defined in terms of object choice), a major project and one of crucial importance for feminists. It is interesting to note that the earliest attempts to do so have been written by theorists in the context of sadomasochism: Gayle Rubin's "Thinking Sex," in which she argues that feminism is a theory inadequate to the task of theorizing sexualities,[75] and Parveen Adams's "Of Female Bondage," in which she wants to show what a separation of sexuality and gender might look like and finds it in the practice of lesbian sadomasochism, which refuses the "forms of womanly pathology organized within the phallic field" and is able to "enact differences in the theatre where roles freely circulate."[76]

But what and where is this "theater" where "roles" can freely circulate? As I will be discussing at length in the rest of this book, the "performative" is too often conflated with a "theatrical" that is insufficiently articulated and often presumed to mean simply "not real life." Theater historians, practitioners, and theorists look at some of this theory with dismay. For those of us who work in theater in all of its aspects know quite well that "theater" is not the *opposite of life*, as it is sometimes posited. Nor does "playing a role" take one out of the ideological circulations of the dominant culture. The way in which "theater" is used as an implied synonym for "fantasy" ignores the complexities of both. What *kind of theater* we are talking about is scarcely ever mentioned. The linguistic "performative" becomes conflated with *performance*, which is then sometimes used interchangeably with "theater." And, ironically, this use of theater ends up becoming metaphorical, thus referring us back to the most conventional definition of theater, the quality that marks it as separate from other forms of representation—that its medium is the *live body*—the "flesh" if you will.

Theaters of the Flesh

While theatrical metaphors were being marshalled to describe sexual identity formations, theater critics and performers were deeply concerned with testing and transgressing the presumptive boundaries between theater and life. In the 1960s and 1970s, when feminism was incorporating lesbians into the movement and defining their profile, theater artists were dismantling fourth-wall illusionism. Herbert Blau cites Richard Schechner's "actuals" and Grotowski's "theatre of sources" as examples of this trend to "replace the illusion of Total Theater with the promise of Total Life."[77] This urge to return to "life" was not peculiar to either discourse, but a widespread western cultural ethos. Radical feminism, like Total Theater, dreamed of a mise-en-scène that was primordial, prior to performance, in which everything could be seen but there was no one watching. Blau speaks of this ideal vision in Rousseau's carnival—a "*mise-en-scène* without a gaze, everything seen and nothing to show. There is nothing remotely like the edge of a stage, as if repression had been lifted in the unconscious, where there is always a stage."[78] This urge to "return to life" further sedimented identification logic.

Our vocabulary of sexualities and genders is obviously thoroughly impoverished as long as it depends upon identity formations.[79] Where, for example, could we locate the fantasy formations of this anonymous contributor to the "Sex Issue" of *Heresies* within the current terms?

> Mon. Fantasized fucking a woman with a penis and not letting her use her penis on me. No sex today.
>
> Tues. Dressed in jockey shorts and a long white dress. Looked for a woman or a man dressed as a woman.

Wedns. Made love to a man with a vagina while I fantasized that I
was dressed as a man making love to a woman.
Thurs. Got fucked by a man and loved it. No fantasy.
Fri. Got eaten by a woman and loved it. No fantasy.
Sat. Played with myself. Fantasized that I was a woman playing
with herself.
Sun. A man, pretending to be a woman, let me eat him. I fantasized
that he was a woman pretending to be a man.[80]

Her "no fantasy" entries record sexual experiences that identify men or
women as object choices. But is it impossible to imagine her other fantasies
realized? Must the flesh always hold on to its status as the real?

Lesbian sadomasochists unsettle the category of lesbians as "women-
identified-women" in both their rhetoric and practice. In the vocabulary
feminism has both inherited and constructed concerning sexual subjectivities, a celibate woman might be allowed into the community,[81] but a definite line is often drawn with women who have sex with men. Pat Califia
says that if she had to choose between being stranded on a desert island
with a vanilla lesbian or a masochistic boy, she would take the boy every
time.[82] But she doesn't then call herself a dominatrix—a term that is usually reserved for the female top in a heterosexual couple. Rather, she continues to refer to herself as a lesbian, insisting that its definition not rely on
the reification of categories that refer to the immutability of body parts.

Califia's standpoint is one that brings us back to the problem of "free
choice." Feminist theory and praxis has a difficult time reconciling with a
poststructuralist notion of freedom as always ideologically mediated. If we
are all caught in the web of ideological causalities, is there any way to think
of freedom that permits more than transgressions that are inevitably pre-
supposed, and indeed permitted, by an ideology that anticipates and incorporates them? Are we all fated to be workers in Derrida's beehive?[83]

The "Impossible" Real

Based on Lacan's seminars in the seventies, Žižek invites us to consider
freedom from another perspective—"free choice as the real-impossible."
Arguing that a subject's relationship to a community entails a paradoxical
moment of "forced choice," which consists in having to "choose what is
already given to him," Žižek claims that, in effect, the community says to its
members, you have the freedom to choose, provided that you make the right
choice; if you make the wrong choice, you lose freedom of choice itself. Of
course one could immediately counter that you might lose membership in

the community if you make the wrong choice, but you wouldn't necessarily lose freedom of choice itself, unless it were a totalitarian system. But Žižek quickly points out that all members of a community are treated "as if [they] had already chosen," and there is nothing "totalitarian" about it. On the contrary, he argues that this paradoxical positioning is constitutive of a community, and any subject who thinks she can evade the paradox is a "psychotic" subject—"one who retains a kind of distance from the symbolic order—who is not really caught in the signifying network." When Žižek says that there is nothing totalitarian about this paradox, he wants to make clear that this situation is not particular to any specific historical/political configuration—"totalitarian" as authoritarian, autocratic, dictatorial. But in another sense, he does seem to mean that inherent to any notion of community is a tendency to totalize—to combine into an entirety.[84]

The question of whether such a tendency to totalize in community formation leads inevitably to a kind of totalitarianism is critical for feminists. Lesbian sadomasochists have certainly accused anti-s/m feminists of exerting an authoritarian power against their sexual identities and practices. The lesbian sadomasochist puts lesbian feminists in a difficult position. They ask to become members of the community while refusing to accept the terms on which the community is built. They threaten not only mainstream feminism's foundation but also its foundationalist fiction of a coherent identity, which may in fact come to the same thing.

Whereas the lesbian feminist was made by feminism on the basis of mutuality, roleless equality, and "natural" desire, in opposition to heterosexual gender inequities, the lesbian sadomasochist seems to play out the worst imaginable heterosexist scenes. Sadomasochism, according to radical feminists, is neither real love, nor free love. Tops often order bottoms to "love" them; they also may pick a submissive from a crowd of masochists, not necessarily on the basis of any qualities that appear to be unique to the individual but simply based on a contest of who qualifies as the most submissive. Certainly within the ideology of liberal or "egalitarian" feminism, as well as in the ideology of romantic love in general, these actions are not permissible. For as Žižek points out, if one is ordered to love someone, it is not "free" love; and if one shops around quite deliberately for someone to love, it is not "real" love. Thus the paradox of the subject within a community is also the basic paradox of love. Žižek writes: "the paradox of love is that it is a free choice, but a choice which never arrives in the present—it is always already made. At a certain moment, I can only state retroactively that I've already chosen."[85] How do we explain this notion of a "free choice" that is always already made, that is at once presumed and produced in the transaction? Žižek argues that the only solution is that some fundamental choice is made prior to our conscious decisions—that choice, in short, is unconscious.[86] The obvious objection to such a position is that such a formulation deprives us of any agency, any ability to intervene in the social field. It is thus easily misunderstood as a dehistoricizing and ahistorical conception. But we do not *not* have access to the unconscious. In fact, Lacan postulates that the unconscious is *not unconscious*, not that is, unconscious in the sense of the popularized Freudian sense of the unconscious.

This unconscious, atemporal choice corresponds neatly to the Lacanian Real, which is not only that brute, inscrutable core or essence, but also the incredible, non-ontological phantasm. Hence, the real-impossible. If we understand by "freedom" the liberating fantasy formations of the latter part of the definition of the "Real," we usually relegate to the former half of the definition the brute facticity of the flesh. But the "Real" as that which falls out of symbolization is not necessarily conjectured as a lack or absence that passively waits to be filled with content. It might also be understood as that which *evades* the frame of representation and its (en)closures. The "Real," in my reading, is precisely the possibilities of the imaginary that are located at the very limits of representation. Or, what representation fails to limit. This is a location where very productive feminist work does—and must, I think—take place.

Simone de Beauvoir says that what Sade demanded of cruelty was "that it reveal to him particular individuals and his own existence as on the one hand consciousness and freedom and, on the other, [the] flesh."[87] In her review of *Coming to Power* and *Against Sadomasochism*, Lisa Orlando wonders if s/m sexuality is not in some way about experiencing ourselves "however illusorily, as pure flesh." She cites a sentence from Charley Shiveley's article in "Fag Rag," which she perceives as potentially outraging but for her, "strangely evocative": "I am not just a human being, I am a piece of meat."[88] But it is not that the body is transformed into flesh in sadomasochism; rather, as I have tried to show, it is that sadomasochistic practice partakes in the paradoxical structure of the Real. Beauvoir locates this contradiction in two of Sade's passages:

> The most divine charms are as nothing when submission and obedience do not come forth to offer them.

> One must do violence to the object of one's desire; when it surrenders, the pleasure is greater.[89]

Of course this sounds like the worst kind of sadistic tyranny, but if we understand that the "object" of one's desire is phantasmatic, that the only "real" object of desire is the desiring-fantasy of the one who desires, then Sade's pronouncements are much more palatable, even liberating. For to do "violence" to one's "object" then is to break open, shatter, stretch, expand, seduce, coerce, force—if necessary—one's *own* ability to imagine alternatives to the rigid, limited, and impoverished sites of desire to which we have constrained ourselves.

Sadomasochism is one of the theories and practices where this kind of "violence" is taking place. It is, if you will, both performance and reality, and neither of them. Or, more precisely, s/m conjures up the contradictory nature of all performance, which strives both to create the truth of illusion and unmask the illusion of truth. The paradox of s/m is unsettling for some feminists because its pleasure is in the paradoxes and contradictions that some feminist theory desires to resolve. And lesbian sadomasochism is particularly disruptive to any feminist agenda that constructs the lesbian body—the body in fact/flesh—as the site where that resolution can rest.

Masochism: Theories and Practices

In this section I will be looking at theoretical discussions of masochism that hold out some promise for feminists who desire to reclaim masochism as an *active* possibility for women rather than a pregiven disposition. I will also consider a variety of ways in which prohibitions on sadomasochistic exchanges *between women* have been erected.

Gilles Deleuze's theory of masochism as an inversion of the Platonic ideal seems to be a useful starting point for feminists theorizing the masochistic position of women in s/m exchanges. His theory is initially quite promising, for it is the only psychoanalytic model that allows for both parties in the exchange to be women, *and* strives to overcome the tenacity of the Hegelian dominant/submissive model.

Deleuze claims that sadism and masochism are distinct perversions with their own particular aesthetics, pleasures, and, implicitly, politics. His thesis throws feminist accusations of the fundamental inequality of lesbian s/m relationships into confusion. For if, in his theory, it is not a relationship between a sadist and a masochist but, rather, two masochists acting out their sexual fantasies, then the economy is not the violence of exploiting differences but a fundamental sameness that grounds the dialectic between them. Masochism might then be basically a "queer" act, based on a relationship that privileges the sharing of similarities.

Each subject in the perversion, Deleuze argues, is seeking the element of "the same perversion, and not a subject of the other perversion."[90] Whereas

Freud considered s/m to be an entity within one and the same individual, the assumption of one role or the other depending on whether the active or passive aspect of her character is more highly developed, Deleuze's argument attempts to take us out of the activity/passivity distinction altogether, beyond the tenaciously gendered dualism. For Deleuze, sadism and masochism are separate dramas, "each complete in itself, with different sets of characters and *no possibility of communication between them*" (my emphasis).[91]

On the face of it, then, Deleuze's argument has tremendous appeal for feminists. First, in masochism "femininity is posited as lacking in nothing."[92] Second, in masochism the father is expelled from the symbolic order through disavowal. Third, the mother figure is invested with the symbolic power of the law. Furthermore, a crucial component of the masochistic relationship is the contract, an agreement that is often formalized (as in Sacher-Masoch's fiction) and a concept that appears frequently in lesbian s/m erotica. The difference between a contract, which presupposes consent, reciprocity, and obligations that do not affect individuals outside its parameters, is contrasted with sadistic institutions, which are of indeterminate duration, extend their power and authority outside the immediate participants, and are involuntary and inalienable.[93] Whereas the contract generates a law, institutions place themselves above the law. The sadistic world is the world of Kafka and Oedipus, where "one oversteps the bounds without knowing what they are."[94] The masochistic relationship is a temporary retreat from that world, not a transformation of it or an alternative to it. For Deleuze, masochism is not revolutionary; rather, it is an escape from the enforcement of individualism.

In her introduction to *Macho Sluts* Pat Califia says that she does *not* believe that we "can fuck our way to freedom," but by listening to the majority opinions of antipornographers, who seem to think that sexual perversions constitute an anarchic force that could destroy the social contract, we might begin to think that we could. She points out that sexual censorship exposes a fear that the perverts will instigate what is *already* a fairly accurate description of our present reality: women routinely subject to male violence, sexually transmitted diseases spreading uncontrollably, children carelessly conceived and uncared for, and nuclear families disintegrating. Her suspicion that what censorship campaigns really wish to protect is the "self-image of the so-called majority," is obvious enough.[95] But what is more intriguing about her observation is the grammar of the censorship panic. For the censoring mechanism here is working by projecting the present into the future through a nostalgia for a past that never existed. Hence the present is always the tense that one cannot comprehend except through a nostalgia for the past or a projection into the future. Leo Bersani's assertion that s/m and other perversions make the center visible supports Califia's observations: "Given the public discourse around the center of sexuality (a discourse obviously not unmotivated by a prescriptive ideology about sex), the margins may be the only place where the center becomes visible."[96]

Both temporally and spatially the censorship campaign is caught in the logic of linear time and a kind of immovable geography. The "margins" in this case are where the "present" becomes located—both spatially and temporally the perversions are constituted as not just oppositional constructs, but *impossible* ones. They lack what the dominant discourse sees as fundamental to normality—an ontological framework. And hence their imaginary "this cannot be" becomes "*this will not be.*"

Klossowski describes the masochistic fantasy as "life reiterating itself in order to recover itself in its fall, as if holding its breath in an instantaneous apprehension of its origin."[97] According to Deleuze, this indicates that the masochist is an idealist who obsessively repeats the phantasmatic moment prior to individuation. Her operative mode is suspense, an attempt to recapture that moment of oneness and hold it in perpetuity. If, as Laura Mulvey has asserted, "sadism demands a story, depends on making something happen, forcing a change in another person, a battle of will and strength, victory/defeat, all occurring in a linear time with a beginning and an end,"[98] Teresa de Lauretis comments that "this sounds like a common definition of narrative, yet is offered as a description of sadism. Are we to infer that sadism is the causal agent, the deep structure, the generative force of narrative?"[99] If so, the masochist's desire for interrupted, incomplete moments, repetitions that overlap, interchange, and reverse but never necessarily coalesce into a conventional narrative, suggests an alternative to the endless repetitions of Oedipus. Her desire acts out the desire for another symbolic order.

Masochism, says Deleuze is the Name of the Mother. But which mother? According to Deleuze, the masochist tells this story: "once upon a time there were three women . . . [who] wage [war] on on one another, resulting in the triumph of the oral mother."[100]

Drawing an analogy between these three mothers and Freud's three Fates of the "Theme of the Three Caskets," the oral or "good" mother is an intermediate figure who becomes the accomplice with or victim of the father. The idealism of masochism swings between the other two mothers—the uterine mother and the oedipal mother. The oral mother's unique combination of severity and sentimentality institutes a new order that Deleuze names "gynocratic sentimentality."[101]

This is the phrase that signals, for me, a feminist pause. And, indeed, from this point on, Deleuze's theory grows less and less promising. We find out that although a man or woman can occupy the masochistic position, the "torturess" (not to be confused with "the sadist") must *always* be a woman. Although the masochistic scenario may be between a man and a woman or between two women in Deleuze's theory, the "top" is fixed and gendered feminine. Interestingly enough, what is *not* possible in Deleuze's scheme is masochism between two men. What then becomes apparent is that Deleuze's masochistic ideal remains primarily a heterosexual affair. At the same time, by making the sexual exchange between men the absent term in his theory, the usually unarticulated "hommo-sexual" economy that upholds the naturalization of heterosexuality becomes visible. And women are potentially freed from becoming exchange objects. Nonetheless, Deleuze's heavy emphasis on the mother/son relationship aims to produce a "new man," who emerges from the ordeal he suffers at the hands of a beautiful and benevolent torturess. In effect, the torturess castrates the son, which is the condition for his rebirth beyond the likeness and the law of the father. The threat of castration of course guarantees the law of the father, exogamous marriage, heterosexuality, and the incest prohibition, a prohibition that also produces the right of men to enact it as a transgression; a theme that I will take up in chapter 5.

While it seems then that Deleuze's masochistic scenario is an alternative to the oedipal drama, it is in fact a *reversal* of it, which leaves women and homosexuals in precisely the same location that they are positioned in the dominant discourse. Furthermore, by ejecting the law of the father, transferring the law to the figure of the mother, and producing a "new" (castrated) man, Deleuze's masochistic scenario shows us what in fact "*makes incest possible.*"[102] Indeed it is incest that is at the heart of the fantasy.

Gayle Rubin was the first to point out that the incest taboo presumes a prior prohibition on homosexuality.[103] I find it astonishing that this point has not made the impact on political theory and representational politics that it so obviously merits. It is almost as if her point produced such a shattering of the social that it has been virtually disavowed. This lucid insight can be developed by proposing that homophobia is, in part, an (unconscious?) intuition that sexual acts between men and between women have the "taint" of incest.[104] It is interesting, however, that whereas the specter of incest that haunts gay male relationships heightens the sexual tension, the conception of lesbian relationships as mother/daughter affairs has tended to imply a desexualization. Many lesbian feminists have strenuously objected to the notion that desire between women is based on a woman's identification with her mother, not because there is a suggestion of incest in such a relationship, but because the mother/daughter bond, due to the cultural deeroticization of mothers, implies that lesbian relationships are sexless.

If, however, it is "incest anxiety" that informs this tendency toward desexualization, lesbians who affirm the eroticism of mother/daughter bonds are particularly threatening, for they do not deny that there is passion in the affair. Indeed, lesbian subcultures have inherited, or invented,[105] a fantasy construct that preempts the "new man" produced by the ordeal of castration. The "butch bottom" is very much a figure who occupies this role as the castrated son; and as a woman, having been "already castrated," she does not have to pass through the "ordeal." Unless, of course, that is her desire. Lesbian butch bottoms then, as opposed to gay butch bottoms or the "new" castrated men, would be much better positioned to *perform* the "ordeal" consensually.

The promise of the Deleuzean model falls away rather rapidly as we discover that the idealism of the masochist places the woman on top *as the fantasy construct of the masochist.* Not only does she facilitate the process of *his* "rebirth"—into a "new man" with "gynocratic" sensibilities, but she is also a derisory figure who becomes the externalized superego of the masochist. In this theory it is still a woman who must "save the world" by saving men from themselves. Freud's formula for sexual difference renders women the beloved and men the lovers. Deleuze merely reverses that formula, so that the "torturess" is the lover and the new castrated man is the beloved. Nothing really changes in this reversal except for the psychic identifications, which are still soldered to gender differences that are wed to the "facticity" of anatomically "correct" bodies. With Deleuze we are still in what Irigaray calls the "blind spot of an old dream of symmetry."[106] As long as we are caught in the web of the idealization of the phantasmatic mother, the repetition repeats without transformation. The Hegelian dialectic overtakes Deleuze's theory despite him. For the torturess ends up positioned as the "master," whose desire can never be realized because it is through her ministrations that he is able to transcend his slavishness. And the one from whom she demands recognition ends up unworthy to give it to her.

The most intriguing aspect of Deleuze's theory is that a woman can be the masochist herself, the one who appears to know that the sexual relationship is non-sense. As Lacan puts it: "what we are saying is that love is impossible, and that the sexual relation is engulfed in non-sense." And he adds: "we are talking about fucking . . . and we are saying that it is not working."[107] It is precisely this "fucking" that is not working that constitutes phallocentric sexuality—the desire *for* desire. Phallocentric sexuality does no *work*; it is unproductive; it makes nothing but more of the same. In my reading Lacan is implying that phallocentric sexuality is capitalistic. It reproduces *itself as a commodity*, which has the "value" of a symptom. The sexual idealist yearns for a prediscursive sexuality, the "flesh" prior to the construction of the body in discourse. Woman, who does not exist in this formula, is the object of that desire, hence the impossibility of the sexual relationship. She is also, however, the fantasy figure of its *possibility*, hence the repetition. Reading Lacan, we might interpret what he is saying this way: Woman is the body that makes non-sense of the sexual relationship, while women are the flesh that threaten to disrupt the dominant discourse on sexuality by posing the fantasy of the prediscursive. When Lacan says that women are "not-all," that there is something in them that eludes discourse, one could interpret this comment as a figure that is psychically positioned in some male imaginaries as "flesh." And yet, in the endless circularity of the phallocratic economy, it is precisely this "not-all" that is repetitiously reconstructed *as the body*. In Lacanian desire the body does not become the flesh, the flesh becomes the body—women become Woman, the elusive object that is necessary to uphold the reproduction of man's desire—hence Irigaray's punning "hommo-sexuality."

If psychoanalytic theory purports to tell the truth about desire, Irigaray argues that the problem is that it stops at this truth, refusing to "interpret the historical determinants of its discourse."[108] She considers psychoanalysis to be a negative theology, since "what is postulated as the cause of desire is lack as such."[109] Is it possible for sadomasochistic sexuality performed between two women to take us somewhere other than inside the circle of this phallocentric model?

Mandy Merck has written that "whether or not we choose to historicize lesbian s/m as a 'new' sexuality emerging out of some as-yet-unidentified conjuncture of the psychic or social, it seems crucial to remember that its literature was composed in the circumstances (and the terms) . . . of the U.S. women's movement in the early 1980s, a period of fabled conflict over the politics of sexual practice ('the Sex Wars')."[110] Merck's question about history arises in the context of her discussion of various theories of lesbian s/m, which she succinctly summarizes at one point in her chapter: "[Parveen] Adams's, which absolves [s/m] from the inequities of both gender (the paternal phallus) and generation (maternal authority); [Julia] Creet's, which emphasizes maternal authority as the conscious focus of both desire and disappointment; and [Tania] Modleski's, which counterposes maternal authority to the gender system it both transmits and contests."[111]

Merck also refers to B. Ruby Rich's essay on the sex wars, and points out that Rich's discussion of "political correctness" in the role of *casus belli* "is matched with an equally notorious opponent"; she cites Rich as saying: "nowhere has this Manichean struggle between updated bourgeois respectability and its opposite become more attenuated than in the debate over lesbian sadomasochism." Merck implicitly agrees with Rich that lesbian s/m is an odd choice as the "bad girl" opponent when heterosexual sadomasochism, given its prominence and its perception as the embodiment of all that is "bad" about heterosexuality, would seem a much more likely site to contest.[112] It is striking to notice that the literature that defends and/or advocates heterosexual s/m is more likely to place it in a broad historical trajectory. The second chapter of Gloria Brame's *Different Loving*, for example, opens with the sentence: "the practices and desires we will examine are as old as eros," and the rest of the chapter traces the historical determinants of s/m practices, back through the nineteenth century with some even earlier historical allusions.[113] Lesbian s/m discussions, however, rarely historicize the practice any farther back than the early 1970s, and most contextualize it, if not assign it as an originary moment, within the sex wars of the 1980s. It is as if lesbian s/m is a relatively new phenomenon, disconnected from other historical antecedents, born *within* the contemporary women's movement. Thus Creet's analysis of lesbian s/m as a feminist "mother/daughter" affair stands out as one of the most historical of the essays. Merck is primarily concerned with how the practice came to be figured as an *ethical* issue, a question that on the face of it seems so obvious that we have forgotten to ask it. Referring to the abbreviation *s/m*, Merck compares the slash (/) to Barthes' *S/Z* or the British journal *m/f*, and remarks provocatively that the slash "suggests opposition without fixed content, content which the appropriately termed 'slash' both stands in for and cuts out. In the case of lesbian s/m, one interesting question is how feminism has read this opposition—how it has, in effect, read itself into it."[114] The "slash" that comes to my mind in this context is Lacan's famous slash *through* Woman, indicating that she does not exist. Merck's suggestion that the slash in s/m is a signifier standing in for something cut out leads us to ask what "content" is absent that the slash marks as a trace. As Merck theorizes, the slash between two terms sets up a rigid opposition and also signifies that there is something *missing*, which could, if retrieved, theoretically account for the slashed formulation. The grammatical sign thus seduces us to search for a missing content—an historical referent. Lacan's slash, by contrast, is a singular one that does not represent a division between but an erasure of the single term—the Woman—*who does not exist.* There is no ontological or historical grounding for the Woman in Lacan's theory. "She" has no referent in "reality," but only a phantasmatic existence in the masculine imaginary. (Women are, of course, another case altogether in Lacanian psychoanalysis).

Although I fully agree that lesbian s/m appeared in the lexicon as a term that emerged into wider consciousness during the sex wars, I am inclined to see and experience it as a phantasmatic construct. Which is *not* to say that it is not *real,* but it is to say that looking for the referent that the slash marks leaves us following not just ghosts but their shadows. The rhetorical debates about s/m have much more substance than the practice of s/m, and that is where the interest of most critics who write *about* lesbian s/m has seemed to lie. Testimonials, interviews, and autobiographical accounts of s/m, on the other hand, are much more interested in the experience of s/m transactions—the psychic and affective responses, their connections and disconnections to *each other*, rather than what they might refer to outside the transactions. I would suggest that the slash in lesbian s/m could refer to *itself.* To think of lesbian s/m in this way is to acknowledge the possibilities of its *self-referentiality*—that is, its performativity, which is the very mode that it has been denied. The slash may also perversely signify the difficulty of and reluctance to focus on lesbian s/m *as a practice,* for, oddly enough, theorists who have risked writing about s/m (most of them within an academic context where the "subject" itself is likely to cause controversy given that academia has no place marked out for this kind of research, no discipline where its analysis can be legitimated) have tended to de-eroticize it by avoiding looking directly at what corporeal and psychical *acts* constitute it.

Lesbian s/m then ironically becomes continually "dis-embodied" even as it is posited as the very embodiment of everything else to which it might refer. This negative embodiment is partly what constitutes its continual fascination. It evokes a doubled and contradictory gesture—to, at once, fill it with content *and* empty it out of all historical traces. The paradox (indeed even the *double* paradox) of its status is that part of what constitutes an s/m transaction is precisely this contradictory gesture of filling and emptying. I will be suggesting that in a number of ways s/m can be understood in just such terms, and that, furthermore, it is in the delicate, transient, and fleeting moment *in between* the desire to empty and fill that the s/m transaction is achieved.

Lesbian sadomasochism is a risky enterprise, a precarious and delicately negotiated act. The mantra "safe, sane, and consensual" is an ideal. No single one of these terms can be easily accessed or guaranteed. Although there is nothing inherent within the ritualized forms of the s/m scene itself that can fulfill such a desire, nor is there any promise that the enactment of the scene between two women in anyway guarantees that the exchange can take us elsewhere than the phallocentric circle, for one or both of the women are just as likely to have fully embraced this phallocentric model as not, nonetheless, lesbian s/m holds open the possibility for an expression of desire elsewhere—one that is *between the body and the flesh*. And that is a site worth looking at seriously, whether one elects to venture into these spaces herself.

Why Psychoanalysis?

Frequently, I have been critiqued by other feminists for engaging with psychoanalysis. I am interested in psychoanalytic models of masochism precisely because within them lesbian sadomasochism is theoretically impossible. This theoretical impossibility is intriguing because it opens a space that points to a certain "Platonism" in the psychoanalytic model of desire itself, for that model presumes a masculine libido as stabilizing, and any effort to account for women's desire outside the masculine model is therefore foreclosed. If for Hegel, as for Lacan, desire is the desire for desire, which constitutes self-consciousness, then what is the "self" that sexuality presumably shatters? Is there not still some notion of a "self" that is apprehended through becoming self-conscious?

Kristeva describes these "double or triple twists of what is commonly called female homosexuality, or lesbianism: 'I'm looking, as a man would, for a woman'; or else, 'I submit myself, as if I were a man who thought he was a woman, to a woman who thinks she is a man.'"[115] Such are the same twists that Bersani, Silverman, (whom I will discuss in chapter 3) Deleuze, and Freud make in the constitution of the sadomasochistic scenario. That is, it is either heterosexual or male homosexual. Kristeva rails against this "sadistic" economy that is "so violent as to obliterate the vagina" and asserts that the lesbian is a product of this economy. Her "vigilant war against her pre-Oedipal dependence on her mother . . . keeps her from discovering her own body as other, different, possessing a vagina."[116] Thus lesbianism is persistently reassimilated into a heterosexual model. Since lesbians of all persuasions do not exist in this economy [Kristeva cannot even write "female homosexual" without indicating its impossibility], and since masochism, in its subversive potentialities, is an entirely male affair, the lesbian masochist is doubly (perhaps even triply?) impossible. And yet, does this theory not rest finally on a notion of the "copy" as the likeness of a model that precedes it, in which the "truth" is accessible through appearances—re-semblances? Chapter 3 will take up this problem at length. Here I want to point out simply that lesbian theorists have produced a number of resistant readings to the Platonic model. For example, from a femme's perspective the erotic charge of the butch is certainly not in her travesty of the heterosexual man, nor is it exactly in her resemblance to him. Teresa de Lauretis has pointed out that the butch/femme couple is erotic not because "it represents heterosexual desire, but because it doesn't . . . it shows the uncanny distance . . . between desire . . . and the representation."[117] It is not, in other words, resemblance that produces the erotic charge as the model/copy paradigm would suggest; and yet, it is not correct either to say that the butch/femme couple does not in some sense produce a resemblance. However, it is I think to be understood as the effect of a resemblance that is exterior and opposed to the internal dissimilitude of the couple that does not appropriate the markings of heterosexuality but disappropriates them. The simulacrum occupies the site of the inappropriate.

The "top" and "bottom" of the lesbian s/m couple might be understood in a similar way. The relationship between the butch/femme couple and the s/m top/bottom is an issue that it is not my purpose to pursue here. But I think I can say without inciting too much disagreement that there has been a tendency to think of the couples as somewhat parallel. The butch is usually thought to be in some sense the "top," the partner who initiates, orchestrates the seduction, and commands the sexual exchange; whereas the femme submits to the seduction and allows herself to be mastered by the butch. The fluidity of these roles has been and continues to be the subject of much discussion within lesbian communities. Of course the assignation of these roles is all about negotiating the power relationships between lesbians, and the disparity between appearances and the reality of the exchange is captured in such lesbian rhetorical commonplaces as "butch in the streets, femme in the sheets."

The more recently constructed roles, butch-bottoms and femme-tops, point to the need within lesbian subcultures to complicate the paradoxes that inhere in sexual/power relationships. There is of course a basic absurdity in attempting to capture the complexities of sexual/power relationships in four categories; but they at least signal the beginning of a proliferation of categories. And they indicate that some lesbians are acutely aware of the inability to divorce power from sexuality and are intent on controlling or containing its excesses by creating some signifying system that attempts to negotiate what one can expect before one enters into sexual activity.

Whereas "vanilla" lesbians tend to be invested in a notion of love that is informed by an inheritance of Platonism's emphasis on the real [or true], lesbian sadomasochists directly defy this tradition, often in the most literal of ways. Thus lesbian s/m would seem to be in conflict with the Platonic tradition that informs the discourse of Western romanticism. S/m, as Deleuze claims, does in this sense overthrow Platonism. And yet, these accounts, both the fictive ones and most testimonials, usually recuperate an ideology of romantic love in their conclusions. Are these recuperations capitulations to the dominant discourse, or are these endings necessary in order to play out the trajectory of a desire that is fundamental to lesbian s/m eroticism? Consider these narrative endings:

> She brought me to my feet [the leather collar] fell to the floor. I rubbed my wrists. They felt curiously light without the bracelets. . . . Her boldness was more appealing than iron chains. Her confidence created an intangible bond between us.[118]

> "What a lucky dyke I am," she thought. "First I get to star in the most scary porn movie in the world, now I come home and find that my best darling girl is waiting for me, so I won't even have to jerk off before I catch up on my beauty sleep."[119]

> "I don't love you. But somebody is going to have to take care of you and teach you what's what. If I slap you around a little, it's to make sure you listen." I talk, she nods, we walk fast. It's cold. I take off my leather jacket and make her put it on.[120]

Although these endings are clearly marked as s/m (even the most "vanilla," the second narrative—realesbians don't "jerk off"), the emphasis on nurturing and continuance is common to most lesbian s/m narratives, fictional or testimonial. The "top" as fantasy/mother, unlike the ideal mother of patriarchal fiction who indoctrinates her daughter into passive conformity, pushes the submissive to test the limits of her endurance, encourages the expression of sexual desire without restraint, and offers a model of assertion—"her boldness," finally, "more appealing than iron chains."[121]

But in addition to this fantasy of a different kind of "mother," what is really striking about lesbian s/m narratives is the emphasis on a different model of continuance. It is possible to think of lesbian s/m as a desire to preserve the lesbian-feminist value of perpetuity, a desire that is perhaps so intense that it risks the appearance of a transvaluation of the terms that dominant discourse erects to serve monogamy. Perhaps s/m lesbians really do want what "marriage" promises but rarely delivers, but they are aware of the necessity for reinventing the possibility for commitment to be sustained. A crucial dynamic in s/m is, after all, suspense, which could be understood as a desire to extend the relationship for as long as possible. Masochists are particularly adept at turning delayed gratification into pleasure, and even when "consummation" occurs, the dynamic is not to arrive at an endpoint but to reproduce the conditions that guarantee the necessity for endless returns.

Desire's Time

In the same interview in which Foucault explodes with laughter at the notion of lesbianism as constructed in the American academy, he is asked to speak about sadomasochism. Thinking about men, he offers the opinion that sexual experiences are so frequent and common that they have become banal, and that s/m is an attempt to introduce a tension that sustains novelty. S/m, he argues, is fascinating because it is a relationship that is at once "regulated and open," resembling a "chess game in the sense that one can win and the other lose."[122] The metaphor may at first confound the desire for perpetuity, for although the game can continue for a very long time, one player must finally lose and one win, unless a stalemate or draw occurs.

But the question of what "losing" means within the s/m dynamic is not at all clear. What is it that is "lost" when the bottom gives up? By giving in to her desire, she is giving up the desire to desire.[123] She may also be giving up the desire for desire, but she is always already foreclosed from that desire anyway. And doesn't the "top" also "give up" when she gives in? One point on which all sadomasochists agree is that the surrender is mutual or it is not s/m.

Foucault argues that the combination of regulation (discipline) and openness has the effect of "intensifying sexual relations by introducing a perpetual novelty, a perpetual tension, and a perpetual uncertainty which the simple consummation of the act lacks."[124] There is an odd parallel here with the way in which lesbian feminists focus on permanence, commitment, endurance. The conjunction that is unusual is in the use of *perpetual* to modify novelty, tension, and uncertainty. Again we are in the realm of rather oxymoronic constructions that are not intelligible from the perspective of Western heterosexual courtship rituals and romantic commitments that link permanency not with change or innovation but with constancy and stasis, not with tension or resistance but with merging, not with uncertainty but with reliability.

But if all desire is the perpetual pursuit of a lost object, s/m is the sexual practice that formalizes desire, repeating its movement with consciousness, deliberation, and ritualized control. Ironically, the dissenting majority's objection to s/m often points to the absence of restraint that is precisely what s/m practice seeks to contain. What many practitioners find so appealing about s/m are the boundaries that it establishes, the rules it institutes, the directness of its negotiations. The fantasy of s/m is partly in knowing exactly what one wants from someone else, what effect a certain behavior will produce, what the consequences of a certain action will be. This is an impossible dream, for desire always exceeds any contractual arrangement.

Yet, s/m could represent a yearning for fidelity. For at the heart of the contract is a desire to guarantee loyalty, and entering into it is an act of faith. Nothing really "binds" the participants except for each other's words. We might understand the actualization of bondage as an attempt to signify the signifiers of the contract. S/m acts out the word as bond—it effectuates the "performativity" of language. It is an acting out of commitment, a willingness to be transformed through the recognition of the other. In this sense it seems to differ little from the traditional values of romantic love, which "vanilla" lesbians purportedly endorse. But much more self-consciously, s/m recognizes the body as the site of these transactions, and it resists the abstraction of the body as a signifier that refers only to itself. It's not about "speaking sex," it's about doing it, and it insists upon the distinction. For the s/m practitioner, the signifier alone is not enough to provide enjoyment. In speech-act theory, the order of the performative banishes the master signifier, hence there is no longer a universal model. Lacan suggests that without the master signifier nothing is permitted ("if God does not exist everything is *prohibited*"),[125] revealing what I have suggested is a kind of Platonic nostalgia in psychoanalysis—a cruel sentimentality that longs for order, control, and discipline.

If Austin's "performatives" are equivalent to Lacan's "full speech," the examples that Lacan offers sound curiously like the language of s/m: "You are my master," "You are the one who will follow me."[126] Mikkel Borch-Jacobsen points out that Lacan understands "full speech" in a "quasi-feudal sense: full, authentic speech . . . is the speech in which one gives one's word, one's fealty (from the same root, *fides*, as 'faith')."[127] In the absence of the universal signifier, someone has to take command in order for action to occur. Predicated on lack, the psychoanalytic economy of desire renders the sexual relation impossible—trapped in the impasse of the "Master."

If psychoanalysis, as Irigaray has suggested, is the "negative of theology," s/m may be a kind of secularized/sexualized perversion of cultural feminism's worship of the goddess, a conjoining of the prostitute and the priestess, more terrifying in its proximity than in its difference. The redemptive rhetoric in some s/m testimonials is strikingly pervasive. For example, in the collection *Leatherfolk*, s/m is frequently described as a healing experience. Redemption figures in these accounts not as parodic distance from the normative order of things but as accessing a "whole" or "real" self that has been fractured or damaged by the imposition of normalizing conventions. In his introduction Mark Thompson refers to s/m as the "healing of wounds that keep us from living fully." He continues in this vein: s/m "cauterizes our hurt, mends our shame, helps clear out the psychic basement, undo memories of the past."[128] Other contributors expand and elaborate Thompson's metaphors, persistently conceptualizing s/m as a journey toward truth—an "ecstatic revelation."[129] When Thompson describes the s/m journey as a "passage from the unconscious underworld to the above world of realization and present light," it is irresistibly tempting to think of this account in terms of the Platonic traveler who makes a journey from the fetters of the senses (the "darkness" of the physical) to the dazzling freedom of the world of the mind. But of course the s/m journey inverts this telos, for it is through the senses that the s/m practitioner reaches the "light of the mind," or rather yet—its "darkness." One tenacious bottom says simply: "When I get there, I get real."[130] Such ardent testimonies are persuasive of its truth for some practitioners. For some, s/m is figured as a rite of passage, an initiation rite, or the acting out of destructive fantasies in order to transcend them. One contributor says this bluntly: "when we act out these fantasies, we, in a way, kill them off."[131]

In this rhetoric s/m becomes reparative or restorative; and the formalization of its practices suggests a ritual that is repeated in order to recuperate losses or heal the wounds of life. S/m, then, implicitly begins to take on the shape of an art form that is counterpoised to life, and in this opposition its acting out becomes an artistic performance that is more "real" than life itself. "Above and beyond the boundaries of time, the boundaries of life and death, there is a greater truth in visions,"[132] Thompson writes. In this way s/m becomes expressed as a journey in which there is no truth prior to the experience but one at the journey's end. Nonetheless, this "end-truth" is somehow always already there, for it is a presupposition of the desire to make the journey itself. In this sense s/m takes on both a redemptive and pastoralizing tone, partaking in the discourses of sacrifice, amendment, atonement. Not, however, in the service of those who have "sinned," but as compensation for those who have been sinned against. It thus perverts the Christian discourse of redemption—for rather than a sacrifice made by one who stands in the place of the "master" in order to redeem the sinners (who "know not what they do") the s/m practitioner disarticulates the "body" as it has been disfiguratively constructed and makes of it "flesh"—

remodeling what matters into a queer speech that cannot be heard without (sur)passing the surface/depth model of "life."

Pat Califia ends her introduction to *Macho Sluts* with a strange juxtaposition about the death of God and the safety of the top: "I don't believe in an omnipotent, omniscient God," she says, because "that would make the world a truly horrible place, beyond human redemption."[133] Yet she implies that a yearning for an absolute is constitutive of sexual desire. Rather than denying it, she suggests a perverse alternative that "turns away" from the phallus as transcendental signifier: "if you'd feel safer spending a night with one of them than you would with me or some other macho slut, I'll remember you in my prayers."[134] Thus she lures the novice, the initiate, to enter into the temple/dungeon where tops compete for the reputation of safest, and it is not just about who aims her whip with the greatest precision.

this time after sex, is not a time for love and its terms of annihilation. it's a time to gather life into yourself and to live
the moments in your cunt, for myself. instead i play
again with the pressure of your prick weighing down
my cervix, the depth of laughter on the same side as
the fear this gives rise to.
if i had a cock that's how i'd fuck, she said.
what do you mean. if.

—Anna Munster, *Kink*

3 • Doing It Anyway: The Impossible-Real

> Analogies depend upon maintaining the space between the lines, the categories of difference, the notions of consistency, the theoretical profile of singularity, purity, and detachment.
>
> —Judith Roof, *A Lure of Knowledge*

The above citation is from Judith Roof's critique of analogical thinking in feminist literary criticism, "All Analogies are Faulty." Roof's absolutism makes me uneasy. I agree that "analogies [can] abstract, separate, and distance terms from their original, perhaps fearsome, referents,"[1] and to Roof's observation that analogical thinking often signals a fear of intimacy I would add that the "object" of this fear is often one's own most intimate "others"— that is, those differences within that are displaced and reconfigured as differences between. Nevertheless, I would be cautious about erasing all analogical processes, for it could lead to a relativism that makes political interventions difficult if not impossible. Even so, one can see why Roof would be tempted to espouse such an absolutist position, for generally analogies can lead to the crudest of comparisons, more often than not based on an economy of the visible/visual that reifies hierarchies and ignores the complex vagaries of the optical field.

Analogical thinking is the staple of feminist arguments against sadomasochism, and it is here that we can see how faulty and politically pernicious analogies can be. In two anthologies published over a decade apart, *Against Sadomasochism: A Radical Feminist Analysis* (1982) and *Unleashing Feminism: Critiquing Lesbian Sadomasochism in the Gay Nineties* (1993), most of the contributors rely on drawing analogies at one point or another in their arguments. Basing their comparisons on sometimes the vaguest resemblances, they level all experiences and histories into sameness, uncritically endorse and privilege empiricism, repeat and perpetuate the notion of an unmediated access to the truth of perception, and, once again, knowing collapses into seeing. Take your pick: sadomasochism looks like and therefore is like—Slavery, the Holocaust, Heterosexist Patriarchy, the Jonestown Massacre. Sheila Jeffreys's classic attack on sadomasochism juxtaposes a description of SS men torturing a gay man to death with advice from a lesbian safer sex manual about how to trim your nails and lube your hand for fisting.[2] Jamie Lee Evans tries to convince us that just as the Los Angeles police claimed that Rodney King could have stopped the beating whenever he chose, so lesbian sadomasochists tell us that the bottom is the one who is really in control.[3]

Whatever the choice of the first term in these analogies, the presumption remains that lesbian sadomasochism is a copy, an iconic reproduction of the oppressive model. This presumption cuts two ways. For the Platonic spectator, lesbian s/m can be derided for merely approximating the original, as Leo Bersani argues that the straight macho man can look at a leather queen and deride him for his poor imitation.[4] Or, as feminists against s/m claim, the lesbian sadomasochist should be chastised for desiring to emulate the model. In either case these spectators assume a resemblance between the model and the copy that presupposes an internal similarity. If one simply looks at the images of lesbian sadomasochism—the whips, chains, handcuffs, needles, razors, and other instruments; the bodies bound, gagged, tied, and suspended; the humiliating postures of the submissives; the military garb—it is easy to see how these representations are read as iconic. But the mechanism for seeing them as such is resemblance, which proceeds from a thing to an Idea. As Foucault reminds us: "Resemblance presupposes a primary reference that prescribes and classes. . . . Resemblance serves representation, which rules over it . . . predicat[ing] itself upon a model it must return to and reveal."[5]

Thinking outside this visual economy, where lesbians can only perform re-semblances, we could regard the value of dis-semblance to lesbian s/m, as impersonations that are not mimesis but mimicry. In her reading of the third section of Luce Irigaray's *Speculum of the Other Woman*, "Plato's Hystera," Elin Diamond gives us just such a way when she argues that Irigaray posits "two mimetic systems that exist simultaneously, one repressed by the other."[6] The first system she calls "patriarchal mimesis," in which the "model, the Form or Ideal, is distinguishable from and transcendently beyond 'shadows—images in the mirror—mere copies.'"[7] This is traditional mimesis, the system that is not repressed. But Diamond ferrets out another system in Irigaray's text, one that subverts the first one, which she calls "mimesis-mimicry, in which the production of objects, shadows, and voices is excessive to the truth/illusion structure of mimesis, spilling into mimicry, multiple 'fake offspring.'"[8]

Homi Bhabha's theory of colonial mimicry as a "desire for a reformed, recognizable Other as a subject of difference that is almost the same, but not quite"[9] is also a useful way to articulate the dis-semblances of s/m. Bhabha's mimicry is a double articulation, a sign that retains the power of resemblance but menaces the authoritative discourse of colonialism by disclosing its ambivalence. Mimicry, as Bhabha describes it, is profoundly disturbing to a dominant discourse because it points out the necessity of producing prohibitions within in order to reproduce. Mimicry repeats rather than re-presents; it is a repetition that is nonreproductive. Mimesis operates in the order of the model/copy. Mimicry performs its operations in the realm of the simulacrum.

Deleuze argues that the simulacrum is "an image without resemblance," but then, not quite. The simulacrum "still produces an effect of resemblance,"[10] but it is a looking like that takes place in the trick mirror where the spectator lacks mastery. The observer cannot dominate the simulacrum because it has already incorporated her point of view. Before the simulacrum, the spectator is mastered. If we think of the erotic interplay of lesbian s/m as resignifications that are no doubt enabled by certain heterosexual or homosexual models but at the same time are dissonant displacements of them, we might move toward a better understanding of their erotic dynamics and better grasp the political and ethical controversies they have raised.

If some feminists insist that lesbian s/m is merely re-semblance, according to the psychoanalytic paradigm, lesbian s/m is only a semblance, at best. Radical feminism and psychoanalysis seem to have little in common. If the former sometimes takes the position that women are masochists who need to have their consciousness raised, the latter theorizes that lesbian sadomasochism is impossible. The convergence of these two seemingly antithetical discourses produces a figure without ground, whose paradoxical (non)existence is the terrain this writing will survey.

Femininity and Ontological Masochism

The essayists in *Unleashing Feminism* continue to see many of the same problems that plagued the women's movement in the 1970s. In *A Taste for Pain* Maria Marcus remembers a women's studies conference in 1972 when Germaine Greer, the keynote speaker, was interrupted by a young woman from the audience who suddenly cried out: "But how can we start a women's movement when I bet three-quarters of us sitting in this room are masochists?" Greer replied: "Yes, we know women are masochists—that's what it's all about!"[11] Although nearly thirty years later, I am more likely to hear the complaint that all women are masochists in the context of lesbians lamenting the scarcity of tops in the community, the mainstream, public image of feminism is still much closer to the attitudes expressed by antiporn/s/m feminists. For example, it is striking to notice that in a recent issue of *Ms.* magazine, the panelists who are brought together to discuss pornography still tend to be dominated by the Mackinnon/Dworkin theory that all pornography promotes and produces violence against women. Although Marilyn French exhorts the panel to stop "tiptoeing around" the issue of censorship within feminist ranks, this panel hedges on the "problem" of porn created by and for women. When Andrea Dworkin is pushed into declaring her position, she says: "they are reifying the status quo. And I think that lesbian pornography is extremely male-identified."[12]

Ironically, while feminists continue to argue with each other about lesbian sexual practices, *masochism*, the term that has become synonymous for some feminists with internalized oppression, has undergone a theoretical renaissance in which the erotics of submission have been reclaimed by a diverse group of scholars as an emancipatory sexuality for men. Leo Bersani's argument, which strikingly concluded that "sexuality—at least in the mode in which it is constituted—could be thought of as a tautology for masochism,"[13] led the way in rendering arguments about the relationship between the fore-pleasures of the erotogenic zones (strongly associated with both femininity and the "perversions") and the end pleasures of discharge (the ejaculatory climax associated with masculinity) irrelevant. However, in his latest work, *Homos*, Bersani criticizes Foucault for "rescuing us from penile tyranny [and] sexual machismo." In this later reading Bersani is concerned that the ejaculatory climax associated with masculinity is requisite for the liberation of male sexuality from sexual machismo: "The body liberated from what Foucault scornfully called the machismo of proud male ejaculation is also the male body liberated from what may be its first experience, at once sobering and thrilling, of the limits of power."[14] Here Bersani is referring to masturbation, a practice, he argues, that teaches the boy his first lesson in qualified mastery, for the hand that would rule is instead disciplined by the penis, and so it was "perhaps in early play with that much-shamed organ that we (sic) learned about the *rhythms* of power, and we were or should have been initiated into the biological connection between male sexuality and surrender or passivity—a connection that men have been remarkably successful in persuading women to consider nonexistent."[15] This is a clever and complex rendering of a reason to "sing the praise of the penis,"[16] and Bersani is quite right that men have successfully convinced women that the jouissance of ejaculation has little to do with male passivity. Men have also been remarkably successful in convincing themselves that ejaculatory pleasure has little to do with passivity. Bersani introduces a utopian reading here that is theoretically provocative but promises something that is a long way from fulfillment. As Bersani reads Freud, sexuality is the dialectic of seeking the end of pleasure through discharge and repeating the tension in order to increase it. Thus Bersani concludes that sexuality is masochistic and that "*masochism serves life,*" for it is what allows the individual to "survive the gap between the period of shattering stimuli and the development of resistant or defensive ego structures."[17] Masochism, far from being a reversal of sadism or an internalization of oppressive patriarchal norms, is, according to Bersani, a survival mechanism.

Although his notion of a sexual ontology is clearly problematic, nevertheless, Bersani's theory has the advantage of freeing sexuality from parental identifications where sexual difference seems to get unavoidably reproduced. Furthermore, Bersani's theory challenges the teleological narrative that ends with heterosexual genital sex. Thus, in his view: "sadomasochistic sexuality would be a kind of melodramatic version of the constitution of sexuality itself, and the marginality of sadomasochism would consist of nothing less than its isolating, even its making visible, the ontological grounds of the sexual."[18]

For feminists who are struggling to articulate a sexual subjectivity that does not submit to the psychoanalytic imperative of an exclusively masculine libido, which ineluctably consigns femininity to a masculinized fetish, Bersani's theory might be welcomed since it takes us out of the discourse of the symptom into a "*nonreferential version of sexualized thought.*"[19] Parental identifications, which inevitably reify Oedipus, are no longer constitutive; and the "lost object," which is relentlessly relegated to a feminized fetish, is diffused so that any object and any part of the body can become an erotogenic zone. This theory does not of course undo the historical/social attribution of masochism to women, but it does suggest a psychic model in which the sexual positions one takes up are not necessarily gendered.

Nevertheless, Bersani implicitly assumes the now privileged masochistic position as a male prerogative and hence, once again, sexuality itself is claimed for men. This move is clearer in his essay "Is the Rectum a Grave?" where he describes the dominant culture's "unconsciously represented—[but] infinitely more seductive and intolerable image of a grown man, legs high in the air, unable to refuse the suicidal ecstasy of being a woman."[20] In *Homos* Bersani extends this scenario by tentatively suggesting that the sexological category of male homosexuality, "a woman in a man's body," though certainly an "imprisoning definition" may nonetheless provide more opportunities for (male) sexual pleasures, since it leaves open the possibilities of fantasizing about a woman's desiring positions. These would include: the wish to be phallically penetrated, the love of himself through the desiring of a boy, or an oral desire that would be best satisfied through sex with a lesbian.[21] While I have no quarrel whatsoever with gay or straight men assuming the various desiring fantasies that are usually attributed to women (and indeed I would agree with Bersani that such psychic mobilities could be salutary for overcoming male sexuality's propensity for dominance), I do find it disconcerting that Bersani openly proclaims that he can only speak for male sexuality, while with his other hand he presumes to know what constitutes a woman's desiring fantasies. Furthermore, and more important, this appropriation of female sexualities is firmly grounded in the assumption of the "real" of morphological differences. For Bersani constantly refers to the act of penetration and the inevitability of the anatomical differences between males and females. Thus his psychic liberatory scheme for men is grounded in a reification of the body as flesh. And though the "flesh" to which he refers is the penis, the "real" of that flesh depends on the assumption that women are at once devoid of that particular "flesh" and constitutive of the ground on which its realness is sustained. Thus for all of his creative recombinations of sexual pleasures and acts, Bersani reinstates the psychoanalytic orthodoxy.

His gay man who assumes the position of a woman's "suicidal ecstasy" is a graphic reenactment of Freud's third form of masochism, "feminine masochism," which Freud also presumes to be occupied by a male subject in a feminine situation. The male subject in this space signifies "being castrated, or copulated with, or giving birth to a baby."[22] Since women ostensibly already experience one or more of the above, the notion of a feminine "feminine masochism" is redundant at best, if not impossible. According to this logic, women cannot *perform* the masochistic role because they *are* masochists. To borrow J. L. Austin's terms, masculine feminine masochism would be performative, while feminine feminine masochism would be constative.[23] Male masochism would not report or describe anything; it would be a doing rather than a describing; it would perform not after but before the referent. Feminine masochism, on the other hand, would merely report an adequation; it would correspond with the "facts" of femininity. If sadomasochism is a melodramatic version of sexuality itself, women have ironically been barred from playing on two stages—the melodramatic and the masochistic—that in all other contexts have seemed to most suit them.

Kaja Silverman acknowledges that psychoanalytic sexual difference relegates female masochism to a virtually ontological condition when she defends her focus on male subjectivity by explaining that the female sub-

ject's masochism is difficult to conceptualize as perverse because it represents "such a logical extension of those desires which are assumed to be 'natural' for the female subject."[24] She nonetheless unproblematically accepts
and repeats the terms of a psychoanalytic symbolic in which there is only
one libido and it is masculine. Women are denied sexual agency because
they are incapable of mimesis. Their options are to take up the position of
passive "normal femininity," or to reverse the position and appropriate
masculine subjectivity and its desires, in which case they can "perform" sexuality, but only through their "masculinity complex." Bersani's desire is
aimed at the pleasures gay men might experience from an alignment with
femininity. Silverman also appropriates femininity, though her project is to
produce a revolutionary subject in a "feminine" yet heterosexual man. Both
of these analyses add weight to feminist arguments against sadomasochism,
for following their logic the lesbian masochist is either enacting the dominant culture's degradation of women or she is playing out the desire to be
a man. In either case, the terms of sexual difference remain intact. These
theories that posit male masochism as emancipatory thus continue to
depend on the impossibility of desire between women. In this context,
truth claims about lesbian sexuality such as this one made by Jan Brown,
"We practice the kind of sex in which cruelty has value, where mercy does
not. . . . What keeps those of us who refused to abandon our 'unacceptable'
fantasies sane is the knowledge that there are others like us who would not
leave because we scream 'Kill me,' at the moment we orgasm. . . . We lied
to you about controlling the fantasy. It is the lack of control that makes us
come, that has the only power to move us,"[25] would easily fall prey to the
argument that lesbian sadomasochists are merely reproducing heterosexist
models or, at best, male homosocial ones.

Practicing lesbian sadomasochists have themselves, however, colluded in
the assumption that s/m is only a temporary retreat, or a thoroughfare to
more "mature" forms of sexual practice. For example, a referent for Brown's
"lies" might be located in earlier rhetoric by s/m practitioners who justified
the acting out of their fantasies by claiming they were means of exorcizing
their real hold on the individual. Tacitly accepting the contention that s/m
lesbians had internalized cultural misogyny, these defenses asked for a toler-
ant reprieve, a period of playing through the fantasies in order to transcend
them. S/m then, ironically, became therapeutic, like a homeopathic cure.

Theatrical metaphors were central to this defense. Susan Farr, for example, described s/m as "pure theater," "a drama [in which] two principals . . .
act at being master and slave, play at being fearsome and fearful." She cites
the clues to the drama in the interchangeableness of the roles and the repet-

itive, scripted dialogue. Even though she acknowledges that much of the scene may be "pure improvisation," it is still "theater."[26] This dialectic between the scriptural and the spontaneous is pervasive in pro-s/m accounts. On the one hand, there is the insistence that the scene is rigidly controlled, with a decided emphasis on the bottom's mastery of the limits. On the other hand, the eroticism depends on the anticipation that the limits will be pushed to the breaking point, that the "scene" will cross over into the "real."

To a certain extent, the controversy about whether s/m is "real" or performed is naive, since we are always already in representation even when we are enacting our seemingly most private fantasies. The extent to which we recognize the presence of the edge of the stage may determine what kind of performance we are enacting, but willing ourselves to forget the stage altogether is not to return to the real, as s/m opponents would have it; rather, this will to forget is classical mimesis, which, as Derrida points out, is "the most naive form of representation."[27] Nevertheless, it is precisely this most naïve form of representation that would seem to be the most desirable of sexual performances. Bersani's objections to the frequent theorization of such things as "the gay-macho style, the butch-fem lesbian couple, and gay and lesbian sado-masochism" as "subversive parodies of the very formations and behaviors they appear to ape," rather than "unqualified and uncontrollable complicities with, correlatively, "a brutal and misogynous ideal of masculinity" [gay macho] . . . "the heterosexual couple permanently locked into a power structure of male sexual and social mastery over female sexual and social passivity" [butch/femme], or "fascism" [s/m], are clearly based on his contention that these sexual practices are not performative. Parody, Bersani states emphatically, "is an erotic turn-off, and all gay men know this."[28] Although Bersani audaciously speaks for all gay men, I would have to agree with him and add that many lesbians know this too. Self-conscious mimicry of heterosexuality is a sideshow; when the main act comes to town, we all want the "real thing," or, more precisely, we all want the Real thing. That is, sexuality is always, I think, about our desire for the impossible-real, not the real of the illusion that passes for reality, but the Real that eludes symbolization.

Whereas early radical lesbians spoke of a contest between "realesbians" and imposters, as psychoanalysis would have it, lesbians are the Real. If the "realesbian" of lesbian-feminism was a socially impossible identity, in the psychoanalytic symbolic lesbians are only possible in/as the "Real," since they are foreclosed from the Symbolic order—they drop out of symbolization. If they can be signified at all it is only as an algebraic x. Given that the "Real" is, in part, the brute, inscrutable core of existence, the "Real" lesbian is in this sense coincident with the "realesbian." Hence as both real/Real, these figures make her "identical with [her] existence—self-identical—raw, sudden, and unfettered," but impossible to "see, speak or to hear, since in any case [she] is always already there."[29] As Judith Butler has put it: "In a sense, lesbian sexuality is not even thought of as the forbidden, for to be forbidden is still to be produced as a prohibited or censored object . . . lesbian sexuality cannot even enter into the parameters of thought itself; lesbianism is here the phantasm of the phantasm."[30]

This contest between the "real" and the "performative" has often focused on the instrumentality of "objects" that are implicitly deemed "unnatural." One sexual practice that has generated enormous controversy among lesbians is the use of dildos. This site of contestation is paradoxical because it refers to a practice that at once is among the most common (mis?)conceptions of "what lesbians do" while at the same time it poses one of the greatest offenses. Since the use of dildos practically signifies lesbianism as such, one could read this objection to their use as an indication that it is not so much what lesbians do that is a matter of concern (most people don't seem to have the slightest idea what we do anyway); rather, it is the very issue of being lesbians that is found offensive. Of course lesbians as well as heterosexual women have always used various instruments for penetration. The Oxford English Dictionary lists references to dildos made of glass and wax as early as the late sixteenth century. Although the word is cited as being of "obscure origin, used in the refrains of ballads," it also was a "contemptuous or reviling appellation of a man," as, indeed, it remains so today. By 1647 it is clear that the dildo refers to an instrument used for a "lady's pleasure," as in this humorous entry: "The very sight of this Madam with a Dildoe . . . put the House into a great silence."[31]

Havelock Ellis refers to the use of dildos by women repeatedly in his footnotes, although he takes care to specify that they were of "foreign" origin and renowned for being used by women outside his Anglo-Eurocentric frame of mind.[32] In other words, to put it bluntly, Ellis found that only women of color—the "real" lesbians, used dildos. Amidst all the discussions about the phallus/penis relationship, it is most often forgotten that the dildo is racialized. Alycee J. Lane asks: "What does it mean, exactly, when white hegemony extends to the production of dildos?" Lane's narrative of her trip to a sex shop to buy a dildo to replace her well-worn standard six-inch mauve model, which her friends complained would be an inappropriate image for her article—"what would women think seeing this used mauve dildo strapped to brown thighs? Honey, please"—is instructive. Interestingly, no dildo strapped to any color thigh appears with the article; rather a simple image of a black dildo appears—one of average size, not the "twenty-four inch, thick as my arm, monstrosities with wrappers reading 'Big Black Dick' " that the cashier shows her when she demands to see a brown dildo. Lane looks around for some "Big White Dick" or "Big Flesh Colored Dick" in vain. So, she concludes, "What's race got to do with dildos?"[33] Her question is, in part, rhetorical; her answer already implied in her seriously humorous narrative. Cherry Smyth begins her article "Crossing the Tracks" with a citation from Jackie Goldsby: "dykes politicize race, gay men eroticize it," then goes on to argue that the intensity with which lesbians "glorify diversity" leads to an objectification of race that is as troublesome as the ways in which gay men eroticize it. Smyth surveys a number of contemporary films by lesbians to show that, while interracial couples are frequently featured, the woman of color is often represented in various familiar stereotypes—"the political spokesperson . . . the infantilized child . . . [but] seldom is race ever discussed or even acknowledged between the lovers or in their social context."[34] Negotiating power within interracial lesbian sexualities, particularly when it is couched in terms of dominance and submission, is particularly tricky. White lesbians often assume that all women of color, particularly black women, are butch (and top butches at that), a complicated recognition that, I think, contains elements of social and historical guilt, which becomes eroticized (hence it is the white lesbian's historical legacy/revisionism and her strategy for overcoming it that makes submitting to a woman of color pleasurable). It is also, however, a trace leftover from the genealogy of race, gender, and sexual identities as they have been historically constructed. For if white women have been socially positioned as the holders of "femininity" and the "keepers" of civilization, a two-gendered system leaves no place other than "masculinity" to be occupied by everyone else. Of course white supremacy doesn't really operate on a "two-party" gendered system but, rather, as a triad in which those who cannot take or are not allowed to take a position on one side or the other occupy the category of abjection (if they are not evicted or annihilated). The abject is subsequently a non- or less-than-human positionality, and white supremacy keeps it open as an active category for channeling all their racially othered as well as their sexual "others." These two groups, however, are not discrete in the white supremacist imaginary. During the sex/culture wars it was not uncommon to hear people saying that homosexuality had come to occupy the place where race was once positioned in conservative ideologies. And statements such as B. Ruby Rich's, that "race occupies the place vacated by gender" (here she is speaking of interracial couples in lesbian films) repeat the gender/race/sexuality divide. I agree with Rich that queers can have a different perspective on race than heterosexuality as an institution has and does, but heterosexuality as an institution is largely an effect (as well as a cause) of white supremacy. When white lesbians strap on those "big black dicks," is the fantasy the same as the dominant culture's mythical eroticization of the black male's hypervirility? Does this myth simply get transferred onto women of color within a lesbian sexual dynamic thereby repeating, in fantasy, the white heterosexual dynamic? Or do white women carry with them into the lesbian interracial exchange the already "masculinized" cultural history of the person of color, disregarding gender since it is a white construct?

One of the issues that is scarcely touched by the New Right in their assaults on representation is race. Although *race* appears in the litany of the Helms amendment, the culture wars are generally perceived as contestations over representations of various forms of sexuality. And race virtually drops out of the discussion during the sex wars, though it does notably appear as a term used by lesbians against pornography and sadomasochism. As I have pointed out before, however, this use of race in the sex wars contains within it an objection to "male-identifications," which then effectively reinscribes "femininity" as the sole province of white women. And in the presumably distinct culture wars, the censoring of the two artists whose work launched the debates—Robert Mapplethorpe and Andres Serrano—was couched in terms of obscenity, blasphemy, sacrilege, and indecency, with little if any attention from the conservatives to the ways in which race was signifying in these representations, despite Mapplethorpe's concentration on photographing men of color in erotic poses and Serrano's "coloring" of traditional images of Christianity.[35] When one examines the contents of *Forbidden Passages: Writings Banned in Canada*, it is first surprising to see that bell hooks's work is included along with a majority of representations of sexuality by white writers and a few women and men of color whose work is clearly about graphic depictions of sexuality. But when one takes into consideration this historical imbrication of race and sexuality, the inclusion of bell hooks in *Forbidden Passages* becomes one of the rarely manifest signs that operating in and through the discourse of sexual identities and practices is a strategically undisclosed white supremacist ideology that achieves its agenda through categorical purification. It is not, then, that the focus has shifted from race to sexuality in the New Right's conservative assaults. Rather, this virtual elision of race is yet another ruse of a white supremacist resurgence that creates the illusion of transference by and through maintaining the "integrity" of the categories of race and sexuality. It is impossible to expect that queer communities will be able to simply sidestep these complex historical inscriptions. But it is all the more important that we attend to them with the utmost caution in order to rede-ploy them with political awareness.

It is rather curious that during the recent "sex wars" dildos have become a site of such heated contestation. As ordinary as they are, dildos (and particularly strap-ons) have managed to divide lesbians into two camps. Heather Findlay points out that critiques of the dildo have been couched in concert with objections to butch/femme and s/m—all three of them ostensibly signifying imitations of heterosexual patriarchy[36] Findlay traces this odd convergence to Freud's theory of fetishism, which, classically, is denied to women. Findlay shows that although Freud's theory of fetishism does not discuss dildos at all, nonetheless representations of dildos in lesbian magazines do conform to Freud's paradigm. Pointing particularly to the "Scorpio dildo products" that reproduce an image in many lesbian publications, Findlay analyzes this image—a dildo resting atop a mirror with a reflection of a penis behind it—as based on a comparison between the dildo and the penis. For Findlay the issue is one of substitution, which is where the two camps diverge. Are dildos "artificial" penis substitutes, or are they sex toys that have no relation to the "real" of the penis? Findlay's most innovative argument concerns the use of harnesses (the strap-ons), which are invariably made of black leather. Although she refers to this discussion as an "aside" in her article, I think it is a significant moment in her discussion. Given that strap-ons seem to be particularly onerous to many feminists, Findlay's point that the harness "may approximate the classical Freudian fetish more closely than the dildo, precisely because . . . the fetish usually refers metonymically"[37] can, in my reading, be taken two ways.

Although Findlay sees the two parts of her argument as confirmations of each other, I think there is another way to read the harness both within and against the theory of fetishism. On the one hand, she points out that the black leather harness "gains its allure from the fact that it is—like a woman's crotch—fleshy and dark," which would reinforce the most classical reading of the Freudian fetish. On the other hand, she points out that the hole in the harness, where the dildo is inserted and removed, "rehearses, in a literal manner, the traumatic primal experience of Freud's little fetishist: now she has it, now she doesn't."[38] Although it is certainly plausible to read the harness in both its material form and its functionality from the perspective of Freud's little boy who sees that the woman has been "castrated" and then reproduces the penis on the body of the woman to alleviate his terror of becoming the same, this is not the same scenario that lesbians enact when they strap it on and take it off. For Freud's little fetishist hallucinates the "return" of the penis onto the body of the woman. Freud's fetishism borders on a psychotic discourse. Perhaps I am being rather too literal-minded about this, but lesbians who use strap-on dildos certainly are playing with material objects—which more often now are made and produced by lesbians for lesbians—not penises that fantastically disappear and reappear. But perhaps this is, in part, a hidden key to the controversy. Findlay quotes an editor of *Off Our Backs*, who refers disparagingly to "games that rely on paraphernalia [and] roles."[39] The use of the word *paraphernalia* is certainly not an idiosyncratic reflex of this one writer but rather a frequent complaint voiced by critics in a variety of venues. The *New York Times*, for example, referred to Mapplethorpe's photographs as depictions of "anal and penile penetration with unusual objects," and the prosecutor in the Cincinnati trial used this as part of his claim that the photographs lacked artistic merit.[40] Perhaps we ought to consider why these devices, as such, are so peculiarly laden with opprobrium.

Dildos have their own specific histories, yet they fall generally within a class of objects that are grouped as prosthetics. What may come to mind immediately when one thinks of the dildo as a prosthetic device is precisely the objection to its use as a penis-substitute. Since the camp of feminists who are so opposed to the idea of a substitute are also generally aligned with the idealization of a "natural" sexuality, it makes sense that the dildo would be an object of derision, sometimes even fear. But let us look for a moment at the concept of the prosthesis.

In his stunning chapter on the use of artificial limbs in the postbellum era and their synedochical relationship to black labor and slavery, Stephen Best draws out some fascinating ideas that might be pertinent to this discussion as well. Best argues that prostheses operate according to a double logic: on the one hand, they "supplement, amplify and extend a naturally limited human flesh. . . . [They] 'lengthen' both in terms of time . . . and in terms of space . . . the human body's reach out into the world . . . extending the human agent's sphere of influence in the world beyond the narrow scope of his or her body."[41] At the same time, they "refashion" the human body and, given that this refashioning is based on a model/copy paradigm (the intent of the prosthesis being to imitate the "lost limb" as closely as possible), the double logic of the prostheses then follows two trajectories (which Best argues are "*seemingly* antithetical" (my emphasis). That is they suggest both "agency and inscription, articulation and interpellation; or, perhaps more simply, a dual type of agency."[42] In the context of Best's argument, where prosthetic devices (he is speaking specifically of artificial limbs fitted for white soldiers after the Civil War) refer in a way that both restores the illusory coherence of white masculinity and narrates the story of that coherency's dependency on the lack of black human agency, the double logic of the prosthesis does pose two trajectories that are seemingly antithetical but that intersect at this historical moment and in this context to produce the same effect: the reproduction of the coherence of white masculinity.

However, taken into a different context, the prosthetic device may operate differently. Or, perhaps it may operate similarly but produce a different political value. If we think of the dildo in these terms, it might be argued that the double logic is indeed merely seemingly antithetical. For certainly the dildo extends and lengthens the capacity for the human agent, but the question of whether it is a technology that does so at the expense of erasing another group's agency and producing it as a lack depends entirely, it seems to me, on the positionality of the perceiver—the location or scene of the psychic fantasy. While there is no question that the "Big Black Dick" version of the dildo reinstates and perpetuates racist and heterosexist mythologies, it is not clear for whom these articles are manufactured. Certainly lesbians of all colors use dildos of all colors, and the black dildo does, it seems to me, resonate with a particular potency that refers to the mythical hypervirility of men (and women) of color. The "Big Black Dick," however, seems to be something of a museum piece. It is hardly a practical, usable item that lesbians actually purchase. It appears more often in the sex shops that are designed to titillate white tourists who come to urban settings to gawk and become aroused by the blatant spectacle of "difference" that these shops invite. Queers do purchase items from these shops, but in the larger urban settings, where there is an identifiable gay and lesbian population, there are usually separate shops for purchasing sex toys, which cater discretely to a gay and lesbian clientele. The geographies of the scene in which these exchanges take place is not only a physical locale but also a psychic one.

Following Laplanche and Pontalis, Elizabeth Cowie reminds us that "Fantasy involves, is characterized by, not the achievement of the desired objects, but the arranging of, a setting out of, desire; a veritable mise-en-scène of desire." Thus fantasy is "more a setting out of lack, of what is absent, than a presentation of having, a being present. Desire itself coming into existence in the representation of lack, in the production of a fantasy of its becoming present."[43] Thus feminists who warn us against "politically recalcitrant fantasies," and appeal "for the discovery of a new feminist eroticism and fantasy, for which we are still waiting . . . will continue to wait, in as much as such a position misunderstands the mechanisms of fantasy."[44]

Foucault speaks of the project to detach erotic pleasure from its "virile form of compulsory pleasure which is jouissance . . . understood in the ejaculatory sense, in the masculine meaning of the word."[45]

As I have already pointed out, Bersani objects to Foucault on the grounds that this "rescue" actually erases the possibility for men to experience the eroticism of submission. Later, in the same essay, Bersani rereads the Wolf Man's dream, in which he awakens from a nap to see his mother and father in "coitus a tergo." Rather than interpreting it as Freud's classic primal scene in which the boy relinquishes his desire for his father through fear of castration (induced by the sight of his penis-less mother), Bersani offers a different reading, one based on the boy's detailed observation that the scene did not induce repression of desire for the father but, rather, as "he had observed [his] father's penis disappear . . . he had felt compassion for his father on that account, and had rejoiced at the reappearance of what he thought had been lost."[46] Based on this revised reading of "The Wolf Man," Bersani concludes his essay by constructing a newly imagined scenario of gay sex:

> We might imagine that a man being fucked is generously offering the sight of his own penis as a gift or even a replacement for what is temporarily being "lost" inside him—an offering not made in order to calm his partner's fears of castration but rather as a gratuitous and therefore even lovelier protectiveness that all human beings need when they take the risk of merging with another, of risking their own boundaries for the sake of self-dissolving extensions.[47]

As a lesbian, I can't help but wonder what it is that women offer each other as such a compensatory gift, especially if, as Bersani declares, all human beings need some kind of reassurance that the boundaries of their "selves" will not permanently dissolve when they risk the merging of sexuality. Furthermore, all human beings clearly do not experience the terror of merging that this scenario promises to alleviate. Indeed, femininity has been characterized as a psychic position in which merging is problematic not because it is so difficult to achieve but because it is too readily assumed. Although Bersani tenaciously ignores the sexuality of women, except to appropriate it in his own phantasmatic versions, he nonetheless introduces a very interesting possibility here, one that most women certainly could not have failed to notice: that in coitus (whether it is homosexual or heterosexual) it is the man's penis that "disappears" and then "reappears" on his body from the spectator's position. If Freud assumed that the primal scene was the site that induced castration anxiety, why should it necessarily have been the mother's body that the child sees as lacking the penis? If the "return" of the penis is not an hallucinatory psychic defense constructed at the sight of the woman's "mutilated" form but, rather, a quite literal child's eye view of the father's penis disappearing and then reappearing, then what happens to the whole theory of fetishism as a prerogative of the male child? The potential here is to restore theoretically the possibilities of "fetishistic" pleasure to women, which, despite Freudian theory, we nonetheless know that women engage anyway. If, as Laplanche and Pontalis have made clear, sexual fantasy is a location, a scene, not an ideation, then we are always in Blau's theater where there can be no performance whatsoever unless one takes into account who is seeing and from what position. Bersani makes clear that he can only speak for "male sexuality" and would no doubt have to qualify that rather large claim extensively. He would, at the very least, have to contend with males, who engage in a myriad of sexual practices and endorse a number of different identities, who do not find pleasure at all in this most "intense experience of [their] body's vulnerability."[48]

Donna Haraway argues that technological extensions of the human body—the "cyborg"—signify a range of "disturbingly and pleasurably tight coupling(s)," rendering "thoroughly ambiguous the difference between natural and artificial, mind and body, self-developing and externally designed" even the "boundary between physical and non-physical."[49] Stanley Aronowitz has argued that technology "throws the old metaphysical integrity of the 'self' into crisis,"[50] echoing Bersani's claim that sexuality itself is a "self-shattering" of the ego, a risk that one takes when one dares to allow one's boundaries to temporarily merge with another person's. But Bersani is speaking of sexual acts and, quite specifically, of the sexual act in which one man is in the "passive" position—is penetrated by another man.

I am suggesting here that the instrumentality of the dildo—as prosthesis, as "an artificial limb," may itself produce a similar self-shattering, or metaphysical crisis. But whose "self" is shattered? Who is experiencing the metaphysical crisis? It would seem that it would have to be the spectator, the one who is watching. It is primarily men and women who have not experimented with dildos, but who are observing images of them in lesbian sex magazines, videos, and sex shops, who are finding in them an optical shattering site. Lesbians who use dildos certainly do not speak of their experiences in these terms. They are either spoken of as playful instruments that are appreciated for their utility, their very ability to appear and disappear (into a dresser drawer) or, more often, they are eroticized as the real thing.

In fact, writers, visual artists, and practitioners have become increasingly assertive about claiming dildos as the "real thing." Although strap-ons are advertised as "toys," inside the narratives and testimonials of lesbian s/m practitioners references to an outside or a "model" are most often discarded in favor of descriptions that simply occupy the status of the real. So, for example, it has become common to speak of "watching her play with her dick," or "sucking her off," or "your dick find[ing] its way inside of me."[51] As one contributor to *Quim* puts it: "When I put on a strap-on I feel male. I feel my dick as real otherwise I can't use it well."[52] Rarely if ever does one find lesbian erotica that refers to the dildo as a joke, an imitation, or a substitute, whether these narratives are explicitly in an s/m context or in the more prevalent accounts of butch/femme vanilla erotica. On the contrary, the erotic charge of these narratives depends on both tops and bottoms, butches and femmes fetishizing the "phallic" instrument. In fact, this is not a recent phenomenon at all. In the now defunct *Outrageous Women*, which was published during the 1980s and was one of the first lesbian s/m magazines, one finds many references to "lesbian dicks," often without the qualifier. What is apparent is that s/m dykes have always considered their dildos to be the "real thing."

Bersani's argument about gay macho depends on this notion of respect for masculinity as a model. But the slide from gay macho to lesbian butch/femme and s/m is too facilely made. Whereas gay macho's "mad identifications" are between gay and straight men, which he argues is a less mediated route to sexual excitement, for within those identifications, "*they never cease to feel the appeal of being violated*" (Bersani's emphasis),[53] the identifications made by b/f and s/m lesbians follow a more circuitous route in which the condensations and displacements are more complex. Most obviously, gay macho's relationship to straight masculinity remains a hommo-sexual affair; whereas lesbian b/f and s/m, as long as we are caught within the logic of this binary, would be hetero-sexual. In both cases, however, the erotic charge can only be articulated within the terms of a symbolic order that depends for its coherency on maintaining the distinction between homosexuality and heterosexuality. Nonetheless, even within the terms of this symbolic order, which I presume is what Bersani refers to when he speaks of sex "as we know it," there is already dissidence—rather than resemblance—in the image of a woman penetrating another woman with a dildo. Although both might be interpreted as a yearning toward "masculinity," in the gay man's case it is a masculinity that the dominant culture at least marginally assigns to him and that he thus might willingly surrender. In the lesbian top's case, it is a "masculinity" that she aggressively appropriates without any prior cultural ownership only then to give it up. If we look at it from the bottom's perspective, there is quite a difference between the gay man who cannot "refuse the suicidal ecstasy of being a woman" and the lesbian who is presumed by the dominant sexual order to already be a woman.

Over a decade ago Monique Wittig implicitly enjoined us to write The Symbolic Order with a slash through the article, just as Lacan writes T̶h̶e̶ Woman, when she made her then startling announcement that "Lesbians are not women."[54] The straight mind, she pointed out, speaks of "*the* difference between the sexes, the symbolic order, *the* Unconscious . . . giving an absolute meaning to these concepts when they are only categories founded upon heterosexuality."[55] Returning to this article, it is interesting to remember that the example Wittig chooses to demonstrate the material oppression effected through discourses is pornography. Pornography, she argues, signifies simply that "women are dominated."[56] Thus Wittig might be aligned with Mackinnon who argues that pornography "institutionalizes the sexuality of male supremacy, fusing the eroticization of dominance and submission with the social construction of male and female."[57] It is just this position that Bersani perversely asks us to reconsider when he temporarily allies himself with Mackinnon and Dworkin only in order to argue for the necessity of proliferating pornography rather than banning it.[58] However, if the ultimate logic of the radical feminist argument for the realism of porn is "*the criminalization of sex itself until it has been reinvented,*"[59] whether one takes up a position for or against pornography on this basis are we not then already acceding to the "straight mind" that can only think homosexuality as "nothing but heterosexuality?"[60]

What has fallen out of these discussions is heterosexuality as a social contract, one that, as Wittig argues, can not only be but already is broken by practicing lesbians. For when we hear of "sex as we know it" or the ultimate logic of antiporn feminists as the "criminalization of sex," this "sex" is always already heterosexuality and, implicitly, a relationship of identity between the phallus and the penis. Lacan reminds us that in Freudian doctrine the phallus is neither an imaginary effect or an object. Still less is it an organ "penis or clitoris, which it symbolizes."[61] However, in her reading of Lacan's "The Meaning of the Phallus," back through "The Mirror Stage," Judith Butler shows that Lacan's denial of the Phallus as an imaginary effect is "constitutive of the Phallus as the very formation of a privileged signifier."[62] At the risk of reductively summarizing her nuanced argument, what Butler's essay seems to conclude is that the Symbolic is always only a masculine imaginary that produces the Phallus as its privileged signifier by denying the mechanisms of its own production.

Lacan's move to locate the Phallus within the Symbolic presumably breaks its relation of identity with the penis since symbolization "depletes that which is symbolized of its ontological connection with the symbol itself."[63] Just as Magritte's painting of a pipe is not a/the pipe, so the penis and phallus are not equivalent.[64] But, as Butler points out, they do retain a privileged relationship to one another through "determinate negation."[65] If symbolization is what effects ontological disconnection, we might ask what happens to those "pipes" that are excessive to representation. Would not those things that cannot take place within any given symbolic not end up accorded a radically negative ontological status? Would they not, in other words, become that which is real and therefore impossible?

When Wittig argues that rejecting heterosexuality and its institutions is, from the straight mind's perspective, "simply an impossibility" since to do so would mean rejecting the "symbolic order" and therefore the constitution of meaning "without which no one can maintain an internal coherence,"[66] she seems to suggest that the straight mind simply denies the possibility of lesbianism. But phallocentrism/heterosexism does not merely secure its dominance through a simple negation. Rather, it needs lesbianism as a negative ontology. It needs its status as both radically real and impossible. In other words, if women had not invented lesbianism (and do not continue to do), men would have had to do so (if indeed they have not.) This is the site of contestation in the theorization of masochism as a male privilege. For it is this new masculine imaginary of submission that posits women's sexuality, and especially the "impossible" lesbian, as the ground upon which such a "masculine" liberation can take place.

That this is the case can be seen in Silverman's reconceptualization of the borders of male subjectivity in which her analysis at once ignores lesbian sexuality and persistently depends on it as yet another instance of a constitutive outside. Determined to undo the tenacious assumption that there are only two possible sexual subject positions, Silverman ends by positing three possible "same-sex" combinations: (1) two morphological men; (2) a gay man and a lesbian [both occupying psychically masculine positions]; and (3) a lesbian and a gay man [both occupying psychically feminine positions].[67] Given Silverman's sophisticated psychoanalytic rendering of the body's imaginary production, it might sound naive to suggest that the latter two positions are morphologically heterosexual, i.e., one of each. Yet she retains the category of two morphological men, so there is obviously still some recourse to a materiality of the body outside its imaginary formations.

Silverman concludes her book by asserting that her third paradigm for male homosexuality has the "most resonance for feminism," which she claims to represent politically. But what is striking is that this is the only place in her analysis where lesbianism is represented. For it is in this most politically productive model of male homosexuality that the "ethereal subjectivity" can be accessed "only through lesbianism."[68] What could this "lesbianism" be if not two morphologically female bodies, which oddly do not appear in her liberating models for "same-sex" desire? The feminism that Silverman speaks for politically is once again a heterosexual feminism; for her ability to make cases for imaginary gay sexualities is only intelligible through the assumption of a lesbian sexuality that remains stable and constitutively outside her recombinations of the relationships between psychic identifications and imaginary morphologies. Thus she depends on the orthodoxy of the impossibility of lesbian desire in order to challenge and break with the other orthodoxies that limit sexual choices for (heterosexual) women. And lesbianism, is, once again, posited as the "flesh" of feminism.

The model that proposes the impossibility of lesbian desire, constructed as two morphological females with psychic feminine identities, is impossible within psychoanalytic terms precisely because there is no desire without a phallic signifier. In order for lesbianism to escape from its stabilizing function as the placeholder of a lack, Butler's fictive lesbian phallus would seem to be indispensable. Yet there is still in this formulation a submission to the psychoanalytic orthodoxy that sexuality per se does not exist without penetration. Lesbian sadomasochists have thought of much more interesting ways to practice dominance and submission.

Consider the following excerpt from "Bad Attitude," which exemplifies the common s/m scene of the top securing (literally) the bottom, followed by a hiatus in which the bottom is left alone for an indeterminant time to contemplate the acts that will follow:

> Will you please fuck me before I go mad? She smiled modestly, then said: "Not yet sweetie. I think you should learn a little patience. I'm going to have some breakfast now. . . ." Lying there helpless and horny, I could hear [her] making her meal. The refrigerator door opened and closed, dishes clinked, the microwave hummed and beeped. . . . I thrust my hips against the pillow.
>
> I writhed, I moaned, I wiggled, I got hornier . . .
>
> Connie returned after 20 minutes. . . . "Did you miss me?" she whispered in my ear.[69]

S/m's (form)ality depends on a stillness, a waiting that is acted out through both the suspense of deferred gratification as well as the reenactment of suspense within the sexual scene itself. Hence the pleasure of holding, restraining, often literally suspending the bottom corporealizes the prolonged psychic negotiation. As opposed to the (illusion of) fluidity in conventional representations of sexual intercourse, the s/m scene is broken up, interrupted. This suggests a different model and value of continuance. For if suspense can be understood as a desire to extend the scene for as long as possible, s/m has at its center a perverse form of fidelity. And even when a "consummation" does occur, it is not an endpoint, or goal but, rather, a means of reproducing conditions that strive to guarantee the necessity for endless returns.

Judith Butler also sees "suspense" as the primary dynamic in pornography: "if the phantasmatic remains in tension with the 'real' effects it produces—and there is good reason to understand pornography as the erotic exploitation of this tension—then the 'real' remains permanently within quotations, i.e., 'action' is suspended, or, better yet, pornographic action is always suspended action."[70] However, Butler's position on sadomasochism, which is only implied in this article,[71] is rather problematic in my reading. She posits the quite credible argument that the antiporn legal statutes (Helms's in particular) constitute their own fantasy in which the central figure is a male homosexual, which the statute prohibits in order to endlessly reproduce for his [Helms's] "own satisfaction." She then asks: "Is this a production of a figure that it itself outlaws from production, a vehement and public way of drawing into public attention the very figure that is supposed to be banned from public attention and public funds? What kind of sadomasochistic performance is this that brings into phantasmatic relief the very object that it seeks to subordinate, revile, debase and denigrate?" And further: "there is no doubt that Helms's fantasy of homosexuality takes place within the scene of child molestation and sadomasochism: let us remember that this is his fantasy, though surely not his alone."[72] This is very tricky language to read, for surely Butler only intends to point out that Helms's fears are also his fantasies and that he (unconsciously) desires the very "bodies," "objects," and "acts," that he intends to ban. Or, in the terms of psychoanalytic fantasy, Helms's "I" (or one of them) takes place on the very scene that he produces as a prohibition. This reading then reinforces my earlier point that it is the fear of intimate desires within the psyche that becomes displaced onto objects rendered "real" (and therefore static and containable) outside the desiring subject, who invents the "real" in order to ward off the threat of his own fantasies.

However, Butler's choice to describe this scenario as "sadomasochistic" is unfortunate at best. The first sentence that I cite above is troubling in its association of s/m as a psychic practice that produces the "object" it reviles, degrades, and denigrates. It would be easy to misconstrue this reading as "evidence" that s/m is about the production of the denigrated object. In a sense, there is some credibility to this claim. S/m practices, as I understand them, do often conjure a "reviled object." For example, masochistic "daddy fantasies" may allow a once abusive father figure to reappear in a fantasy scene, where the "abuse" may appear to be reproduced by the top who is positioned in the role of "daddy." In some sense this repetition does work in the service of "outlawing" that father figure in order to reinvent him within the psychic fantasies of the lesbian bottom. This, however, is a very delicate negotiation that requires a tremendous amount of trust and understanding between the partners. It strikes me as dangerous to bandy about the term *sadomasochism* from one context to another without being very specific about how the term is being used. The second statement cited from Butler's article is even more worrisome. For to say that Helms's fantasy of homosexuality takes place in the scene of child molestation and sadomasochism could imply that the "real" homosexual does not engage with either of these practices. Or, it could be to say that some homosexuals do indeed engage these fantasies—"let us remember that this is his fantasy, though surely not his alone," Butler emphasizes. So who then are those others to whom she refers? Butler comes precariously close to instantiating the very distinction between fantasy and the "real" that her article otherwise brilliantly deconstructs. Sadomasochism, however, seems to appear as the sticking point in this argument. She writes that "sadomasochism is presumed to be clearly and collectively identifiable in its distinction from other sorts of sexual activities," (the word "presumption" signaling that s/m is in fact not clearly identifiable). But at the same time, she follows with a comparison of s/m to homoeroticism, which she takes as a term that "concedes the indeterminate status of this sexuality, for it is not simply the acts that qualify as homosexual under the law, but the ethos, the spreading power of this sexuality, which must also be rooted out." The effect of this comparison, despite the word *presumed,* is to render homoeroticism the privilege of being indeterminate, while sadomasochism becomes stabilized within but also against the fluid, permeable, mobility of homoeroticism.

Now suppose we agree with Bersani's argument that phallocentrism is "above all the denial of the *value* of powerlessness in both men and women,"[73] and consider what value women might find in powerlessness. I would agree with Tania Modleski that from a heterosexual woman's perspective there might not be much to value in powerlessness. But from a lesbian perspective things look different. Although Modleski acknowledges that lesbian sadomasochists' arguments must be taken seriously, and she points out the unresolvable contradiction between the acting out of power and the presumption of consensuality, I take exception to her assertion that "*some* of the most important marks, indeed the defining features of s/m

[are] the infliction of pain and humiliation by one individual on another."[74] What is important to point out here is that Modleski subtly posits the same distinction as Silverman between the "feminist" reader and the "lesbian." The former is a heterosexually gendered subject; the latter is something like an exception to the feminist "rule." Thus, once again, the lesbian becomes the constitutive outside—the necessary exterior—that facilitates the feminist argument.

Powerlessness, in Bersani's argument, seems to mean little more than submitting to penetration. When he takes anatomical considerations into account, he refers to human bodies that are constructed in such a way that "it's almost impossible not to associate mastery and subordination with intense pleasures."[75] If the value of powerlessness is equivalent to being penetrated, note that the "woman" in Bersani's imaginary must be either a heterosexual female or a gay male, who presumably share the "self-shattering" experience of being penetrated. However, the ecstasy of that self-shattering, according to Bersani, is in the becoming of woman, which the heterosexual female does not share with the gay male. Not because she already is a woman but because she has already become one (in most cases). Not because she has been penetrated but because she is female and hence interpellated as a woman. Understood in the context of Bersani's appropriation of femininity as the ecstasy of being penetrated, experienced by a man, the old cultural assumption, occasionally still current in some settings, that a girl becomes a woman when she "loses her virginity" is exposed as the desire of a masculine imaginary that projects its own repressed desires onto the bodies of women. Not only does Bersani then retain an equivalency between the phallus and the penis, he also reinforces a morphological conflation of the vagina and the anus. At the same time, he insists upon a phantasmatic gender distinction that depends on these anatomical parts as referents. Bersani's argument, then, surely exceeds his intentions. For while he means to value the powerlessness of both men and women, it is paradoxically between these two penetrable orifices, which are at once the same and different, that on their front/to/back axis the illusion of an impermeable male body is sustained. As D. A. Miller puts it: "only between the woman and the homosexual *together* may the normal male subject imagine himself covered front and back" (my emphasis).[76]

If, as Butler argues, Lacan retains a relationship of identity between the phallus and the penis through "determinate negation," it is also possible to understand the valorization of a masochism that is explicitly male as further consolidation of this relation of equivalence. For male masochism, which presumably relinquishes the phallus by occupying the being of woman, would necessarily assume that she is the one who does not "have it." In other words, it is only by giving it up that one gets it. Hence the continuing postulation that female masochism is impossible depends on the assurance that she has nothing to give up. The female masochist would have to give up something that she does not have; and if she were represented as giving it up, then it would have to be admitted that the phallus is nothing more than an imaginary construct. According to Freud's narrative, women are presumed to have once "had" the penis. The phallus/penis as "lost object" always refers us to the past of a woman's body and the dreaded future of a man's body. Hence the cultural horror associated with "becoming a woman."

While the paradox of actively submitting has been theoretically unbound from the mode of simple contradiction, it has been so in the service of liberating a certain pleasure for men. A sexually submissive woman is just a woman. A sexually submissive man, however, is now a "masochist," who is "man enough" to submit to becoming a woman. The active pleasure of masochism remains a man's prerogative, any way that these theorists look at it.

The most thoughtful, sophisticated, and affirmative discussion of masochism that I have read is written by a woman—Eve Sedgwick's "A Poem Is Being Written." Her essay weaves through a complicated series of psychic negotiations as she examines the histories of her sexuality. She does, however, identify as a woman, though she scarcely leaves it at that. Her account begins with the memories of her nine-year-old self—Eve Kosofsky—someone who "is allowed to speak, or I to speak of her, only here in the space of professional success and of hyperconscious virtuosity, conscious not least of the unusually narrow stylistic demands that hedge about any language that treats one's own past."[77] Near her conclusion, Sedgwick explains that though she does identify as a woman, her identification as a gay person is "a firmly male one . . . and in and among its torturous and alienating paths are knit the relations, for me, of telling and knowing."[78] Her essay ends in the present moment of the writing. What fascinates me, among other things, about this essay, is that what she identifies as her pleasure in the "visibly chastised" becomes a part of her imaginary, consciously, in what seems to be the moment of her firm gay male identification. For if, as I have been arguing, performative masochism is theoretically impossible for women (and this I take to mean a female who is identified with femininity psychically), then Sedgwick's essay raises again the question of whether masochism, for women-identified women (as opposed to lesbians, who are not by any means necessarily identified with femininity) can be a choice rather than a mandate. In other words, *must* there be a secondary revision to *perform* the masochistic role? And is femininity somehow barred from such a secondary revision? To put it slightly differently, can one attain conscious access to the structure of masochistic pleasure only through representation?

While Sedgwick's essay richly complicates this question, it remains troubling that "women" appear to be trapped in a position in which they are incapable of acting out masochistic fantasies (or even having them) without reinstating our "ontologies." This leaves "femme" lesbians in the primary process, in the realm of the instincts, where we are rendered incapable of secondary revisions. It leaves us in the "theater," but not in command of mimesis, much less mimicry. It returns us to the blank page on which history is inscribed, barred from the creative process. Like the fixed point on Donne's compass, it is the feminine position that guarantees the [male] traveler's return to meaning by representing faithfulness to his origins. The one who waits is not permitted the faculty of oblivion that Nietzsche considers necessary to "strong health" and to the possibility of apprehending the present. Like the garment Penelope weaves by day and unravels by night, the one who waits is made and unmade in order to ward off intrusions from others who would declare the death, not merely the absence, of the loved one. Barthes can declare that it is "Woman who gives shape to absence, elaborates its fiction," and celebrate the "miraculously feminized" man who "utters the other's absence."[79] If a man is "not feminized because he is inverted but because he is in love,"[80] a woman who is in love with (and waits) for another woman would not even have attained the subversive possibilities of inversion, much less a miraculous transmutation of historical gender roles. Male and female masochism necessarily takes place on different stages; not because there is an essential difference but because they have different histories.

Sedgwick's analysis of her own masochistic pleasure is a complex and riveting document. The first half of her essay, on "spanking and poetry," is a "relatively ungendered" memory of being spanked as a child and of the "act's careful orchestration of spontaneity and pageantry" that took place " 'simply' over the parental lap."[81] Her memory of the scene, as she remembers it actually occurring however, is transformed in her imagination into a much more restricted mise en scène that closes in on the immobilized lower body of the child bent over a table scaled precisely to size and shape. The stage on which the spanking in her imagination occurs is a proscenium, designed to

> eject from the *tableau* or table itself, along with every figure but the figure of the part of the child, the entire visible mechanism of the gaze to

which the child is exposed, the graphic multicharacter drama of infliction and onlooking, the visibly rendered plural possibilities of sadism, voyeurism, horror, *Schadenfreude*, disgust, or even compassion.[82]

In effect then, this fantasy reframing affords the child being spanked a kind of invisibility that is ironically made possible at the moment that she is most visibly exposed. This is precisely the mechanism of realistic (proscenium arch) theater, which creates for the onlooker the illusion of seeing all precisely because she cannot see what, according to Blau, she most wants to see—that which is just outside the frame. If this kind of theater also creates for the spectator the illusion of watching without being seen, it does so in much the same way as Sedgwick's fantasized tableau, by concentrating the spectator's optical field on a site in which the mechanisms of the gaze are held outside the spectator's line of vision. This is the theatrical scene that works diligently to produce the illusion of reality and thereby, depending on the spectator's position in relationship to the stage, most blatantly displays reality as illusion. It all depends upon how one is positioned to look. Sedgwick takes up this point in her provocative analysis of the "view from behind,"—in theatrical terms, the background, backstage, the place that the spectator is not allowed to look but also, arguably, the place that we most desire to see—for this is the space where the theater creates its suspense (spatially) and the anticipation that creates our pleasure (an anticipation that is always, in realistic theater, unfulfilled; if, by chance, it should accidentally be made manifest, it is virtually guaranteed to disappoint us, *if* our pleasure is *in* the suspense). As Sedgwick's reading of the constitution of her own sexual pleasures reminds, it is in the intricate tensions between what can and cannot be seen that desire is staged. As she puts it, it is in "the relations of telling and knowing."[83]

In Blau's search for "universals of performance," he states emphatically that there is no point in discussing the topic at all without asking "*who* exactly is doing the discerning—and whether inside or outside [an issue] so critical . . . *in* performance that the problem itself can be considered a universal."[84] The proscenium frame, the space within which most "realistic" theater takes place, is an apt site for Sedgwick's masochistic fantasy. For it is here that the "real" and "artifice" are most violently yoked together, here that the visibility/invisibility divide is at once most powerfully enforced and most radically undone. It enacts the paradox that the more formal, contained, and constricted the mise en scène, the more likely the spectator is to experience the illusion as truth. And in order for the performer to create this illusion for the spectator, she employs techniques designed to erase her self-consciousness as much as possible. Thus more consciousness of performance produces less self-consciousness, which is in itself a paradoxical, counterintuitive construct, as I will elaborate later in reference to an s/m narrative, "The Duchess of L.A."

As Sedgwick points out, the title of her essay, "A Poem Is Being Written," is an obvious allusion to Freud's famous essay, "A Child Is Being Beaten," written in the "shifty passive voice."[85] The voice in Freud's essay is shifty, not only because it is "passive" but also because in the second phase of Freud's three-step fantasy, the anonymous child who is being beaten becomes the "I" of the one who produces the fantasy: a child is being beaten is replaced by "I am being beaten by my father." It is also shifty because Freud's title does not refer to the one who administers the beating. The complete representation of the first phase is: "My father is beating the child." Sedgwick translates Freud's banal observation that children might replace earlier memories of being beaten in grade schools with fantasies derived from reading in higher grades "books whose contents gave a new stimulus to the beating fantasies,"[86] with a correlation between memories of being spanked and the form and scene of writing poetry. Notice then that Sedgwick shifts Freud's tenses. In Freud the grammar of the beating fantasy moves from a later period to an earlier one—the past is reconstituted in fantasy from a later experience. In Sedgwick's fantasy, if the spankings occurred prior to the writing of the poetry, the tenses move in the opposite direction. Or, if the writing of poetry was taking place at the same time as the spankings, then the scene is shifted from one context to another, and the spankings and the writing of poetry are made analogous or even nearly consonant. Freud's explanation of masochistic fantasies takes place in the traumatic space of the present. Sedgwick, on the other hand, lifts the spanking fantasy out of the traumatic space, and if one were to have to choose a psychoanalytic term that would best describe her transmutation of the scene it would certainly not be trauma but perhaps sublimation, another psychic mechanism that, from a psychoanalytic point of view, is awarded to men only.

And yet, there are in Sedgwick's essay some moments that could be read as significations of traumatic spaces. Sedgwick's memory of her own childhood is free of trauma—"my big sister and I and our little brother were good and well-loved children and were not abused children, and it matters that this narrative is about an attentive, emotionally and intellectually generous matrix of nurturance and pedagogy";[87] nonetheless, the excerpts from Sedgwick's poetry, which make up a significant section of her narrative, include some passages that could easily be read as the voice of a traumatized child, adolescent, and young adult:

that's me—that naked trunk that's bent and tied
over the abdomen-high table, waiting for stripes;
. . . That's me, all these weary nights
waking to my own screams five and six times before dawn
afraid to fall asleep, afraid to wake and find
a note of summons slipped under the door . . . ("Lost Letter")[88]

. . . helpless to turn away the new love, helpless to
accept it, helpless to keep the adult
from panicky silences or sudden inattention,
the child finally invents from its own baffled
heart a new, expensive theatrics:
a hallucinatory mimicry
of the adult, by which within the child
a second adult is made; whose function
being to put under the child's control what is
strangest . . . ("Trace at 46")[89]

"I'll wash the child," he'd voice.
A few fresh coals woke the resentful fire;
the red-gilt tub, for once, was warmed,
the child among her father's fingers more
and more wooden, deeply chilled . . . ("The Warm Decembers")[90]

And from the same poem:

. . . Nothing was kept
secret from her or revealed to her;
the things she put together were both more
than wanted, and less than at any rate
Henry had feared.[91]

These poems, in these moments, allude to the experience of a traumatized child, both in the present moment of its occurrence and in the aftereffects. In "Trace at 46," the double, the introjected other whom the child invents as an(other) within herself (often the adult him or her self) to create the illusion of controlling the scene is invoked. A witness who becomes, in a sense, the spectator is the one who can narrate to the "survivor" the poems, or paint the images, to create an intelligible "history." It is *as if*—the magic words of realistic theater—she were no longer the one to whom "*it*" occurred, for she can see what is outside her own ocular space. On this periphery, she *can* see the view from behind, backstage. Since the relationship between the "perpetrator" and the survivor is generally (though certainly not exclusively) male-to-female, then we might speculate that the girl's introjected other is psychically masculine. If it is indeed the survivor who has access to secondary revisions, to the making of representations, then who is it who writes the script? One of the things that Sedgwick accomplishes in this essay, a combination of theoretical analysis and personal testimony, is to complicate any simple notion of causality, that is, a *necessary* correlation between sexual abuse and its repetition through eroticized fantasies. Furthermore, these poems *are erotic*, not despite their juxtapositions of sexual coercion and sexual pleasure but, daringly, because of it. As Sedgwick elaborates in her structural analogy between poetic meter and the rhythmic, regulated cadence of the beating fantasies, there is a visceral pleasure common to them both.

I. A. Richards's description of the physiological effect of meter is instructive for Sedgwick's correlation between spanking and poetry. Richards argues that the pleasure of meter is "not due to our perceiving a pattern in something outside us, but to our becoming patterned ourselves. With every beat of the metre a tide of anticipation in us turns and swings . . . the pattern itself is a vast cyclic agitation spreading all over the body, a tide of excitement pouring through the channels of the mind."[92] Thus the effect of apprehending metrics could be understood as analogous to the heightening of tension that, Bersani has argued via Freud, is inevitably experienced as sexual. Paul Fussell points out that one of the ways that meter can "mean" is by producing a "ritual frame" and thus "enclos[ing] experience . . . like a picture frame . . . remind[ing] the apprehender unremittingly that he is not experiencing the real object of the 'imitation' . . . but that object transmuted into symbolic form."[93] In this way we can understand Sedgwick's spanking fantasy—the one contained in the proscenium—as a kind of artistic rearticulation of the remembered act. The spanking becomes the poem, and the poem constantly recalls the spanking but repeats it with the intervening control of Sedgwick's desiring fantasy. Thus the lyric poem "was both the spanked body . . . and at the same time the very spanking, the rhythmic hand whether hard or subtle of authority itself."[94] The revision of the spanking allows Sedgwick to transform memory into a pleasurable text, one in which she can "abstract the body of one's *own* humiliation; or perhaps most wonderful, to identify with it, creating with painful love and care, but in a temporality miraculously compressed by the elegancies of language, the distance across which this body in punishment could be endowed with an aura of meaning and attraction—across which, in short, the *compelled* body could be *chosen*."[95]

In this fantasy space, the body is aestheticized. Sedgwick's fantasy is a representation of desire itself as the object—the desire for desire. The particular shape it assumes, the severe economy of the framing device that banishes all other characters, creates a "free switchpoint for the identities of subject, object, onlooker, desirer, looker-away."[96] But these positions circulate within a closed space where everything is interior to the fantasy/frame. Her fantasy is thus precisely a representation; for, as Barthes puts it: "representation is . . . when nothing emerges, when nothing leaps out of the frame: of the picture, the book, the screen."[97] Sedgwick's revisionist fantasy creates a text of pleasure but not a text of bliss. Barthes makes this distinction:

> Text of pleasure: the text that contents, fills, grants euphoria; the text that comes from a culture and does not break with it, is linked to a *comfortable* practice of reading. Text of bliss: the text that imposes a state of loss, the text that discomforts . . . unsettles the reader's historical, cultural, psychological assumptions, the consistency of his tastes, values, memories, brings to a crisis his relation with language.[98]

For a queer woman, like Sedgwick, whose identifications are with gay men, the fantasy passes through the cultural/historical soldering of femininity with passivity. Nonetheless, it depends on a recognition of that divide, even as it traces out a detour through it. Her masochistic fantasy does not exceed the closure of representation and therefore does not appear to take place outside the "impossibility" of masochism for women. Sedgwick's *essay*, however, is certainly a text of bliss, for it discomforts, unsettles, and takes language to the point of crisis. It is not only "about" crisis; it performs that crisis linguistically. Even granting that desire is constituted by the absence of the object, Barthes points out that the Greek *Himeros*, the "burning desire for the present being" is not the same thing as *Pothos*, the desire for the absent being."[99]

The text of bliss encounters a subjectivity in the "contradictory interplay of (cultural) pleasure and (non-cultural) bliss;" here is the "subject at present out of place, arriving too late or too soon (this too designating neither regret, fault, or bad luck, but merely calling for a non-site): anachronic subject, adrift."[100] This discomforting text, the text that imposes a state of loss, could be the homosexual scene as Sedgwick describes it: "Nothing—no form of contact with people of any gender or sexuality—makes me feel so, simply, *homosexual* as the evocation of library afternoons of dead-ended searches, 'wild' guesses that, as I got more experienced, turned out to be almost always right."[101] In other moments, she locates the scene of her homosexuality in her richly provocative comment: "A will-to-live, per se, has seldom in me been more than notional, often aggressively absent: its place taken, when it is taken at all, partly by an also aggressive will-to-narrate and will-to-uncover, each with a gay male setting. That this is a vulnerably off-centered psychic structure—dangerous to itself, but, potentially, homophobically dangerous as well—is clear to me. The *clarity* of that particular danger is, I sometimes think, the most homosexual thing about me."[102]

Not only does Sedgwick's relationship to the death instinct align her with the mythically male homosexual (see chapter 4 for fuller discussion) but also her desire to narrate, uncover, and take pleasure in the solitary activities of searching, discovering, and circumventing through her willed creativity the dead-ends of that singular journey are activities traditionally associated with masculinity. It is in her anxious evocation of the homophobic danger of her particular psychic identifications that she assumes a pleasurable loss, a description of her desire that is not unlike the one that Foucault ascribes not only to himself but to gay men in general.

Interviewing Foucault, James O'Higgins is reminded of Casanova's expression: "the best moment of love is when one is climbing the stairs." O'Higgins cannot imagine a homosexual making such a remark, and Foucault agrees. The homosexual, Foucault returns, would be more likely to say that "the best moment of love is when the lover leaves in a taxi."[103] These remarks occur in the context of two men discussing promiscuity, the "love them and leave them" attitude that our culture presumes is somehow constitutive of gay male desire. Perhaps above all else it is this myth of gay male desire that has caused an historical and cultural breach between gay men and lesbians, the latter deploring the behavior on the basis of its perceived disregard for the value of "true" love and fidelity.

Foucault explains that "recollection rather than anticipation of the act"[104] assumes such importance for gay men because of the ironies of a history that has made sex between men easily accessible and readily available. Among the peculiar paradoxes of the closet is that the public courtship rituals that have characterized heterosexuality are rendered minimal for gay men. For women these courtship rituals are a bit more accessible because the heterosexual population cannot read them as readily between women. The idea then of the beloved object always being slightly outside one's grasp in heterosexual/romantic courtship rituals imitates (or is imitated by?) the desire always to see that which is just beyond the frame of one's optical field in the theater. Gay men have historically replaced this desire, according to Foucault, with the "wink on the street" and the "split-second decision to get it on." Hence the paucity of eroticized anticipation among gay men.

Prominent myths of lesbian desire as impoverished, hystericized recollections claim almost the exact opposite. Lesbian and Gay historicists and theorists have gone far toward debunking such myths, but they still retain a tenacious hold in the cultural imaginary. The pervasiveness of this perceived difference has played largely in the s/m debates. For lesbian sadomasochists have been the most prominent spokespeople, among women, for the deemphasizing of fidelity, the advocacy of group sex, the pleasure of multiple and simultaneous partnerships, and the explicit descriptions of sexual acts. Thus they are easily rendered "male-identified," since these myths are accredited primarily to men and especially to gay men. Whereas the behavior is considered normative if lamentable for heterosexual men (witness the lyrics to almost any popular song from the 1950s onward), it is a sign of the degradation of love by a class in the case of gay men. The history of gender no doubt produces then a different valence in the idea of "missing" among gay male and lesbian relationships. The eroticization of absence is a pleasurable suffering that yearns both for a space that can never be filled and for the fulfillment of that space. This absence/presence dialectic is ubiquitous among all imaginable forms of sexuality. But depending upon which gender and sexual orientation one speaks about, it takes on quite different values. That the first term, *absence*, is not merely a negativity but a sign of positive erotic value is a misrecognition that misses the fact that absence is presence in recollective pleasure.

One can almost imagine the scenes of rapid exchanges of sexual acts among gay men as a speeding-up—through urgent repetitions—of the dialectic of appearance/disappearance. The shift in the tempo of the exchange foreshortens the return of the first term. Following Freud, we would have to read such exchanges as a desire for mastery, for the "best moment of love" is when one lover leaves and the other is left alone to reconstruct the act according to the terms of his own fantasy structure—to "master" the real of the exchange without the interruption of the distracting presence of the other. One could also read this pleasure as mastery in the sense that the lover who is left then has the challenge of causing the "object" to return. In this scenario the one who is "left behind" is, ironically, the one who has the power of the seducer. However, there is another way, I think, to understand this eroticization of leave-taking—the pleasure in overtaking the lover's inevitable absence, a pleasure that takes the form of submission, acquiescence. Precisely, the masochistic flight forward.

In 1982, when this interview took place, Foucault could still say that "most homosexuals feel that the passive role is in some way demeaning."[105] That "some way" was of course then, as it is now, in the passive role's historical association with being in the "feminine" position. Foucault thought then that s/m had somewhat alleviated this problem, through the switching of roles and the insistence on the presumably passive partner's command of the sexual act.

I would suggest, however, that the "passive" role is more about an attempt to "lose" (self)-consciousness, rather than the "shattering of the self" (by which Bersani clearly means the ego). Hegel explains that self-consciousness is the "entry into the native realm of truth." As opposed to the movement of knowing, self-consciousness "is the reflection out of the being of the world of the world of sense and perception, and is essentially the return from *otherness*."[106] Paradoxically, people who are self-conscious are not really focusing on themselves but, rather, on the mirrors of the others who are watching them. They make bad actors in the realistic theater (and bad sexual partners). It is as if a performer were watching her spectators watching her perform. Thus self-consciousness is precisely what one has to lose in order to focus on oneself. It is a "truism" that women are more inclined to this form of self-consciousness than men, having been socialized not only to attend to the needs and desires of others but also to watch themselves being watched and conform their images to the ways in which they imagine themselves being seen.

Jane DeLynn's story, "The Duchess of L.A.," is precisely about how an s/m encounter between two women is a "gift" from the top to the bottom of the loss of such self-consciousness. The narrator in this story is initiated into a mild s/m scene by her friend, Linda, the most sought-after dominatrix in the community. The narrative takes us through the bottom's initial disgust when confronted with her friend's perverse desires to recognition of her own deeply resistant desires. Linda takes her friend to a lesbian s/m bar where there is a playing space. The narrator is cool and detached, considering herself to be rationally above the infantile eroticism of the women in the bar. She scoffs at their conventional attire, finds them unbearably ugly, and thinks of herself as a dispassionate observer. When encouraged to participate by delivering a few blows of the whip on an anonymous submissive, she does so, reluctantly, only because Linda tells her that declining would not be proper etiquette in the bar and that the other participants might be discomfited by her distance.

Linda's experience allows her to locate her friend's resistance to her own pleasure almost immediately. For what Linda sees, that her friend cannot see for herself nor overcome without assistance, is that the narrator's self-consciousness is constructed through a hypersensitivity to the desires of others. Telling her that failing to engage in the practice will cause distress for the others is a trick of Linda's seduction, a top's trick—facilitating the passage to a bottom's desire by locating a switching point where the bottom's resistance can be overcome. The narrator's self-consciousness, precisely that which makes her uncomfortable, is that switching point. Linda sees that her friend is limited in her capacity to fulfill her own desires by a crippling awareness of what others want. This makes the narrator disconnected from her body, and what the top teaches the bottom in this scene is how pronounced and self-inhibiting this disconnection can be. Furthermore, she shows her how to do something about it by seducing her into relinquishing control, allowing her "self"(consciousness) to disappear by applying a variety of psychic and physical stressors.

The narrator begins to feel a few flickers of arousal as she experiences empathy with the anonymous woman whom she is persuaded to whip. When someone else takes the whip from her, she is about to leave when Linda pulls her back and suggests that it is now her turn. The narrator resists, but Linda points out to her that her disconnection from her body is not allowing her to read her own signs of desire.

She grabbed my arms and pinned me against a wall near where we were standing. She was strong, but perhaps if I had really tried I could have pushed her away. But I shut my eyes and let her continue to caress me.

LINDA: "You want me to, don't you?"

NARRATOR: "No."

LINDA: She laughed. "You sure fooled me."

NARRATOR: "Not here."[107]

Linda then gives her friend a series of directions, each one in a cool, deliberative tone that is often mistaken as the top's "indifference." But DeLynn's narrative shows us that the top's stance is in the service of allowing the bottom to push past her own resistances. With each command the narrator slips back into self-consciousness, which displays itself again and again at each moment that she begins to experience pleasure. Linda then blindfolds her "so that [she] doesn't have to see what is happening," cutting off the most debilitating of our senses that produces self-consciousness, then tells her to unzip her pants. The narrator does so, but then she immediately falls back into the self-consciousness that is blocking her body's pleasure: "I felt foolish with them slightly open, and did not know whether I should push them down more or not. I didn't want to ask because that would look too eager. I almost wished my hands were tied so I would not have to worry about these things."[108] Linda sees then that she will have to take firmer control, as at each juncture the narrator is incapacitated by her compulsive concern with the effect she is having on others. Linda pushes the narrator's pants down around her ankles; the narrator worries that her underpants are torn or stained. Linda leads her to a pommel horse and bends her over it; the narrator fears that she will sneeze or have to blow her nose or urinate. Finally Linda calls in the other women in the bar for assistance. What they take from the narrator is language and her "I"—that is, they begin to speak for her and of her in the third person: "she's really wet . . . see how she wants it . . . she'd probably beg for it if we stopped." Linda: "Go ahead, touch her, she doesn't mind."[109] The narrator finds this objectification soothing and comforting, thinking that it was the way people spoke about her when she had done something remarkable and she has to extend no effort to become the object of attention. When the group begins to spank her, she has one last burst of self-consciousness as she wonders to herself whether she should cry out when the blows land on her thighs and buttocks. But at this moment she catches herself thinking this way, and realizes that her mental process is not at all about s/m "etiquette" but rather about how to ensure that the spanking continues. Afraid that they will stop if she cries too much, but wanting them to know that they were hurting her, her own pleasure is constantly interrupted by thoughts about what they desire. Then she realizes the true absurdity of her situation, not that she is draped naked over a pommel horse while a group of women she doesn't even know are spanking her, but that even in this most extraordinary situation she is obsessed with what kind of response she was "supposed to make."[110]

Many women would certainly recognize this kind of self-conscious behavior in more "ordinary" scenes. To cite just one example, women who teach self-defense methods to other women find that overcoming their students's self-consciousness of how they are being perceived, even in a life-threatening situation, is a difficult obstacle. Feminist therapists are also no doubt distressingly familiar with the difficulties in working with women who cannot focus on themselves no matter how much they are clearly suffering from failing to do so. The setting and content of this story might be unusual to many women, but the psychic process that the narrator undergoes ought to be quite familiar.

Linda lectures the narrator and applies a series of repetitive, regulated, cadenced, strokes that allow the narrator to enter into "a different kind of space, the one that exists while you're in a dream or watching a totally engrossing movie, and there's nothing to do but witness the events going on all around you."[111] Linda is teaching the narrator how to be her own witness, her own spectator. When the spanking stops and the lights go up, the narrator feels bereft, "as if I had been chucked out of paradise."[112] She realizes that she really is not such a "nice girl," and she is both relieved and disappointed by this recognition. This story is particularly adept at demonstrating the way in which s/m scenes deal with issues that are common to many women, whether they choose to work on them through therapy, meditation, dialogue with other women, or physical encounters. The scene certainly does not pretend to effect any kind of magical cure. Notice that the narrator remains ambivalent about finding out that she is not such a "nice girl." But at least she has a few moments of recognition that she is not. And perhaps this can be the beginning for her of a different kind of self-awareness that is not self-consciousness. What this story also shows clearly is that sexuality is a scene, a psychic location that can be effected by a material setting. And that setting is going to be different for different women. Most important, this scene is, in fact, a consciousness-raising event for the narrator, for what she learns is that she must be her own spectator. What matters is who is looking. Indeed, what defines the "I" is the one who looks. Through whatever method, if that witness can be made internal, then a fundamental feminist precept is accomplished.

That is not to say, however, that lesbians do not imagine and practice sexual "scenes" that do not come closer to fitting the presumably "gay" paradigm of recollection, as Foucault described it. Another of DeLynn's stories, "Butch," quite clearly fits this "gay" model. Tired of "being even a little bit in charge," the narrator of this story completely surrenders control to a butch she meets in a bar. The butch refuses the narrator's offer to make love to her and leaves her tied up on the sofa with a dildo inserted firmly in her anus. The alternation between cruelty and tenderness is nicely captured in this story as the butch leans down to kiss the narrator quickly on the mouth, then says: "I'm going to leave you like this." Although the narrator protests: "It hurts. But the more it hurt, the more I liked it." After the butch leaves, the narrator lies in bed listening to country music—"songs from a region [she] wished she had been able to escape from rather than move towards." It occurs to her then that she must nonetheless like this, "why else would [she] keep going to bars, if not to find it." Part of the pleasure the narrator experiences in this story is the ambiguity about the butch's return. When she asks her if she will return, the butch answers: "Maybe. You never know."[113] The *not* knowing becomes a kind of pleasure in itself, the pleasure of suspens(ion). The poignancy of this story is precisely in its anonymity (neither of the characters are named), its transience, and its rejection of the pleasure associated with the imperative to reproduce the scene. There is no promise made, and thus none to be broken.

These few examples cannot begin to justify the enormous variety within lesbian s/m accounts. The notion that the "leatherscene" is homogeneous is blatantly belied by the literature, both fictive and testimonial, on the subject. Nonetheless, there is a tendency to collapse this richly varied experience into an oppositional construct and thus reinstate a spurious binary between "vanilla" and s/m lesbians, which are hardly distinct categories. Despite the fact that s/m appears to have become commodified and therefore a spectacle of consumption for the masses who do not participate in this particular form of consciousness-raising, we still must make a distinction between the ones who are watching and the ones who are participating and watching themselves. Of course, the latter are also watching themselves being watched, and this affects the internal dynamics of the s/m subculture, but that does not mean that the subculture has become what its spectators see when they look at it from the outside.

In her essay, "The Student and the Strap: Authority and Seduction in the Class/Room,"[114] Sue-Ellen Case makes an argument against s/m, and the strapping on of dildos in particular, that emphasizes class differences. Case finds lesbian s/m to have become "chic" and "fashionable." Both in "underground 'zines as well as in posh academic settings," Case finds that the dildo-bedecked dyke is presented as alluring, and perverse, while the earlier dykes, the "dowdy" ones who had no value on the market, have no allure. She compares reactions to the dowdy dykes with the reactions of American tourists who traveled into (what once was) East Berlin and commented on the drab, boring, gray appearance of a city devoid of enticing shops and seductive advertisements. The old (non)fashionable dyke, according to Case, was not just nonfashionable but nonfashioned. She had no sex toys and did not play with scenarios of power, but she has been obscured by terms such as *essentialist* or *feminist*, whereas the leather dyke has gained visibility through her association with gay men. This is the repetition of a very old argument, one that accuses the lesbian of "male-identification" if she performs any acts whatsoever that do not conform to the expectation that she represent the "real thing" in the feminist imaginary. Not only is such an argument deeply problematic for the reasons that this book has consistently set out—that representing the "real" of the feminist movement is a position that relegates the lesbian to matter, to the ground upon which all else can be imagined and nothing is possible for the lesbian in the realm of fantasy— but also because the accusation of "male-identification" reifies sexual difference absolutely. If men can appropriate femininity but women are barred from playing on the stage of what the dominant culture deems masculine, then the binary terms of sexual difference and the heterosexual/homosexual dichotomy have no fantasy space, not to mention any possibility of multiplying the possibilities of new forms of sexual pleasures. Case is quite right to see that Pat Califia comes close to a libertarian position in some of her arguments and that the problem of lesbian "invisibility" presents a scenario that demands the appropriation of the phallus in order to enter the order of the visible. However, in my view lesbians are not and never have been invisible. Once again, to belabor this most obvious but nonetheless constantly elided point, it all depends upon who is looking and from what position. I would agree with Case absolutely that making lesbians visible within the optical field of the dominant order is not a particularly valuable project. However, the confusion of "invisibility" with psychic, phantasmatic "impossibility" does constitute an area of genuine concern. For it is the latter that shuts out and down the sexual fantasies of women, and arguments such as Case's contribute to that process by further cementing a spurious divide between the old-fashioned dyke and the new leather dykes. In chapter 4 I will discuss a story that is based precisely on this false division and show how these two groups have much more in common than their social constructions can even begin to indicate.

Case argues further that the leather scene is based on a politics of individualism, whereas the radical feminist is interested in coalitions. The dildoed dyke is for Case an "ad man," that is, she is interested only in her appearance and the erotic moment for her occurs when she sees herself being seen in the photographs that appear in the lesbian magazines. It may in fact be true that another erotic moment occurs for her when the photo display appears, but what is quite obvious about Case's argument, though I admire it for its focus on class (an issue that is rarely discussed in relation to sexuality and its practices) is that she is the one who is looking at the leather scene from a position outside its internal dynamics. Her identification with the "dowdy dykes" (who are implicitly in her view the "real thing") is manifest throughout her writing. Case's argument is about representations of the leather scene, and there is no doubt an obvious problem with appropriation of the leather s/m lesbian subculture by the mainstream media, where it has indeed become something of a "fashion subculture." But to make the leap from this appropriation to the "real" of the subculture is a gross oversimplification. While Case and others are claiming that the leather scene is the ultimate in commodification and male-identification, lesbian magazines that dare to depict "kinky" sex acts between women are struggling to stay in existence. As I have already mentioned, *On Our Backs*, the longest-standing and most middle-of-the-road lesbian sex magazine, has recently gone out of business. Copies of *Bad Attitude* are being kept out of sight, as they once were in the 1980s, in my local bookstore in a large urban city. The Canadian "Butler" laws have shut down bookstores and confiscated all manner of lesbian and gay publications. The playing spaces on the Internet are at serious risk for being closed down as "pornographic." And meanwhile lesbians are entering into mainstream publications in an unprecedented way—certainly not, however, as leather dykes; rather, as the innocent, charming, smiling, all-American girls on the cover of *Newsweek*,[115] or the "butch/femme" couple (k. d. lang and Cindy Crawford) on the cover of *Vanity Fair*.[116] (Not too long after that cover appeared, Cindy Crawford took out a full-page newspaper ad declaring her heterosexuality.) Most ironically, Case is arguing for the commodification of a subculture by looking at its representations by the dominant culture. Standing on the outside looking in, of course this is all that one can see. Pat Califia once reviewed Camille Paglia's book in which Paglia is posed in leather gear standing outside a pornography shop. Her review ended with the advice to Paglia that she stop posing in front of the store and go inside if she really wanted to know what she was talking about.[117] Case is herself, paradoxically, buying into the very interpellation of the lesbian leather scene that she so fervently desires not to purchase.

Colleen Lamos's celebration of *On Our Backs* argues that "on one level [its] success demonstrates the unflagging ability of capitalism to respond to changing demands from emerging consumer groups, however queer."[118] On the other hand, Lamos addresses the concern with the "spectacle of undesignated readers peering into the pages"[119] of the magazine. She cites a number of theorists who praise the multiplicity and permeability of pornographic literature without examining just how this is produced and what constitutes the cross-over audiences, as well as feminists who continue to criticize the disappearance of typological categories. Lamos makes an argument with which I am in total agreement when she says that:

> The generic differentiations within pornography are the residue of discredited sexological typologies and naive notions of a text's or film's implied reader or spectator as well as the effects of class- and sex-based production and distribution systems. These generic categories rest upon the presupposition of a clear, even innate difference between hetero- and homosexual (or other) desires.[120]

Lamos's article takes the stand that what we are looking at in the "postmodern" lesbian is the "end of lesbianism as we know it—as a distinct, minority sexual orientation. Lesbianism was born in the panic of sexual/gender definition at the turn of the twentieth century. As we approach our own fin-de-siècle that panic has not subsided."[121] The dildo remains the figure that most powerfully signifies that panic, hence its place in the center of the hot contestation between what Case calls the "dowdy dykes" and the fashionable leather lesbians. We could perhaps argue endlessly about the dildo/penis/phallus relationship, but Lamos's historicization of these debates brings us up to the present moment, where the dildo no longer signifies as a substitute, a parody, or even a prosthesis.

Lesbians who regard their strap-ons as the "real thing" have instigated a representational crisis by producing an imaginary in which the fetishistic/hallucinatory "return" of the penis onto a woman's body goes beyond the "transferable or plastic property"[122] of the phallus to other body parts by depicting a phallus that has no reference to the "real" of the penis. The lesbian dick is the phallus as floating signifier that has no ground on which to rest. It neither returns to the male body, originates from it, nor refers to it. Lesbian dicks are the ultimate simulacra. They occupy the ontological status of the model, appropriate the privilege, and refuse to acknowledge an origin outside their own self-reflexivity. They make claims to the real without submitting to "truth." If the phallus was banned from feminist orthodoxy because it was presumed to signify the persistence of a masculine or heterosexual identification, and tops who wore strap-ons were thus represented, as Butler points out, as "vain and/or pathetic effort[s] to mime the real thing,"[123] this "real thing" was at least two real things, which were only each other's opposites. There was not much difference between the straight "real thing," and the lesbian "real thing," since the latter was only the absence of the former. Both these prohibitions converged on the assumption of an identity between the phallus and the penis. Without that identification, the top who wears the strap-on is not the one who "has" the phallus; rather it is always already the bottom who "has it" by giving up what no one can have. In the lesbian imaginary, the phallus is not where it appears. That's why so many butches, as most lesbians know, are bottoms.

dedicated to Bob Flanagan, 1952–1996

4 • Death and the Referent: The Queer Real

"I am totally submissive to her. She is the kind of woman I have fantasized about all my life. But this is no fantasy, this is no game, it's the real thing."

—Bob Flanagan

I am at the Performance Space in Sydney, Australia. It's July 16, 1994, and I have just found out that Anna Munster will be on my panel, "Performing Sexualities." My body is trembling. I don't know whether it's from emotion or the cold. There is no heat in this building, and I am freezing in what my new queer girlfriends call this "mildest of all" Australian winters. I bet they say that to all the girls.

On the other hand, I am about to perform, and I am sitting next to a woman whose work, most of it published over the years in *Wicked Women*, the Australian lesbian s/m magazine, I've just read during the twenty-four-hour hallucinatory flight from New York to Sydney. Perhaps I am still hallucinating? The only thing that convinces me that "I" am really here is my shaking body. So I remember it as real. As I read Munster's work, I am thinking to myself: this is "the real thing." Is it because she really "does it," as opposed to just spectating—"I am not a horrified on-looker"[1] she reminds us—or is it some indefinable, uncapturable quality in her writing that makes me believe in her? Is it because I identify with her? If so, I guess that means that *I'm* the one who, for me, is really the *real thing*. I am very pleased when I read my paper after she finishes hers, though the audience has nothing to say to us at all—they sit there either in stunned silence, intellectual bewilderment, emotional exhaustion, or perhaps just frozen from the cold (of course they might simply have been bored).

Anna and I survive the interminable postpresentation silence by cheerfully chatting with each other about body fluids—blood, piss, and tears. I am pleased by what seems to be a mutual recognition. It makes me think that she thinks I'm real too. At least my narcissism is up and running, I see. Then I realize what it is about her work that makes me think of it as "the real thing." It's not just that I know that Munster is an active participant in the Australian lesbian and gay sadomasochistic subculture, though that is important too. But mostly it is about her writing.

Much of it is not easily recognizable narrative, unlike most prominent United States women's writing that presumably speaks from a similar subculture. And, more important, some of it is virtually non-narrativizable. The tenacity of narrative makes the pleasures of *realism*. But writing that resists narration seems to evade or exceed representation. Instead of producing realism, work such as Munster's falls out of symbolization—it reaches toward that constitutive absence that Lacan calls the "Real." Munster writes a piece called "The Violence in Fish," after having lived in Japan for two years, going insane, eating a lot of sushi, and making a video about fish and knives. It ends:

> **now, again, from the other island I dream continuously of living through another time, another time of speaking, of speech with fish, of words sprawling out of the fish's mouth, of fish spoor planting itself in the gaps of my teeth, of the sharp edges of a marauder's jaw, and** not of these inadequate gestures this deserted hovel of representation, in which the pain and violence of joy have yet to be executed. in which the language of fish has yet to be invented[2] (bold in original)

That this text was originally produced in the form of a video may help to explain why it strikes me as so imagistic, with its first part in bold, followed by a commentary on the longing for a place/space beyond the impoverishment of representation. In her piece "I Want a Gorgeous Icon," Munster cites Baudrillard—*images have become our true sex object, the object of our desire*.[3] Although the subject of the lines I quote from Munster's "The Violence in Fish" could be characterized as "fish," one can scarcely go beyond that to imagine a fully dramatized scene. Furthermore, the relationship of her "fish" to the referent "fish" in the real world is oblique at best. The illusion of referentiality seems to be precisely what Munster's writing strives to avoid.

In his chapter "Surrealism Without the Unconscious," Fredric Jameson argues that

> if interpretation is understood, in the thematic way, as the disengagement of a fundamental theme or meaning, then it seems clear that the post-modernist text—of which we have taken the videotape . . . to be a privileged exemplar—is from that perspective defined as a structure or sign flow which resists meaning, whose fundamental inner logic is the exclusion of the emergence of themes as such in that

sense, and which therefore systematically sets out to short-circuit traditional interpretive temptations.[4]

At the conclusion of his chapter Jameson playfully tells the story—"once upon a time"—of the semiotic history of modernism and postmodernism. It is a story that postmodernist theoreticians know well, but I would like to repeat it at some length in order to think about how to position Munster's work, and the work of other queer performers, in relationship to this history and to the death *of* referentiality.

Once upon a time at the dawn of capitalism and middle-class society, there emerged something called the sign, which seemed to entertain unproblematical relations with its referent. This initial heyday of the sign . . . came into being because of the corrosive dissolution of older forms of magical language by a force which I will call that of reification, a force whose logic is one of ruthless separation and disjunction. . . . Unfortunately, that force—which brought traditional reference into being—continued unremittingly, being the very logic of capital itself. Thus this first moment of decoding or of realism cannot long endure; by a dialectical reversal it then itself in turn becomes the object of the corrosive force of reification, which enters the realm of language to disjoin the sign from the referent. Such a disjunction does not completely abolish the referent, or the objective world, or reality, which still continue to entertain a feeble existence on the horizon like a shrunken star or red dwarf. . . . this semiautonomy of language is the moment of modernism. . . . Yet the force of reification . . . does not stop there either: in another stage, heightened . . . reification penetrates the sign itself and disjoins the signifier from the signified. Now reference and reality disappear altogether . . . [and] we are left with that pure and random play of signifiers that we call postmodernism.[5]

In both her theoretical writing and her prose/poem pieces, Munster would certainly seem to be on the side of the disjunction between the sign and the referent. She writes in a quasi-hallucinatory prose style, and in the piece from which I quoted she says that she was "insane" when she wrote it.

Elsewhere I have argued that lesbian writing often partakes of something like a psychotic discourse by definition, since the very term *lesbian* has the privilege and the peril of (non)existing in what passes for The Symbolic Order.[6] Munster's work, however, appears to be different. The space of her work lies somewhere *in between* the modernist disjunction of sign and referent—for there are some "shrunken stars" in the horizon of her writing—and the postmodernist pure and random play of signifiers.

Significantly, Munster's work is firmly (un)grounded in a lesbian identity. So that rather than the hallucinatory return of the impossible-real lesbian in more conventional writing and performance, where the hallucination proceeds from a reading of the text that is *outside* the frame of reference of the writing itself, Munster's writing and performance emanates from an inner space in which she struggles to articulate a language of her experience *already aware* of its impossibility in the universe of signs that constitute the dominant culture.

Because realism (the illusion of referentiality) and the real have often been conflated in perception, writing that resists thematization is often marked in a variety of ways: not only as modernist or early postmodernist but also as narcissistic, the presumption being that it emerges from a consciousness that is closed to audience participation. This latter charge is of course primarily due to the perceptions of readers, or spectators, whose social context places them *outside* the framework of a particular set of signs. In performance, and particularly in contemporary queer performances, the semiotics of narcissism takes some curious turns. In earlier chapters I have discussed performativity in linguistic, social, and cultural contexts, focusing on the ways in which theater and performance become—metaphorically and/or metonymically—idiomatic informants in a variety of contested sites. Now, I will examine some scenes of performance already marked as such, albeit "queerly" so, and look at audience responses to these queer operations.

A story Anna tells at that meeting stays with me all these months later. She had staged a performance at a sex subculture party in an ongoing series of queer theatrics at dance parties. Anna played a psychologically precarious female patient who is catheterized by a "slightly disturbed male doctor."[7] The catheterization was a simulation. The empty catheter bag was swapped for a full one, *out of sight of the audience*, then the bag was ripped open and its liquid poured out over the audience. Classical mimesis—the "most naive form of representation"[8]—fulfilled its promise. Munster reported that for weeks after the performance she heard *nothing* but criticism for failing to perform "safe sex" in a queer venue. Of course, Munster *had* in fact filled the bag with Lucozade. So the performance *was "safe," but was it sex?* The audience was not, as they believed, doused in piss. But as Munster said, they "bought the theatrical illusion,"[9] a curious thing to purchase. Nostalgia perhaps? Or a yearning for innocence that no one ever really had, made especially poignant in queer communities by the danger of exchanging bodily fluids and the memories of an earlier time when one was oblivious to that pleasure's potential for destructiveness. What I am suggesting here is that the content of this particular performance triggered some psychic responses of anger and fear that ironically, perhaps, manifested in a reversal of the most basic tenet of theater—that it is illusionistic.

Even my undergraduates laugh when I tell them about the spectator who rushed on stage to replace Hamlet's hat because it was a cold night out there waiting for his father's ghost. They think it's hilarious that anyone could be so silly as to try to save Desdemona from Othello's strangling embrace. And they don't blame Mr. Garrick one bit for banishing the audience from the stage of the Drury Lane in 1763 in order to put a stop to such interruptions as the one made by a gentleman who, evidently overcome with pity, stepped from behind the scenes during a performance of *King Lear* and threw his arms around Mrs. Woffington as she played Cordelia.[10]

And yet they still often enough repeat such misrecognitions when the subject of the play has to do with sexuality. Like the students in one of my summer classes who kept referring to the women in Sartre's play, *Intimacy*, as "naked ladies." When I reminded the class that the women were covered from neck to ankles with white sheets, they responded, "well, yes, but they were naked *under* those sheets!" A new twist on the "Emperor's New Clothes"? When I teach Tim Miller's *My Queer Body*, these same students become obsessed with wanting to know if the man in the audience whose lap received Miller's naked body was forewarned. Was he a "plant"? Was he one of Miller's friends? Was his permission secured prior to the performance? This is what they want to know: Was that particular moment "real" or *staged*? They are unperturbed by the scene in which Miller strips naked and has a conversation with his penis, commanding it to get erect, demanding that in this time of the AIDS epidemic gay men not give up their rights to pleasure and desire. They receive Miller's various monologues about his sexual history and experiences as if they are the unmitigated truth, and they respect him for his forthrightness, his honesty, his bold revelations of behavior that mainstream America censors. And they think it just fine for Miller to sit naked on a man in the audience, as long as it was a performance. They expect performance artists to tell the truth, but when it comes to physical acts, they want to be assured that they are staged. What if it were "the real thing?" I asked them. That was easy for them to answer: then it was invasive, crossing a line into the obscene and the immoral.[11]

One can see the same phenomenon at work in responses to Karen Finley's performance art. For all of her bold, painfully graphic speech about the horrors of sexual abuse, governmental indifference to AIDS, incest, rape, and a host of other issues that address race, class, gender, and sexual minorities in a tone that unmistakably conjures the genocidal bent of mainstream

Americans toward these "othered" people, it has been Finley's acts of *physicality* that have engendered the greatest controversy and have made of her an object of opprobrium and a target of hate from the fundamentalist right. One remembers that it was the smearing of chocolate on her body that first brought notice of her work to the NEA-bashers. And of all of her performances, it is perhaps "Yams Up My Granny's Ass" that some people have found most offensive. And not because she speaks about hideous abuses of the elderly in nursing homes in this monologue but, ostensibly, because she smears canned yams on her naked buttocks. The letters that poured into the *Village Voice* for weeks after Finley's show displayed an obsession with what she actually did with the yams: did she merely smear them on? Did she insert them into her anus? Were they cooked or uncooked? Was it possible to anally insert an uncooked yam? And so the letters went, on and on without any mention of the *speech act* and its contents that accompanied this demonstration. Once again, the image—conveyed through the physical action—subsumed the speech. Or at least it seemed to do so.[12]

Then there is the case of Ron Athey in the United States who generated another NEA brouhaha. In much the same way that the work of the "NEA Four" performance artists was ludicrously sensationalized, Athey stood accused of dripping HIV-positive blood—real blood not stage blood—onto his audience's heads. Weeks after Athey performed "Excerpted Rites Transformation" at Minneapolis's Walker Art Center, a writer for the *Minneapolis Star Tribune*, who had never seen the show (shades of Karen Finley and the *Washington Post*), reported that spectators were stampeding out of the theater to avoid being contaminated by HIV-positive blood dripping from bloody towels that were sent "winging above the audience on revolving clotheslines."[13] What Athey actually does is part ordeal art, part purification ritual, part sadomasochistic enactment. Some of those purported "bloody towels" were installed in a Soho gallery in New York.[14] They are prints on paper made from blotting the blood of Darryl Carlton, an artist who performs with Athey. Athey makes twelve cuts into Carlton's back, reopening already existing scars, in a stair-step formation that is a traditional African tribal pattern, and a triangle to symbolize queer. Assistants blot the blood with paper towels, hang them from a clothesline, and wind them out over the audience. The prints are bagged in plastic immediately after this section of the performance. Carlton is HIV-negative anyway. If it matters, which it shouldn't, but evidently it does.[15]

The most blatant example of queer performativity's relegation to the "real" that I want to cite is Arlene Croce's notorious (non)review of Bill T. Jones's dance performance, "Still/Here." Croce, the leading dance reviewer for *The New Yorker*, refused to attend Jones's performance and claimed that she did not intend to review it. Instead, she filled her column with a vitriolic diatribe against "victim art," referring to "Still/Here" as a "messianic traveling medicine show," and complaining that *she* was victimized by being confronted with a performance that she was unable to attend because it was "beyond the reach of criticism." Her objections to Jones's work were based on three fronts: (1) "Still/Here" incorporated videos of people with AIDS who talk about their illness; (2) in doing so, the performance "crossed the line between theater and reality," making it unassailable to criticism; and (3) the combination of points one and two has made critics like herself "expendable." It is almost as if Croce believed that by attending the performance she herself would be annihilated, and that by not attending, but rather naming the dance performance not-art, she was preserving her own identity as a critic.

Croce's review of Jones raised an outcry; many people responded with eloquent rejoinders to her fundamentalist dismissal of the work. I want to point out, however, that once again there is in this example a curious conjunction between art that is deemed "too realistic," i.e., too *real*, and art that works with images of sexualities and death. "Dying an art form?" Croce asks derisively, "Why yes, I suppose dying can be art in a screwily post-neo-Dada sense (Dr. Kevorkian, now playing in Oregon . . .) But this is not the sense intended by Bill T. Jones. . . . If I understand 'Still/Here' correctly, and I think I do [despite the fact that she did not see it!]—the publicity has been deafening—it is . . . designed to do some good for sufferers of fatal illnesses, both those in the cast and those thousands more who may be in the audience."[16] Frank Rich pointedly rebuffed Croce by asking if she would refuse to watch the autobiographical work of Dennis Potter ("The Singing Detective") who did a final interview on television on the subject of his cancer; or would she not look at Goya's "The Croup," a representation of a diphtheria victim, or read Oliver Sacks's "A Leg to Stand On," an account of his surgery?[17] Through these examples, Rich quite rightly points to Croce's homophobic and racist aversion to Jones, which she names with the euphemistic nomination "victim art" and tries to cover with allusions to other dancers, like Pina Bausch, whom she implies are simply not good artists but who have amassed a wide following simply because they focus their work on "dissed blacks, abused women, or disfranchised homosexuals."[18] Tony Kushner, whose own work, *Angels in America*, was implicitly referred to by Croce as another example of this proliferation of victim art, also responded with some excellent points: that the very artists whom Croce now glorifies were once attacked by reactionary critics like herself for being vulgar, "insufficiently reticent," and spiritually impoverished. Kushner also smartly remarks: "Ms. Croce finds Mr. Jones guilty of over-responding to multiculturalist and community politics and, at the same time, of narcissism, which is a neat trick."[19]

These and other excellent rejoinders were powerful rebuttals. But what the countercritics seemed to have missed is the connection Croce was making between the "real" of this performance and the tie between sexuality and death. Rich comes close when he ends his column by saying: "To the extent AIDS is responsible for yanking death out of the American closet, history may show that the epidemic has changed our culture in much the same way that the cataclysmic carnage of World War I transformed English literature. However it turns out, this is the story of our time. Amazingly, Ms. Croce has missed that story, just as surely as she has failed to see that dying is part of art because it is part of life."[20] But I don't think Croce *has* missed that story. In my reading of her column, she did not mis(s)understand Jones's performance at all. Indeed I think she skipped it because she understood it only too well. What Croce's actions and language signify is her participation in the dominant order's *refusal* to allow AIDS and its representations to enter into discourse. That is, Jones's incorporation of people-with-AIDS into his work is rejected by Croce as nonartistic, which is to say "real," and thus she willfully participates in what Tim Dean has explained as a *social psychosis*: "AIDS is encountered not only as the discourse of the Other in a return of the repressed that constitutes the repressed as such (the structure by which we understand a neurotic subject); it is encountered also in the real as a consequence of its wholesale repudiation by a society that refuses to admit a signifier for AIDS and is therefore analyzable according to the structure by which we understand a psychotic subject."[21]

It is the connection between Croce's objections to Jones's work on the basis of her nomination of it as "victim" art *and* its critical unassailability on the basis of its "realness" that makes her response complicit with a social psychosis. For notice that Jones's work *is* art for Croce as long as it is preceded by the adjectival "victim," whereas it is, at the same time, *not art* due to its crossing of the boundary between theater and reality. So, is "Still/Here" a particular *form* of art that Croce dislikes, or is it not art at all? Both/And. How can we understand this impossible response? It is insufficient to say simply that Croce's homophobia gets her so rattled that she makes confusing contradictions. As Dean points out, though psychoanalytic orthodoxy states that psychosis is a defense against homosexuality, psychosis understood as a "loss of reality" (i.e., heterosexuality) is too simplistic.[22] Certainly Croce is not out of touch with reality; on the contrary, she is too much a *part of reality*. As Dean puts it: "psychosis is not a question of a maladjustment to reality, a reality from which the psychotic subject has taken too great a distance; rather, psychosis is a question of the real that is too proximate, a real from which sufficient distance has not been obtained."[23] Croce keeps her distance from Bill T. Jones and his representations of people who are terminally ill—"I have not seen Bill T. Jones's 'Still/Here' and have no plans to review it."[24] But she does review it. She re-views it, without first viewing it, as an unspeakable, extradiscursive act, a dance that cannot be symbolized, a dance that falls out of her repertory of the symbolic. Again, to cite Dean: "AIDS is a condition of the *body politic*, an index of the socialized body of the American subject caught in a network of signifiers that renders it vulnerable to AIDS precisely because, by refusing a signifier for AIDS, it faces the prospect that what is foreclosed in the symbolic will return in the real."[25]

This latter part of Dean's statement is of course Lacan's famous statement—*what is foreclosed in the symbolic will return in the real*. On first glance, Lacan's Real, that which falls out of symbolization, and Croce's real—the boundary crossed between theater and reality—would seem to have little in common. But when Croce says that Jones's performance was too realistic, she doesn't mean dramatic realism—the illusion of reality— she means *life*. Here again is this bizarre contradiction: Croce is saying that because Jones's work deals with death, it is too lifelike. So, she does know what Rich thinks she is missing—that death is part of life. But she knows even more than that, unconsciously at least, she knows that death is in some way life's supreme achievement. Perhaps Jones's work was just *too* *"good"* for Croce to confront? Perhaps she feared that her own critical skills, and thus identity, were insufficient to the task of taking on a performance that was *that* transcendent.

Dean reminds us that Lacan's term *foreclosure* is his translation of Freud's *Verwerfung*—"also translatable as 'rejection,' 'repudiation,' or 'exclusion.' "[26] He summarizes Lacan's complex thinking on the question of psychosis by saying that "the being of the subject is not where it thinks it is; rather, the subject's being is located at the heart of what it excludes."[27] In a way, then, Croce *did* attend "Still/Here," even though she was not there. But as one of the performers who wrote letters to the editors of *The New Yorker* pointed out: "I found it ironic that Ms. Croce describes the workshop participants as 'dying people' who 'aren't there' when in fact most of us are alive and still here."[28]

Jones's "Still/Here," Athey's blood-letting performances, Munster's catheterization scene, Miller's choice to sit naked on the lap of an audience member, Finley's yam-smearing: all of these queer performances aroused

very strong responses that had to do with the "realness" of the performance. In Munster's case, artifice was mistaken for the real. In Athey's case,
the blood was real, but the terror was fueled by the fantasy/conflation
of "deviant" sex/performance with HIV. In Munster's performance, by
switching the catheter bag *offstage*, she deliberately played to a credulous
audience that may have been duped precisely because they were *not*
expecting/ "realism" in a queer/s/m performance venue, so they took the
act for the real.

Athey, on the other hand, insists quite emphatically on the "realness" of
his performance. He says: "my work is based on physically, dynamically
altering the body. I cannot fake cutting. My theater is controlled actual
experience."[29] Athey's spectators support this perspective. Mark Russell,
director of New York City's P.S. 122, describes Athey's work as "a rite of
passage, a cleansing trial," in which "artifice would not be appropriate."[30]
This is not true only of Athey's blood work. When he presides over a dyke
wedding ritual, a member of the audience just has to know if Julie and
Pigpen, the couple, are lovers in real life. Athey tells "true" stories of his
boyhood; the piercings he performs on himself and others are real. C. Carr
reports that a spectator behind her at Athey's performance shouted: "It's
not entertainment. It's something more."[31] And Athey describes his own
work, his blood work in particular, as "the loudest form of expression, for
when you're beyond words."[32]

Getting beyond words seems to be the thing, the point, the "real thing."
As Elaine Scarry has written, that place *beyond* words is a place we call
pain.[33] Scarry's study is quite emphatically about *physical* pain, as is Athey's
piercing/cutting blood work, and as is sadomasochism. Although many, if
not most, s/m practitioners say that s/m is *not* about physical pain but
about power, I think the tendency to disavow s/m's physicality is due, in
large part, to a a history in psychological/psychoanalytic studies of denying
that the masochist actually desires to feel pain. Long before it became a
feminist controversy, an extraordinary effort was made to argue that the
masochist's objective is *not* to experience pain, as if pain were something
absolute or transparent, rather than contextual and constructed.

Wilhelm Reich, for example, recounts being cured of the erroneous
impression that masochists actually sought pleasure through pain when he
was treating a masochistic man in 1928. Having resisted, through a number of sessions, his client's entreaties to be beaten, Reich finally relented and
administered two hard blows with a ruler. The client yelled aloud and never
made such requests again, though "his lamentations and passive reproaches
persisted." From that moment on, Reich concluded that "pain is far from

being the instinctual goal of the masochist. When beaten, the masochist, like any other *mortal,* experiences pain."[34] Based on this one incident, Reich concluded that the whole industry of sadomasochistic representations, as well as the actual instruments and performers procured to satisfy s/m desires, is constructed on a faulty edifice.

Theodor Reik also concluded that "masochism—as well in its realization as in its phantasies—leads to situations which are pleasant and have nothing to do with pain."[35] Reik's analysis is, however, a little more subtle than Reich's, for he admits that though pain itself is not what the masochist desires, there are certain *effects* associated with pain that are pleasurable. Returning to Freud's earliest conjectures on the relationship between the aggressive instincts and masochism, Reik champions the thesis that Freud would later reject: that masochism is the result of sadistic impulses turned inward. Thus Reik argues that the masochist aims for pleasure, *like everyone else,* but the sexual gratification is detoured through certain experiences in which the masochist achieves a subversive triumph in what appears to be a defeat. In both of these accounts, the words and phrases that I have highlighted point toward a humanistic/universalistic model of behavior. Reich must believe that his client is "mortal": Reik feels compelled to say that masochists are "just like everyone else," with a slight detour. Deviations are comprehensible and tolerable; *differences* are not. I suspect that lesbians who practice s/m are sensitive to this cultural inability to accept that people *feel* sensations differently.[36] I'm not suggesting that s/m is about pain per se; rather, I'm saying there is no such phenomenon as pain per se. As obvious as this point must be, I feel compelled to emphasize it; for in a culture such as mine, that upholds the death penalty and is complicit in various forms of heinous international torture and war, the idea that most of its citizens cannot tolerate the thought that some people experience pleasure through acts that others would experience as painful seems an absolutely bizarre displacement. If we can understand that some women do not like to have their breasts stroked even lightly, while others like to have their nipples pinched, then why is it so difficult to take the next step and understand that some women like to have their nipples clamped?

Elaine Scarry's study is illuminating in this regard, for some forms of pain, or intensifications of the body's surfaces, are severe enough to lead to the loss of language. And indeed, s/m sexual practices often lead toward that place, if they do not fully accomplish it. From a Western perspective, this is apparently perceived as always a terrifying and violent experience. That it can also be a form of meditation, deep relaxation, or beneficial sensory deprivation seems to be incomprehensible, especially if it is accompanied by a sexualized euphoria. If, as Scarry has argued, pain *is* the place where language leaves us; or, to put it slightly differently, if the leaving of language is what we call pain, then my question is this: Why are these *queer* artists carrying the place of the inexpressible, the place of pain, in performances that have elicited an uncommon concern and unselfconscious new naivete about representation? What is this purchase on/of the "real"—or is it the "Real"?—in queer performances about?

Munster has this to say: "queer performance is literally saturated by a desire to understand and pose the body as raw material, the body unmediated by the form and consumption of spectacle."[37] She links this desire with the complicity of a drive that permeates gay and lesbian identity politics—the drive toward *visibility*. Maybe we all know by now in the global academic discourse that "the screen is not simply a field for display but is simultaneously a device which eradicates, which screens out what is not fit for public consumption,"[38] but there is still an overwhelming urge to mark a stationary place, to appeal to a referent, to have recourse to a/the "real thing." What are the implications of that mark, that referent, becoming located on queer performative bodies?

It strikes me as particularly interesting, and relatively unnoticed, that these performances, which have become so vexed for their realness (actual or presumed) are firmly within the parameters of a vast discourse that is nonetheless recognizable as queer/autoeroticism/sadomasochism. In other words, we are talking about "scenes" that have either been taken *for* real, with or without the artist's complicity, or have been assumed to be real.

A similar dynamic is at work in the performances of the late Bob Flanagan, the renowned "supermasochist" who was, until his death in January of 1996, one of the longest survivors of cystic fibrosis. In a fairly simple cause and effect pattern, Flanagan attributed his masochistic desires to the clinical procedures that he was forced to undergo as a child, which were often quite painful. Some of his masochistic performances were even close to replicas of his childhood experiences. For example, he attributes his desire for bondage to being restrained as a baby while needles were placed into his chest to withdraw the accumulated mucous.

Physical therapy for children with cystic fibrosis often entails the therapist pounding on the child's chest to dislodge the mucous, sometimes in an inverted (hanging) position, sometimes over the lap of the therapist. Hence we have images of Bob as an adult lying prone over the knees of his mistress and long-time lover, Sheree Rose, who is spanking him with a paddle in front of an audience. Or pulleys attached to Flanagan's ankles that would gradually lift him out of his hospital bed (in a performance called "Visiting

Hours") until he was hanging by his ankles. Flanagan also explicitly remembers cartoons, films, and toys that he connects with his masochistic activities. In "Visiting Hours," a toy chest is displayed full of such childhood memorabilia as doctors' kits, operation games, boxing gloves, and other standard children's toys mixed with cultural icons such as a crucifix and s/m paraphernalia such as handcuffs and riding crops. These articles mingled in such proximity present both a shocking juxtaposition *and* an unmistakable recognition that there is more continuity than the dominant culture cares to admit between categories that are constructed as if they are discrete: sexual fantasy and organized religions, childhood "innocence" and adult "maturity," the body as an object for medical restoration and the body as a site of orgasmic pleasure. Notice, too, that this intermingling breaks down the barriers between the generations, suggesting that childhood and adulthood are not separated by some mythical rite of passage (like puberty for instance). This simple recognition may be one of Flanagan's most transgressive acts, for, as I will discuss at length in chapter 5, the abolishment of generational differences can connote a violation of the founding taboo of the culture—incest. When Flanagan advertises a show with the simple slogan, "Bob Flanagan is Sick," accompanied by an image of a smiling infant lying over the lap of a nurse who is poised to insert a rectal thermometer, he powerfully and succinctly invites us to reconsider the history of pathologizing "deviants" as *products* of dominant cultural norms rather than as perverters of it.

One of the fascinating aspects of Flanagan's masochism is its extraordinary simplicity, according to the connections he makes himself. For example, he attributes his ability to transform pain into sexual pleasure as originating in one particular memory. One of the effects of cystic fibrosis is that it interferes with pancreatic and digestive functioning. Hence Flanagan suffered from severe stomachaches as a child. This was his first conscious memory of transforming pain into sexual pleasure:

> Because of my early, really horrible stomach-aches, I would rub against the sheets and the pillows to soothe my stomach and this became more and more erotic—I started to masturbate that way; slowly it all blended together. One way of taking control of the stomach-ache was to turn it into an orgasm.[39]

Although it's certainly not unusual for a child to discover genital pleasure by rubbing against the sheets of his/her bed, Flanagan, remarkably, seems to have been able to translate nearly all of his childhood experiences into masochistic pleasure. For example, he went to Catholic catechism classes through junior high school and was able to relate his own suffering to the crucifixion of Jesus. Of course this is also not at all uncommon. One knows in the s/m subculture that Catholics are particularly prone to relating saintliness to suffering, and the "Stations of the Cross" are excellent primers for future masochists. What is remarkable about Flanagan's experience, however, is that once he became older and began to feel guilty about comparing himself to Jesus, (again, it was not merely the fantasy association that worried him but his imitation of Jesus's suffering by tying himself up in positions that resembled the cross), he did not begin to resist his masochism. Instead, he began to listen to *Jesus Christ Superstar* and whip himself the full thirty-nine lashes during the sequence of the "Trial Before Pilate."[40]

Linda Kauffman has described Flanagan as a "father-confessor without shame, one who has no interest in promoting behavior based on *guilt*."[41] While I agree with the latter half of her statement, Kauffman does not make a clear distinction between shame and guilt, which are very different emotions. My own impression of Flanagan's work is that it *is* shame-based, and I would describe him as shamelessly shameful. Despite the fact that such a construction is logically "impossible," I have been arguing throughout that this is what s/m activity is frequently about—living in, experiencing, and (re)creating paradoxical contradictions. First of all, I can't imagine a top or bottom who would not agree that humiliation is a paramount ingredient for the eroticism to be evoked. If a bottom were to achieve true "humility," however, the sexual charge would likely disappear. Kauffman's argument that Flanagan is more or less just a "normal" (notice how she emphasizes his heterosexuality and his long-term, monogamous relationship with Sheree Rose) guy whose sex play and performances are best understood as illustrations of the "posthuman, for he illustrates step by step how the human senses—taste, touch, smell, hearing, and sight—have been utterly reorganized by medical technology"[42] makes an interesting point. However, the tendency of her article is to deeroticize and/or heterosexualize Flanagan's masochism; to explain his sexual excitement by comparing it to the large, relatively hidden, subculture of highly successful, powerful, heterosexual men who regularly go to dominatrixes for masochistic play. Such men have a "strong compulsion to repudiate masculine authority" by engaging in infantilizing and/or feminizing behavior, or are men who are fleeing from "adult responsibilities, failures, impossible social problems, unhappiness, complex relationships with women *and* with other men."[43] Although Kauffman disassociates Flanagan's sexuality and his art from "commercial" s/m (by which she seems to mean heterosexual), she nonetheless promotes him as a kind of "commercial"— someone who instructs, illustrates, demonstrates, and makes the undigestible elements of our society visible and palatable. Flanagan himself, however, indicated little if any interest in educating the masses about his sexuality and work. *All* that he seemed to care about really was devising ingenious ways to improve his sexual pleasure and heighten the intensity of his orgasms. If this included the pleasure of being observed as he practiced these sexual acts, this was not in the realm of performance per se. On the contrary, Flanagan said that he became a performance artist rather serendipitously, after he became involved with Sheree and her passion for documenting their relationship on video and through journals. When he did "take s/m out of the closet and into the museum," as Kauffman says, it had nothing to do with his desire to entertain or educate spectators. Rather, it had everything to do with Flanagan's discovery that some of the acts that had grown stale through repetition could be recharged if he added the dimension of exhibitionism to them.

As a child Flanagan would hide in the bathroom or his bedroom and improvise sadomasochistic play—whipping himself with Ping-Pong paddles, mummifying himself in blankets or bags, building his own private pit and pendulum in the bathtub, walking around the backyard naked in the middle of the night and defecating behind bushes. These activities produced an erotic charge precisely because of the suspense that he might, at any moment, get caught—and implicitly punished—by his parents. At that time, however, all of his efforts were geared toward *not* being actually seen, while fantasizing that he might accidentally be seen. Later, when he began to perform publicly, the first instance was a surprise party in which some of his friends had arranged for Sheree to spank him over her knee (one hundred strokes) while his friends cheered her on. Flanagan was reluctant to participate at first (like all bottoms he wants to control the scene meticulously), but he went ahead with it because it was *too embarrassing* to refuse, given his reputation. He found, however, that he enjoyed it very much. There is evidence everywhere in Flanagan's writing that his sexual proclivities are imbued with a rich sense of shame.

Of course this sounds as if I am playing right into the hands of the s/m protesters. However, I do not think that it serves us well to avoid or apologize for such an obvious "truism" of s/m sexual practice. Shame, or humiliation, is quite simply a pervasive element in s/m. Although I cannot make this claim for everyone, it is certainly possible to think of shame differently than ontologically. One can experience shame without "being ashamed." Shame can be situational, it can be erotic, and there is no reason to conceive of it as ontological.

Eve Sedgwick and Adam Frank have produced a brilliant reconsideration of shame through their reading of the work of Silvan Tomkins, whose first publication on the theory of affect was published in a volume edited by Jacques Lacan. Sedgwick and Frank argue, following Tomkins, that "the pulsations of cathexis around shame, of all things, are what either enable or disenable so basic a function as the ability to be interested in the world"[44] If, paraphrasing Tomkins, a barrier emerges that reduces or depletes interest or pleasure in the world, and shame is the affect that rebounds to reactivate this interest, then it is credible that Flanagan would have begun to perform his masochistic sexuality in public in order to introduce an element (the spectators) that might have recharged his shame. He himself speaks of being a very shy, very private person who only began to perform when some of his activities had lost their sexual edge through repetition. Furthermore, what Sedgwick and Frank argue in this article is instructive for understanding s/m generally. For, as they say, if the emphasis in Tomkins's account is "on the *strange* [my emphasis], rather than on the prohibited or disapproved . . . [then] the phenomenon of shame might offer new ways of short-circuiting the seemingly near-inescapable habits of thought that Foucault groups together under the term *repressive hypothesis* [emphasis in original]."[45] The strange in Tomkins theory might be likened to Freud's notion of the "uncanny," in which what was once *unheimlich* becomes *heimlich*, or, better yet, the *unheimlich* is *already heimlich*. S/m sexuality often has exactly this dynamic: the strange and the familiar are not oppositional. But rather than thinking in terms of the strange *becoming* familiar when "the repressed returns," we might understand them as concepts that alternate in rapid oscillation during an s/m scene, or as affects that, contrary to our usual ways of thinking about them, do not exist in contradistinction to one another but are rather closely related, hovering on an edge or borderline where they are sometimes indistinguishable. Sedgwick and Frank see shame as a "switch point for the individuation of imaging systems," as the necessary accompaniment to positive affect—"only a scene that offers you enjoyment or engages your interest can make you blush"—and as an affect "characterized by its failure ever to renounce its object cathexis"[46] I could cite numerous instances of s/m fiction, poetry, and testimony and point out that in each case shame is an ingredient in the erotic charge. I will select only one, however, for my purposes here, for it is a story that pretends to show that one can have pleasurable sexual experience *without* all the "baggage" of s/m. Appropriately, it is entitled "The Old-Fashioned Way," a story that either inadvertently or ironically (it is rather difficult to tell which) includes an s/m dynamic in what appears to be not so much an anti-s/m representation but a narrative that first presumes that the use of "dirty talk" and bags of sex toys connotes s/m, then strives to undercut the value of such activity. What the story actually shows, in my reading, is that s/m is not about the paraphernalia and the transgressive speech with which it has come to be associated in mainstream popular culture; rather, it is about the unexpected element, the *switching*, in whatever form it might assume, which takes the participants by surprise and produces a form of pleasure that emanates from finding oneself suddenly *unguarded* and, it would seem then to follow, pleasurably embarrassed.

The story is by Lucy Jane Bledsoe, in a collection entitled *Tangled Sheets: Stories and Poems of Lesbian Lust.* The plot is very simple. Elizabeth and Erika are roommates. Erika is a "twenty-three-year old sex radical," who "hates anything associated with seventies feminism"[47] She has multiple piercings, including a ring in her clitoris, and a drawer full of sex toys. Elizabeth is thirteen years older, presumably a "product of seventies feminism," and likes to do things the "old-fashioned way." Erika, who is "not shy," or so she claims, seduces Elizabeth, who goes along with it out of curiosity but isn't really particularly aroused by Erika. After Erika collects all of her sex toys and talks dirty to Elizabeth, calling her a "sexy, trashy little whore," and a "cheap piece of meat"[48] she fucks Elizabeth with a large lavender dildo. Neither of them come. Then Elizabeth persuades Erika to allow her to try, and she brings Erika to a volatile orgasm by licking her nipples, running her tongue around her clitoris and putting one finger in her anus and three fingers in her vagina. Simple—the old-fashioned way. The point of the story appears to be obvious. Sex radicals (or sadomasochists) have gotten lost in the "high technology" of the sex industry. What a woman wants, as Elizabeth, the narrator, first reminds us then shows us, is "real passion" and close attention to her body's responses.

Well, yes. But, the story actually has an s/m dynamic, which shows that these are not mutually exclusive aims. First of all, the "top"—Erika—is "topped" by the "bottom"—Elizabeth. Second, Elizabeth teases Erika (whom we know *is* truly aroused by Elizabeth) not only before but especially during the sex scene. She licks around Erika's clitoris ring, but refuses to actually touch Erika's clitoris until Erika is screaming for it: "I wanted her to get so desperate she *had* to ask me"[49] This is something that Erika usually finds *humiliating* to do (asking for it); furthermore, we are told that Erika's "ears redden" when Elizabeth begins to talk about fucking her. And, most important, Elizabeth is motivated to fuck Erika by three emotions: "At first I was embarrassed. Then I felt sad for her because she hadn't transformed me into a liberated sex machine like she said she could. Finally, I felt angry. Erika and her friends really believed they'd invented hot sex and radical politics"[50] If this story is meant to be an endorsement of seventies feminist principles about love-making, it misses the mark by a long shot. A "real" seventies feminist would hardly endorse making love that is driven from shame, sadness, and anger. Perhaps Bledsoe intends all that I am suggesting, but the story is ambiguous. For even as it shows that so-called vanilla sex and s/m are not really oppositional, it does critique s/m's "special effects" *or*, at least, insists that one can practice s/m sexuality *without* the special effects, which everyone knows anyway except for the media that promotes the subculture as consumers of various forms of equipment. Significantly, although the narrator indicates that Erika pulls a whole drawer full of sex toys out before they begin, the only one that we see her actually use is the giant lavender dildo, which she calls "the whale." *This* is the item that is missing when Elizabeth fucks Erika successfully. So for all the talk and images of dildos that have amassed in more conventional literature by and for lesbians, it still appears that the dildo can be the one item that somehow represents a kind of artificiality that is treated with suspicion and opprobrium. But the real fake thing in this story is Elizabeth's relationship to her own professed ideas about sexuality. She says that she has no objections to talking dirty, as long as you love the person, and that hot sex has to emerge from "real passion." Yet, are we suppose to believe that Elizabeth has developed a sudden "real" desire of the type she names for Erika, after Erika fails to sexually arouse her? Maybe so, but the story does not makes this in any way clear. In fact, if anything, this story is a kind of "revenge" narrative. Elizabeth fucks Erika only to show her that she can do it better, and that *her* generation was superior in their knowledge of sexuality. Interestingly enough, this is one of the few stories that actually presents the top, Elizabeth, as a kind of sadist, whose pleasure is unmistakably found in truly humiliating Erika and, in a sense, punishing her for her implied critique of Elizabeth's generation of lesbians. Despite what Elizabeth says about true love and real passion, they are shown to be incommensurable in this story. Erika is scarcely a "victim" in this narrative though, for in a sense she *does succeed in topping Elizabeth*. After all, she is the one who gets what she wants, even if it wasn't the way she thought she would get it.

Narratives such as this one make the distinction between sadism and masochism extremely complex, even though the narratives themselves do not at first appear to be very complicated or well written. Although it is endlessly fascinating to speculate about the etiology of masochism, what intrigues me more is the perception/reception of these acts, the social context in which they are performed or reported, and their relationship to "theatricality" and the real. Flanagan is particularly interesting in this regard, since beyond all the other performance artists, whom I can only briefly and selectively discuss in this chapter, Flanagan's work is the most unremittingly "real." The only time he ever mentions performing an act in public that tricks his audience is when he nails his scrotum to a wooden board, a procedure that he knows does not really hurt but that appears to the audience to be excruciatingly painful. Some onlookers have even fainted when watching this act, which gives Flanagan a kind of gleeful (sadistic?) pleasure. Significantly, this is the *one* act that is most often noted when Flanagan's work is mentioned—the only one that is "fake," or that appears to be fake. For though it doesn't really hurt, Flanagan does do this privately as well. His pleasure in doing so is derived from the *sight* of his scrotum splayed out and nailed down, so one might surmise that he places himself in the spectator's role when he performs this act in private. Otherwise, as Kauffman points out, while Flanagan "was inspired by Rudolf Schwarzkogler who 'had himself photographed (supposedly) slicing off pieces of his penis as if it were so much salami,' " these acts were staged "whereas Flanagan's actions are real. He pierces the penis, attaches weights, clothespins, fishhooks, baby dolls to it and nails it to a board."[51] Flanagan always insisted upon the realness of his acts, whether they were performed privately or publicly.

For example, when discussing his participation in s/m parlors, where he would spend a hundred dollars or more for a single session in a contractual relationship, he persistently expressed his disappointment. He was "never much into the verbal [humiliation] because it wasn't real; it was all an act." In heavy whipping scenes, however, "it didn't matter if it were phony because [he] still had to endure it." Nonetheless, he "really wanted this to be real with a real person, without paying for it . . . as part of a *relationship.*"[52] Sheree Rose was thus the woman of his dreams. For she was really into it. She truly enjoyed humiliating and punishing him. Not always for the right reasons in Flanagan's opinion (no relationship is perfect)—but the fact that she really was a "bossy" woman who enjoyed making men do what she told them to do, pleased him enormously.

During his 1994 installation, "Visiting Hours," at the New Museum in New York City, I visited Bob and Sheree while he was lying in his full-scale reproduction of a hospital room and spoke with him about the issue of spectatorship and his performance of the "real." He verified my suspicion that members of his audience were invariably concerned with whether or not the acts he performed were theatrical tricks, or did he indeed drive nails through his scrotum, lie on a bed of real nails for hours, endure a string of clothespins attached to his body then snatched off suddenly. The answer to these questions is of course both yes and no. Flanagan certainly could not have been experiencing the *same* sensations that his interlocutors might if they performed the same acts on their own bodies. Yes, he really nails his scrotum to a wooden board; no "you" would not feel the same way if you did it to yourself. In an interview with Deborah Drier, Sheree Rose comments:

> We're playing with the idea of what's real. People say, "this is so *real,* this is really Bob," but it isn't exactly. When people see Bob in the hospital bed, it's Bob Flanagan they're seeing, it's also Bob Flanagan *playing* Bob Flanagan. And it's only the part of him that he's revealing at that moment, not the totality. When Bob goes up in the air he goes motionless and quiet, and so does the room. He's a real person, but at the same time he's also this object hanging there, and playing with that concept makes people really uncomfortable.[53]

Flanagan comments: "A woman came in while I was suspended and stood watching me. Then I breathed and coughed, and she said, 'How do they do that?' She thought I was a hanging sculpture."[54].

Flanagan's public acts thus raise in a very clean way the question of what constitutes performance. Is the presence of a spectator, who is not directly involved in the acts themselves, enough to make the "real" performative? People have *always* attended performances in order to have vicarious experiences, but I can think of no time in the history of theater, except perhaps for the period of high naturalism (and that had more to do with the objects in the spectacle), during which spectators were concerned to ascertain to what extent the performance was real. The medieval mystery cycles went to great lengths to set their stage with great authenticity, but as far as we know no spectators who watched the actor playing Judas get caught up in and nearly strangled to death in the elementary flying machinery designed to represent his hanging actually came to the play anticipating such a performance! There is, I'm suggesting, something quite "queer" about these responses, and I suspect it's not incidental that they are occurring in and around the context of performance that is marked as queer in that other, nominative, sense. These queer performances, in other words, are either insisting themselves on a recognizable referent, indeed a near collapse between sign and referent, *or* they are *expected* to make that collapse and found lacking if they do not. While I would agree with Munster up to a point, that queer performance is literally saturated with a visceralness that is connected with the drive toward lesbian and gay visibility, such an interpretation puts the onus of this phenomenon on the queer performers themselves, suggesting that due to a rather passé political agenda they are degrading their own form of work. I think, however, that there is a way to think about this differently.

One could, of course, simply wonder what difference this all makes. For after all, for the postmodernist, the referent is *always* the illusion of referentiality. Are we not merely talking about what *kind* of performances these queer artists are making, rather than whether they are real or performative? My interest in this question is twofold: first, whether or not we accept the postmodernist dictum of the arbitrary or free play of signifiers, which refer only to each other, there is nonetheless a fixation on the real(ity) of these performances that is tenacious, perhaps naively—but perhaps not. Second, and relatedly, there is the argument that the semiotics of theater is different from linguistic performativity. And it is these two that are often confused, or used interchangeably in contemporary discourse theory. Citing Judith Butler's widely used discussions of the performative, Eve Sedgwick points out that *performative* is often used as if it were synonymous with *theatrical.* Butler, however, insists upon the performative's "double-meaning of 'dramatic' and non-referential," and Sedgwick points out that "performative" then "carries the authority of two quite different discourses, that of theater on the one hand, of speech-act theory and deconstruction on the other." These are very useful and important distinctions to be made in what has become something of a chaotic (because so undifferentiated) use of the term *performative.* I want to contribute further to this chaos by at least questioning Sedgwick's assertion that the performative partakes of the "prestige" of both these discourses, for from my point of view theater is *not* a discourse that is prestigious. In fact, the antitheatrical prejudice is historically long-standing. In academia particularly, theater, as a discipline is usually the most under-funded and least prestigious of the fields, often only included as a "program"—a poor cousin to English literature departments. This devaluing of theater, as one of the terms associated with the performative, is worth considering in the proliferating discourses of the performative. I agree with Sedgwick that "more can be said [indeed *much* more] of performative speech acts than that they are ontologically dislinked or introversively non-referential." And I think that one area where this inquiry needs to go is in the way in which "theatrical" is most often conflated with theatrical realism and the way in which this conflation leads to all sorts of confusions when someone refers to an act (linguistic or otherwise) as theatrical.

Sedgwick's suggests that we might not want "to dwell . . . so much on the non-reference of the performative but rather on (what de Man calls) its necessarily 'aberrant' relation to its own reference—the torsion, the mutual perversion, as one might say, of reference and performativity."[55] Theater scholars and practitioners have been telling themselves and their students for decades, and continue to do so, that what makes theater different from all other art forms is the presence of living actors. Patrice Pavis writes:

It is ideology—through the phenomena of recognition and eroticism . . . which attracts us and draws us into the spectacle. Hence ideology and the social context superimpose, on the fabric of a work of art, a living trace of the *spectator's* reality. In the ideology given form by the artistic sign, just as in the body lent by the actor to his character, there is always a "physical residue" which cannot be semiotized. . . . It is first and foremost this body and the living and unpredictable person that we have before us. The "physical residue" could, for example, be the pretty legs of the actress which have an erotic effect on me; it will also be, on an ideological plane, what I recognize in the fiction that corresponds to my own ideological situation.[56]

The actress's pretty legs are of course themselves ideologically constructed and thus recognized. Nonetheless, there is a difference between the second recognition (of the pretty legs) and the theatrical illusion of referentiality in which the actress's legs are not one of the signifiers that make up the fictive world of the performance. Unlike the more common argument that theater, alone of all the art forms (and this is no doubt partly what lends it a rather degraded status in contemporary theory), does represent its referent, Pavis takes a diametrically opposed position. His argument—"the linking of a text to an ideology extraneous to it is not merely a process of recognition (of the signified); it is, rather, a semiotic mechanism, connecting text to a field of discourse (that is a discursive referent)"[57]—may seem a rather banal point to repeat now, yet it is still very much the case that in academic theater studies the position of recognizing the signified retains a very powerful hold, for in large part this is presumably what constitutes theater's difference from other art forms. It is also the case though that in semiotically sophisticated discussions of art, and particularly in work that has focused on gender and sexualities, the concept of "theatricality" is still frequently deployed in contexts that indicate some kind of *return to the referent* and thus the "physical residue," or what I am calling "the flesh." This is so, I think, particularly in regard to the work of solo or performance artists. Again, Pavis writes:

The *autotextual* is the self-contained, self-referential level whereby a text claims autonomy and adopts the perfectly rounded form of a monad, thus fending off outside influence, intertextual or ideological. This type of self-referentiality . . . is to be found in any text which calls attention to the processes it employs. In the theatre, where it takes the form of theatricality, it is the crux of the illusion/disillusion dichotomy, hovering between the "real" and the "theatrical."[58]

While we are making distinctions between performance and performativity, it is also vital that we not collapse performance into the theatrical. In other words, we need to be able to distinguish between the performativity of various modes of the theatrical, as well as the performativity of performances. Performance may carry *both* meanings—performativity and theatricality—but they are not exclusive. A performance need not be dramatic (where the dramatic signifies referential or representational), nor are all nonreferential performances *not* dramatic. The performances of the queer operators I have discussed above tend to muddy these distinctions, and in doing so they foreground the problem of the relationship between performance and the "real" and invite us to reconsider a history of cultural controversy that has been, in part, wrecked on the notion of a theatrical realism that is always only a particular set of conventions designed, precisely, to create the illusion of referentiality. Theatrical realism then works both edges of the controversy, for it is simultaneously the theatrical site that most discloses and most veils the relationship between the staged and the performed.

Munster, Miller, Finley, Athey, Jones, and Flanagan could all be said to engage in performances that are *autotextual* in the sense Pavis describes. What remains perplexing about responses to their work is that in the "hovering between the 'real' and the 'theatrical' " it would seem logical that the "real" would come to rest on the side of their speech, whereas the "theatrical" would rest with the "physical residue"—the acts that they perform with their bodies and the various objects that they use to enact these performances. That, however, has not been the case. Rather, when these performers display acts of physicality, they generate controversy (often quite negatively) about the "real" of the performances. These acts not only stigmatize the performers as not-really-artists (real artists don't smear chocolate on their bodies, pierce themselves with needles, lie on beds of nails, douse the audience with piss, talk about terminal illness, etc.) but they also affix to their work a rather paradoxical relation of sign and referent. These performers do not create the "illusion of referentiality," nor do they disjoin the sign from the referent. And certainly they are not read as if they are engaging in the free play of signifiers or the death *of* the referent. On the contrary, it seems that their work is linked with a kind of referentiality that collapses any distinction between sign or signifier and referent. Their performances are received as if the signifiers *are* the referent, and the referent becomes *the thing itself.* What we are looking at here, in contemporary queer performance art is something like *death AND the referent,* rather than the death *of* the referent that we know so well.

It is odd enough when one stops to think of it, that queer sexualities, and especially those that can even be remotely connected with some idea of sadomasochism, are absolutely permeated by theatrical rhetoric. One (two, three, or more) people *do* "*scenes.*" They do not "have sex" like "normal" people. Nonkinky heterosexual sex acts rarely if ever are described as *doing scenes.* Although one can easily imagine a straight man referring to sex with a prostitute as a scene. It seems that the antitheatrical prejudice, which has been functional and pervasive at least since Plato, is an operative paradox in such performances. For, on the one hand, by virtue of the very fact of their theatricality these practices occupy a denigrated space in our cultural imaginary. On the other hand, practitioners of s/m sexuality have found some means of defense against the onslaught of both the New Right and some feminists by appealing precisely to that theatricality that is otherwise demeaned. Depending then on the context, these performers may find themselves saying something like this: "it's not real, it's *only* a performance," in an appeal for tolerance.

Sadomasochistic, or any kind of "perverse" sexuality is about *doing.* Whereas "straight" sex (whatever the preference of the people involved) is about *having.* Now this is an obvious but, I think, crucial and fascinating difference. For, the notion of "having sex" signifies at once that "sex" is something one can own, and that it (sex) was there *prior to the performance.* The s/m sensualist, quite contrarily, in *doing* a scene *makes* sex in the performance. Unless, of course, the scene is a realistic one, in which case there is an illusion of reality constructed, which is to say that the scene makes possible the fantasy of a referent—a truth or reality prior to the performance. Even this naive realism, however, is performative. If straight sex (by which I mean not necessarily heterosex but any sexual acts that claim to being unmediated by culture and ideology) has been presumed to be the "real thing," then what are we to make of this tendency toward *denial* of performativity in queer performance?

These queer performance encounters with the real lead me back to the controversies within feminism about the place of lesbian s/m. What strikes me as missing from these ongoing debates is a consideration of them in terms of *performativity.* Here I do not have space to take up the issue of what these debates, in themselves, rhetorically perform. What I would like to do in the space that I have is to consider how one might read the controversies about lesbian s/m differently, and hence push past an impasse that has been fortified by over two decades of very repetitive arguments. I do not want to ask whether s/m is real or role playing; rather, I want to take as a given that we are always already on stage, whether or not we are recognizing its edge, and ask what *kind* of performance lesbian s/m might be.

It is my contention that sadomasochism is the site of such highly charged controversies among feminists not because of the "violence" that it purportedly perpetuates and condones but because it is comprised of a group of sexual acts in which the eroticism is evoked precisely in the ambiguity between the real and the performed, that "autotextuality" that Pavis claims is the "crux of the illusion/disillusion dichotomy."[59]

Changing the Scene (Again)

Tracking "universals of performance," Herbert Blau does so in the service of pursuing "the thing which appears in that subjunctive moment when whatever was there before becomes a performance. Or, so far as it is imaginable, that which in performance is other than that which is *not* performance, the cipher which marks it off from, shall we say, life? or shall we say, death?"[60] While performative discourse has come to include everything that was once referred to as everyday activities, and the distinction between "doing" and "acting" is so murky as to be nearly indecipherable, there is nonetheless, as Blau points out, a "crucial particle of difference . . . between just breathing eating sleeping loving and *performing* those functions of just living; that is, with more or less deliberation."[61]

Feminist positions both for and against s/m sexual practices seem to be in pursuit of the moment when something presumably *authentic* occurs. But lesbian sadomasochists seek that moment *within* the performance. Accepting that we are always already in representation, even when we are enacting our most private experience, the lesbian sadomasochist is aroused by the dialectic of appearance/disappearance and the pleasurable suffering that constitutes the persistent failure to master its implacable necessity.

The cipher that marks off the distinction between performance and "life or death" figures in sadomasochism in the "becoming nothing" that the ritual enacts. The body of the bottom is the place where this marking is inscribed. Tops facilitate this passage and serve as the guarantee of returns. The dialectic is between the body—the home of the culturally constructed "self"—and the "flesh"—the abstracted desire for something that is not performance, is prior to performance, or beyond performance. The following passage from Pat Califia's story, "The Calyx of Isis," captures this oscillation:

> she began to erase herself. She began to give up the idea that she had anything to hide or any right to demand pleasure instead of pain. She

began to crumble herself at the edges, fade into air, render herself will-less and invisible. . . .

Liar, screamed the first lash of the whip, and she was suddenly unable to be anywhere but here, bound to this wooden cross.[62]

In Califia's story Roxanne is delivered bound, gagged, and bundled in a body bag to mistress Tyre's dungeon. Roxanne is the principal player in a ritual designed by her lover, Alex, to test her fidelity. Alex has enlisted eight other tops to assist her in testing her lover's endurance. If Roxanne passes through the ordeal designed for her, she will belong to Alex, whose ownership will be signified by piercing Roxanne's ears, nipples, and labia with Alex's rings. What Alex needs to know, in order to trust Roxanne's love for her, is how capable Roxanne is of surrendering.

Her submission, however, is not a sign of Roxanne's abjection but, rather, a test of her strength. Not the courage to withstand pain, but the ability to give up, temporarily and under ritualized conditions, her notion of her "self" as an autonomous ego. Alex wants to know if Roxanne can withstand becoming "dehumanized"—erase (her)self—and trust that Alex and her accessories will bring her back to the ground that necessarily reasserts itself in reality. The world is too much with Roxanne; Alex wants to narrow her vision, heighten her other senses, telescope her experience so that she learns to focus. The route to taking Roxanne "outside herself" is, paradoxically, by asserting intense pressure on her body. The pain ironically affords her sensory deprivation/transformation. Roxanne is practicing coming and going, falling and returning, leaving her body and becoming nothing other than her body, repeating the movement until she understands that there is nothing other than this movement.

Masochists are great educators, Deleuze claims. It may be difficult to comprehend how this woman who is rendered completely immobile while eight tops practice their specialities on her body—whipping, piercing, clamping, in addition to oral, vaginal, and anal penetration—could be the educator of the scene. But what Roxanne demonstrates is the ability to inhabit her body as an instrument that is at once, "her" and "not-her." Roxanne is performing the "between" of between the body and the flesh, and it is in this dialectical movement that Alex learns that her desire for control can always only be an illusion—a performance that will not bear repeating and whose very condition is a failure.

Alex can only own Roxanne if she can succeed in making meaning of her. The truth/fidelity that Alex so intensely desires can only be achieved in death. Roxanne thus shows the tops how to live, how life is the repetition of this movement between the body and the flesh, the swerving in and out of fantasy and reality, the surrendering to the necessity of the dialectic of appearance/disappearance. If there is nothing to trust, nothing to be faithful to except the inevitability of this persistent failure, there is nonetheless a tenacious desire to perform again and again. This repetition of the performance is an acting out of the hope that a different structure of value could emerge—an elsewhere—beyond the dialectic, a different kind of knowledge/experience that escapes the closure of representation.

Lesbian sadomasochistic sexual practices, as described and defined by practitioners, consummately enact Blau's first, and most important, "universal" of performance—the consciousness of performance. Minimally, any act that can rightly be called a performance contains cues, what Blau calls "marks of punctuation which are inflections . . . of *consciousness*."[63] Although all "acts" are performances, in a performative act the participants must be aware of themselves as actors in the very moment that they are performing. In contradistinction to the realistic method, in which the actor strives to disappear into the character she is performing, the s/m performer takes up a position in relation to her "self" and the role she plays that is much more akin to the Brechtian gestus. Thus, being somewhat alienated from oneself is a precondition for s/m performance. The vacillation between forgetting and remembering one's self in performance is the measure whereby we determine what kind of performance is being enacted. There is something, however, in between forgetting and remembering that haunts all performance. Blau calls it "theater, the truth of illusion, which haunts all performance whether or not it occurs in the theater."[64]

It is this theater that I think is the ghost in the machinery of feminist debates concerning sadomasochism. Although it encompasses a wide range of practices, the movement of sadomasochistic sexuality is toward a delicate, precarious borderline where testing and transgressing the line between the real and the phantasmatic deeply troubles a feminist movement invested in consciousness and clarity. If consciousness of performance is the first and most important of Blau's universals, "Calyx of Isis" is exemplary in this respect. In fact, Blau is even more emphatic: "there is no performance without consciousness."[65]

What is striking about many s/m narratives and testimonials is the extent to which the sexual act is determined in advance, rigorously negotiated, planned in excruciating detail. Even the reactions of the participants are anticipated and prepared for as much as possible. In this sense s/m sexuality obviously contradicts the notion of romantic love-making in which spontaneity is equated with the natural. This is a tenacious myth. One

thinks how difficult it has been for feminists to achieve such simple recog-
nitions as the right for a woman to ask, simply, for what pleases her in a sexual exchange, or to guide her partner through certain motions that she herself must know better than her partner will please her. The evident heterosexism of such incalcitrant attitudes is manifest; it is the masculine ego that
must be preserved above the woman's pleasure at all costs. S/m violates this
mystification of sexuality. In addition, the negotiations of s/m are in the
service of safety, both physical and emotional attempts to guarantee that
the consent of the parties involved is secure. But rather than a deerotociz-
ing gesture, these deliberations prolong and heighten the erotic exchange
itself. In this sense they are not merely preparatory; rather, they are indica-
tions that sexual desire is already in play before the "acts" are enacted. In
fact, the speech acts emphatically enact the libidinal exchange. The scandal
of seduction, Shoshana Felman argues, is "not so much in the fact that the
linguistic is always erotic as in that the erotic is always linguistic."[66] Felman
explains that this is why language, for Lacan, is always an "obscenity," for
the "human sexual act always connotes the speech act."[67]

In "Calyx of Isis" some of the verbal exchanges seem to be presented for
readers who might need reassurance that lesbian sadomasochists are not
oblivious to the ethics of feminism. For example, Tyre, the madam of the
calyx, instructs her transsexual secretary to provide funds for a lesbian
mothers' collective, gives permission for an anthropology professor to
bring his students on a guided tour, and frets over the costs of cotton swabs
needed by the Well Woman Body Care Center that provides a weekly clinic
at the calyx to do Pap smears and STD tests. She also points out that they
keep dental dams in good supply. But these speech acts are heavily tinged
with an erotic exchange between Georgia, the secretary, and Tyre. They
expand and multiply the varieties of eroticism the calyx accommodates:
voyeurism dressed up as intellectual inquiry, clinical exams as potentially
arousing, safer sex as abundance rather than deprivation.

The negotiations also serve to make Alex articulate what the performance
is for. What she hopes to accomplish through it, besides giving Roxanne a
fantasy that many bottoms hold, is knowledge about what motivates her
own desire for the "special session." This elicits from her an examination of
her own sexual history and desires. And she realizes that what she desires is
actually quite conventional: "Maybe romance and S/M don't mix, but I
want a woman . . . who will stick by my side, somebody who really needs
and likes what I do."[68] The performance is thus about the acquisition of
Alex's knowledge about herself, an educational experience. Alex is not learning how to trust Roxanne but how to trust herself and her ability to let go,

whether or not she believes that one person will be there to catch her if she falls. She must learn to trust that the pleasure is in the falling and the undecidability of the other's presence. She tests her own ability to withstand the pain of separation. Although she begins by believing that marking Roxanne's body will secure herself against that pain, what ends up being more instructional for her—what the masochist as great educator teaches her—is that one can only believe in trust, not believe it. Trust and fidelity are only symptoms, and there is no hidden content behind them to be discovered. On the contrary, the symptom reveals only that there is nothing to be seen. As Lacan points out, "the difference between believing *in* the symptom and believing *it* is obvious. It is the difference between neurosis and psychosis. In psychosis, not only does the subject believe in the voices, but he believes them. Everything rests on that borderline."[69]

This is a distinction that feminists quite rightly suspect; for after all, has not nearly every feminist accomplishment been a matter of resisting "reality?" Where would feminism be if we had not believed "the voices" that come from elsewhere than the dominant culture's speech acts? Furthermore, as I will discuss at greater length in the last chapter of this book, the divide between neurosis and psychosis is far too simple in this formulation to explain women's experiences, especially in regard to sexual experiences between women. What is of value in Lacan's formulation is the concept of the "borderline"—where "everything rests."

"Calyx of Isis" is a narrative that is very much about negotiating the perils and pleasures of that borderline. The psychotic structure of belief is something the story works to undercut, and at the same time it expresses a yearning, a longing for its possibilities. Although there are multiple references to the failure, even the undesirability of fidelity, it is at the same time the goal toward which the narrative obsessively aims.

If Alex were only interested in testing Roxanne and her endurance of pain, if Alex's eroticism was cleanly defined as a sadistic urge toward mastery, then she might as well have put Roxanne through this ordeal herself. The fact that she enlists eight other tops while she watches is highly significant. Again, this is not simple voyeurism. Alex explains that she doesn't really understand the concept of belonging and that she thinks the real test is "can you give it away? And if you loan it out can you get it back?"[70] She is also then testing her own powers of seduction, which she needs to have interrupted, momentarily, so that she can repeat the seduction until she trusts herself to accomplish it. This is a much more complicated strategy for insuring continuity than extracting promises from someone that can never be kept. Rather than lamenting the failure of commitment, Alex and

Tyre work together to create a performance in which "failures" are built-in mechanisms that facilitate the possibility of endless returns.

Thus there are two seemingly opposite concepts of pleasure in this narrative. What has been dubbed "vanilla" sex by lesbian sadomasochists is scarcely absent from s/m narratives. Even in a story as hard-core as "Calyx of Isis," tenderness, trust, commitment, fidelity and equality are strongly valued. One moment in the story powerfully dramatizes Califia's contention that "tops are the most compassionate women" she knows. Following a session in which Kay and EZ simultaneously fist Roxanne vaginally and anally, Roxanne asks for a break to urinate. Kay insists that she do so in their presence. "Water sports" are the most intimate of sexual activities. Engaging in them requires a loss of inhibition that is tantamount to relinquishing one's hold on the coherent "self" that marks the transition from infancy to adulthood. When Kay "opened and closed her hand, rotated her fist, and made [Roxanne] piss again"[71] for the first time in the scene Roxanne suddenly "wanted to quit."

This moment instigates immediate reassurance by all of the tops; it marks an interruption in the scripted performance, and it brings Alex out of her role as spectator:

> Strong hands in leather gloves materialized all over her body. They were covering and caressing her face, her ribs, her belly, her arms and legs, her hands and feet. A soft tongue began to lick gently at her tears. . . . Then another face descended—Alex coming toward her abraded lips . . . . Their lips touched, merged, and Alex's tongue opened her mouth. Cool water trickled down her throat. She sucked, and Alex fed her a little more water. . . . The leather-clad hands continued to soothe and massage her. Alex gestured. One by one, the women came forward and gave her sips of water from their own lips. She murmured with contentment. Everyone withdrew leaving her alone with Alex.[72]

The intimacy in this scene is more than consolation for having violated Roxanne's privacy. It certainly indicates how dangerous s/m sexuality can be (although terror can suddenly be elicited in any sexual play); and it does constitute a moment of "failure" in the scene when one of the tops oversteps Roxanne's limits. But it is also a failure that allows Roxanne and the tops to know more about where Roxanne's psychic limitations are located—how much of her "self" she is able to erase and under what circumstances. Also, this failure permits a narrowing of the distance that Alex has been keeping from her. If we think of this scene in terms of speech act theory, it is certainly an infelicitous performance, among the category that J. L. Austin calls "misfires," and, specifically in this case a "misinvocation," which occurs when the "procedure in question cannot be made to apply in the way attempted."[73] It is important to stress, however, that such misfires allow for a change to occur, for something to happen that could not have otherwise. As Felman points out, the "act of failing opens up a space of referentiality— or impossible reality—not because *something is missing* but because *something else is done* or because something else is said: the term "misfire" does not refer to an absence, but to the enactment of a difference."[74]

Like Lacan's "misrecognitions," misfires are moments when a "truth" emerges. They are thus creative moments that serve life and allow for the possibility of continuance. And indeed the scene does continue after the misfire, but with each participant more aware of her limitations and thus better able to play as close as possible to the edge without invoking terror. Rather than retreating, the tops intensify the pressures on Roxanne's body, and the tops are closer to each other with Alex having moved from the margins closer to the center. Knowing that Alex is the controlling presence, Roxanne is now able to plunge more deeply into erasure, and her falling can have a wider scope. The traumatic space has been reorganized, but only by traversing it.

"Calyx of Isis" moves toward a commitment that is beyond the inevitability of the broken promise. The acts performed indeed stretch toward something beyond the limitations of language. This yearning is acted out as a sacred rite. It is not unlike what Lacan calls love:

> A creature needs some referent to the beyond of language, to a pact, to a commitment which constitutes him, strictly speaking, as an other, a reference included in the general or, to be more exact, universal system of interhuman symbols. No love can be functionally realisable in the human community, save by means of a specific pact, which, whatever the form it takes, always tends to become isolated off into a specific function, at one and the same time within language and outside of it. That is what we call the function of the sacred, which is beyond the imaginary relation.[75]

Lacan argues that the necessity for love is introduced because the object of Eros must submit to the "primary imaginary relation" and be inscribed in it. This primary imaginary relationship is in the narcissistic framework. And though the object relation can transcend it, "it is impossible to realise on the imaginary plane."[76] The desire for recognition as a separate self, an object that is other than the projections of the narcissistic ego, then demands a certain submission on the part of the desiring ego. Love becomes a matter of being able to put oneself in the place of the other without narcissistically incorporating the other. In the parlance of contemporary psychotherapy, to love successfully one must be able to respect and appreciate one's own and the other's boundaries. It is thus a division, a separation, and a wounding of the ego that constitutes love. And it is unremunerative—love does not pay nor collect a debt. It is Irigaray's fantasy about a love that would be neither "gift nor debt."

When Roxanne passes the test in "Calyx of Isis"—"she was wearing Alex's rings now. Permanently. Forever"[77]—the exhausted pack drive away together in Tyre's limousine (an image that both mimics and mocks the traditional heterosexually wedded couple who leave the community to begin their journey into coupledom alone). Tyre jokingly asks Alex: "Where can you go from here?" Only half-jokingly, Alex quips: "Sell her?" Tyre nods, thinking to herself: "Would it be a permanent transfer of rights, or would there be a time limit?"[78] They know that the promise of eternity is disconsonant with life. Roxanne has been bound, gagged, chained, pierced, but she has not been immobilized. On the contrary, the ritual whose endpoint was designed to ensure permanency has released the entire community, mobilizing their desires. They are exhausted but not satiated. Roxanne never has her "one final gigantic orgasm that would be so dramatic and beautiful that they would stop this whole thing and take her down."[79]

Alex's joke about selling Roxanne may sound like a crass duplication of the "traffic in women," and thus a reinstatement of patriarchal commerce. However, as Tyre stares at Roxanne sleeping on Alex's shoulder, she is both bewildered and exhilarated by the possibility of a love that cannot be afforded. Even as she tries, she cannot "calculate the fair-market value of that much love." The market that Roxanne has been on might be understood as a different kind of commerce, one that Irigaray concedes is "Utopia? Perhaps. Unless this mode of exchange has undermined the order of commerce from the beginning."[80] In this different economy Irigaray imagines that "use and exchange would be indistinguishable. The greatest value would be at the same time the least kept in reserve."[81]

The repetitive closing and opening of Roxanne's body, the contractions of her multiple orgasms, represent the very movement of the s/m structure itself. The positing of an identity in difference blurs the lines between the individual and the community. "One is never separable from the other," Irigaray writes: "You/I: we are always several at once. And how could one dominate the other? impose her voice, her tone, her meaning?

One cannot be distinguished from the other; which does not mean that they are indistinct."[82]

Although each of the women is carefully differentiated in Califia's narrative, their individualities blend in Roxanne's state of mind during the scene:

> as each member of the pack worked her over, the pack itself—as an entity—became a more powerful force in her imagination. The women seemed to loom nearer and taller, their voices more forceful and resonant. . . . There were long moments when it seemed to [Roxanne] that only they existed, and her life force had flowed into them. She was like a vessel being emptied into the sea, or a shadow melting into evening. But she was also a current of energy that held the pack together—the point at which they crossed and focused[83]

At one point in the narrative, Roxanne can no longer distinguish whether the hands that are touching her are leaving or entering her body. In moments like these, the text strains to approximate something like a pure libidinal flow that leaves the consciousness of performance behind. In these embraces the s/m performance almost finds the promise of eternity. But it can always ever be almost, as close as possible to the edge without falling. "It is exactly what goes out of sight," Blau points out, "that we most desperately want to see. That's why we find ourselves, at the uttermost consummation of performance, in the uncanny position of spectators."[84] Rilke says it this way:

> And we: spectators, always, everywhere,
> looking at everything and never from!
> It floods us. We arrange it. It decays.
> We arrange it again, and we decay.
> Who's turned us around like this,
> so that whatever we do, we always have
> the look of someone going away? Just as a man
> on the last hill showing him his whole valley
> one last time, turns, stops, and lingers—
> so we live, and are forever leaving.[85]

To be the mirror that reflects—to bend or throw back the image of one's self—is the lover's promise. It is broken not because the lover never intends to keep her promise (the category of the performative that Austin calls "abuses") but because the mirror is a duplicitous instrument. What it appears to cast forward is always a folding back. What the mirror expresses or shows is a recollection, an after(thought). It thus tells us that what is with us (present) is behind us. In the lover's re-collecting gaze, we suffer from reminiscences.

The abundance of theatrical metaphors in s/m testimony and theory is not casual. The "scene" or "scenario" is a staple concept repetitively evoked in s/m rhetoric. In Theodor Reik's massive study of the etiology of masochism, he persistently returns to performance metaphors. Reik's "provocative" feature in masochism is the "showing or wanting-to-be seen [which is actually] a means to invite the sexually gratifying punishment."[86] Masochism, he argues, must have a public: "in most cases it has the character of a performance and frequently it does not dispense with a certain theatrical flavor."[87]

As his analysis develops, we see that Reik conceives of masochism as theatrical because he is thinking of the male submissive's desire for suffering at the hands of a dominant female as a disfigured, or distorted, enactment of his unconscious desire to change places with her. Hence the male masochist, "whatever he does represents a performance, a kind of enacted scene."[88] For Reik masochism is symptomatic of desires that are repressed and hence susceptible to reversals into sadism. In one of his examples, when the masochistic "reversal was undone, when he now took his evening strolls through the streets he nourished the phantasy that he was a lust-murderer on the lookout for his female victims. When he now went for a walk with a girl he sometimes felt the impulse to change a tender movement into a brutal injuring one. He doubted, as he put his arms around her neck, whether he did not want to strangle her in reality."[89] Reik thus believes in masochism as a symptom that conceals the prevailing conception among analysts that "the homosexual-feminine attitude toward the fathers may hide behind the facade but it is of no decisive importance."[90] If male masochism is the symptomatic expression of femininity, as Freud suggested, Reik argues that "it certainly is distorted and caricatured," and as such it "has the meaning of a performance."[91]

Thus we can see in Reik's analysis of masochism a belief in the truth concealed by the illusion. His search is geared toward locating a "hidden aim"; his etiological analysis presumes a model from which all the manifestations of masochism are tracked through detours. Like the anti-s/m feminists then, Reik's rhetoric is haunted by the truth/model behind the illusion. Reik rescues masochism from the "real" by theatricalizing it: "it is in accordance with the theatrical element in masochism that it seldom becomes a matter of 'deadly earnest' as with the sadistic perversion."[92] The masochistic desire must then, however, remain in the realm of fantasy (theater), for if it emerges into the "real" (practice), the masochist would perhaps not be in "deadly earnest"; rather, he would be in deadly danger, since the sadistic perversion is not theatricalized. The fantasy of masochism, for Reik, is classical theater—a dialectic between concealment and display in which the wanting to be seen is in tension with the desire to be hidden.

It is this truth behind the illusion that the anti-s/m feminists wish to expose and contain when they insist that acting out the fantasy is both self-destructive for the participants and potentially harmful for all women. While acknowledging the pervasiveness of both sadistic but, especially, masochistic fantasies among women, they will insist that realizing these fantasies is giving in to internalized misogyny.[93] Trapped in a reproductive model, these feminists cannot imagine that repetitions might be transformative. Acting is necessarily an "acting out" that merely duplicates the original. Their logic leads to efforts to maintain rigid boundaries between fantasy and practice, failing to recognize that there is no illusion as naive as the illusion of unmediated experience.

The pleasurable suffering that is enacted in lesbian sadomasochism is much more than the paradoxical desire for pleasure detoured through pain. These narratives also enact the pathos of the impossibility of love, the conflict between desiring-fantasy's shattering of the self and the necessity for returning to a coherent self in order to take one's place in the symbolic order, and the persistent fantasy of something that exists beyond language. Or, to shift to another register, the constancy of a belief in something that is before or other than performance. Linguistically, this would be the persistence of a belief in the constative even as the performative devours any effort to hold onto a commensurableness between the speech act and a referent that is not constituted in the performative.

S/m sexuality pushes hard against the referent that feminism needs to make its truth claims. But s/m also longs for a referent, for something that provides an anchor, or ground, beyond representation. As Artaud wanted a theater that "to the degree that life is unrepresentable [was] meant to be the equal of life,"[94] I think that lesbian sadomasochism is a performance that yearns for an experience that is beyond the closure of representation, and it seeks that beyond through the apparently paradoxical method of discipline, regulation, prescription. Artaud's visionary theater of cruelty would have banished mimesis and returned the theater to something that was prior to or beyond imitation. He theorized the effective annihilation of theater, in the name of theater, to create a theater that would be the equal of life. More than any other theoretician of performance, Artaud sought the "thing in itself."

Derrida describes Artaud's longing in a way that would complement a feminist agenda: "Artaud also desired the impossibility of theater, wanted to erase the stage, no longer wanted to see what transpires in a locality always inhabited or haunted by the father and subjected to the repetition of murder."[95] Most feminists, I think, would share this desire for a scene not haunted by the law of the father, a way out of the endlessly repetitive oedipal drama. But the way out, if there is a way out, is not through accumulating testimonials about the "truth" of our illusions. Rather, it must be through performing the illusions, producing, multiplying, and traversing them. Those who are watching the performance of sadomasochism and condemning it are like the spectators at a play who think they are outside the spectacle. The appeal to "natural" expressions of sexuality is like the illusion of the spectator who believes that she is merely "living." The struggle is not to avoid repetition but to repeat with differences that are transformative.

Whether we are spectators or performers, time is of the essence. That is to say, our temporalities indeed define whether we are conscious of ourselves as inside or outside the performance. The image that the mirroring gaze of the lover casts promises to "fix" us, to offer us constancy and coherency. It is an image that creates the illusion of atemporality—hence the romantic discourse of lovers who experience the sensation of time standing still, or inhabiting a space that has magically lifted them out of time. This "being in the moment" promises us "being," the sensation that we will last, through and because of our love. This exchanging gaze of lovers fulfills another of Blau's "universals"—the protraction of time. To protract is to draw out, extend, lengthen in duration. In performance it operates as a "mode of deconditioning, bringing performance back to "life."[96] Blau explains that certain "accretions of everyday life" impede, or are "felt as impediments" to performance. The determining of time in performance is a paradoxical movement. First the behavior that is not performance is recognized. Then, in order to create the illusion of "natural movement," the behavior must be unlearned, deconditioned, so that it can reappear as if it were already there. Blau uses the familiar example of Stanislavski's struggle to teach his actors how to walk on stage to exemplify the distinction between "just doing" and performing the "doing" so that it appears to be already done: "Stanislavski [said] that the hardest thing for an actor to do on stage, though he has been doing it all his life, is to walk." The natural movement has to *die* in order that it can be *reborn* in the performance: " 'Kill the breathing! Kill the rhythm! repeats the dancing Master.' "[97]

In Reik's analysis of masochism, time is also crucial. What he calls "the flight forward" is both an overtaking and overcoming of the anxiety that had been pursuing the masochist. If anticipation is the dominating mode of the suspense, here we are still in a linear temporality. The leap into the perverse scene, however, constitutes a bridge across the gap between the past and the future. It is a leap that can always be only one of faith. The scene takes place in what appears to be the "present," but if it is a present indicative it is a performative one in which the "I" is ek-static—a being put out of its place.

But this time is not to be confused with the willful forgetting of classical theater. If the performative time of s/m is understood as psychoanalytic, the bliss that is an "ek-stasis" is more like Nietzsche's "oblivion," an active forgetting. Nietzsche's oblivion is "not merely a vis inertiae . . . but an active screening device" without which there can "be no happiness, no serenity, no hope, no pride, no present."[98] Active forgetting "represents a power, a form of strong health."[99] Oblivion, Nietzsche argues, is a faculty designed to solve the problem and the paradox of promising. In claiming to anticipate the future, the promise tries to make the future present, or past—as if it had already been. Promising thus always takes place in psychoanalytic time—the future that is already. In Lacan's reformulation of Freud, "what takes place . . . is not the past definite of what was, because it is no more, nor is it the present perfect of what has been in what I am, but rather the future anterior of what I will have been for what I am in the process of becoming."[100] Catherine Clément explains that it was Lacan "who by fooling around with tenses found in grammar that needed resource, the form whose function it is to span the gap between past and future and link the two firmly together: the so-called future anterior, the future that comes before like the poetic life imagined by Baudelaire."[101]

If history and performance cannot be repeated, that is not to say that they cannot be altered. Lacan's "Real" is impossible, but through psychoanalytic time, it becomes the "real-impossible." For if the "Real" is a psychic space that cannot be occupied, it is because it is not ocular. That is, it does not take place in the time or space of the ideological illusion called "reality" because it exceeds a specular economy. Nonetheless, it does produce "reality-effects," not in spite of but due to its extra-metalinguistic status. The future anterior is the grammar of the Real. It is also, I think, the tense of masochism.

The masochist does not merely equate pleasure with pain nor does she strive for pleasure to succeed pain; rather, if we follow Reik's useful concept of the "flight forward," we can comprehend masochism as "pleasure and discomfort welded into simultaneity"[102] and hence moving toward a period of repose not unlike Bersani's reading of Baudelaire's erotic somnolence, or, in Califia's words, the moment that "we all fall asleep at exactly the same moment."

The movement toward this period of recovery or repose is achieved through a paradoxical gesture that Reik characterizes as a "peculiar in-between thing," for it is at one both "approach and escape."[103] It is important to recognize this contradictory movement as simultaneous, for during the suspense phase it is only a vacillation. But the masochist's aim is to make them consonant and bind anxiety.[104] The longed-for repose can only be achieved by passing through a phase where the anxiety will assert itself even more profoundly, as will the pleasure. And this is the point where the masochist will make the leap of faith into the "flight forward," where anxiety will not be merely parried but bound. The movement from the phase of suspense to the flight forward begins with the emergence of masochism into practice; a transformative moment, when what was once feared is no longer both sought after and avoided, i.e., held in suspense but translated into pleasure.

Of course this is not always successful. Indeed it is extremely difficult to achieve, for it is common for the masochist to retreat from the "practice" back into the suspense/fantasy phase when the anxiety overcomes the pleasure. It is even more common for one to resist ever making the move into practice at all, for obviously the number of people who will admit to sado-masochistic fantasies far exceeds the number of actual practitioners. Once the movement has been made, however, a retreat from it could well leave the masochist stuck in the suspense phase where the "acting out" is no longer a process of working through but a monstrous miring in a traumatic space that cannot be traversed. It is for this reason, among others, that I find it important to argue against the assault on sadomasochistic sexual practices. For, especially among feminists, such assaults can produce shame, guilt, and fear in women who are perhaps on the very verge of exploring s/m or have begun to dabble in its possibilities, and thus propel them back into an anxiety phase from which they may never emerge.

Reik's emphasis on masochism as a process, not an unchanging entity, is very important. For in the suspense phase the pleasure/pain dialectic is an alternation: "now the one and then the other."[105] Whereas once the flight forward has been achieved, "the one and the other have become one and the same"[106] and the dread of integration can be overcome. Equally or more important, the process is not linear but spiral: the movement from "fantasy to reality," from the suspense factor to the "perverse scene," blurs the boundaries between the conscious and the unconscious (which are in either case always already blurred). But the key mechanism in Reik's analysis is not the lifting of repression or the reversal of an instinctual aim; rather, for Reik, masochism "becomes the switching point to bliss and to salvation."[107]

Felman argues that the necessary link between the promise and "marriage" is that "every promise promises *constancy* . . . consistency, continuity in time between the act of commitment and future action."[108] In this formulation we are once again trying to capture our image in a mirror that is always already broken. If "constancy" is the structure of the "constative," then the promise is the "promise of language to refer, to make sense."[109] Lacan's notorious statement that the "sexual relation is nonsense" could then be understood to mean that the sexual relation does not make "meaning." Looked at this way, constancy is not a very desirable attribute, and the promise is held open that the sexual relation will not "die" in the closure of representation.

If the one who promises is the seducer, she tricks the one whom she seduces into thinking that the performative is constative. That is, seduction is a "trap," which consists in "producing a *referential* illusion through an utterance that is *self-referential*," the "illusion of a real or extralinguistic act of commitment created by an utterance that refers only to itself."[110] The promise produces a belief in the constative—the order of meaning/truth. Such a belief is a yearning for something that rips through the fabric of reality. We could think of it as a mourning for referentiality, the grief expressed for the loss of something one never had. If narcissism = death, in postmodern theories, so does referentiality. Or, to put it slightly differently, death is the referent, the moment when time stops—the present. As Jonathan Dollimore points out, "death is always already there, which is why . . . future death, and the decline that leads ineluctably to it, are vividly imaged as the truth of the here and now."[111] Because perverse sexualities fall out of symbolization or, as Dean puts it, are foreclosed from signification, they are ineluctably associated with death (the ultimate referent).

Thus, paradoxically, the perception of these performances (performance itself being an art form that takes place in the here and now) as real (by which their detractors mean life-like instead of art-like) produces a confusion between the very boundary that is presumably the only one that remains unassailable—life and death. From this perspective, one can see why such performances have generated such enormous anxiety in the fundamentalist Right, whose efforts to censor them have an apocalyptic fervor. Ironically of course, it is their own refusal to allow these acts to signify that has produced the return of the Real in the fantasia of the dominant order's Symbolic. Foreclosed from the Symbolic, they return in the Real—as the real. As "life" that is death—death to the coherency of a Symbolic Order that constitutes itself as whole by producing its own constitutive outside within.

In my reading, s/m sexuality in general, and the autoreflexive/erotic performances of the artists whose work I discuss at the beginning of this chapter, mimic this psychic and social configuration. But the form and structure of these performances do not confirm its truth. Rather, they explore its limits and boundaries in ways that disrupt the hegemony of this order. By mining its surface, they undermine its depth.

The distinction between the top and the bottom in s/m sexuality appears to reify a binary that, in part, explains why some feminists find these practices so odious. If "top" and "bottom" correspond to the dyad of surface/depth, the former may be likened to what Deleuze calls the "surveyor of surfaces we thought we knew so well that we never explored them"; in fact, we might say that the top becomes that surface whose role "is precisely that of organizing and displaying elements that have come from the depths."[112] Bottoms consistently describe their experience as plunging into the depths—leaving their bodies, falling, losing consciousness. Tops speak of the huge responsibility and risk of becoming the one who must pull the bottom back to the surface before she becomes lost in the depths. Deleuze claims that Lewis Carroll's surfaces cannot communicate with Artaud's depths. Yet Deleuze has himself already acknowledged that one always finds fragments of the depths in the surface.[113] It is the depth model that demands a certain purity, an element that is unmixed, that does not promiscuously mingle. Such a quest for the pure or absolute cannot be other than a desire for mastery. As Kojeve reads Hegel on the master/slave dialectic, he finds that mastery is always an impasse, because the desire for recognition comes from one (the slave) who is ultimately not "worthy" of giving it to her. Once one has achieved mastery, there is no more desire because there is no possibility for recognition. The one who desires mastery (of the other) becomes paralyzed because she cannot recognize the desire of the other, having subjected or incorporated her.[114]

The apparent correspondence between the top and the master is not this Hegelian dialectic. On the contrary, what is constantly reiterated in s/m narratives is the top's extraordinary attentiveness to the slightest variations in the bottom's permutations of pleasure and fear. Here, for example, is an observer's account of his first witnessing of an s/m scene:

> Bottom endures, bound in sightless concentration on two rings of fire. His sighs grow quicker and louder till his chest is heaving and drenched in sweat, low bellows coming now, his jaw angled and mouth rounded as though sucking a cock. Now the motion of the riding crop is swift and sharp. Top stops abruptly, cradles bottom's

head in his hands, kisses him deeply . . . nipples between his thumb and forefinger. I stood watching among a group of leatherguys, each of us aroused at the sight of one man leading another through twists of tenderness and turns of severity, and at the blindfolded trust of finding a lover again at the heart of the maze.[115]

Although Deleuze claims that surface and depth are incommunicable, located in his own commentary is a moment when these two worlds coincide. Brief, precious, infinitely worth waiting for, and endlessly repeatable, it is that moment when "the little girl skirts the surface of the water, like Alice in the pool of her own tears."[116] For it is in this moment that she is neither surface nor depth. Her body still partially submerged but her head breaking through the pool of tears, Alice inhabits the borderline for a split second. This breaking of the waters is the breach in language, where one catches a glimpse of full speech.

The top does not merely wait on the shore, dispassionately observing the descent and resurgence of the bottom. Nor does she simply facilitate that movement. She comes and goes there with the bottom. Neither anticipation nor recollection, it is not waiting for what could be nor remembering what has been. Neither real nor phantasmatic, but a sexuality that is self-conscious about the ways in which fantasy constructs the real by posing the illusion of authenticity, s/m strives to hold, while forever failing to capture, lovers mingled in that tense more impossible even than the future anterior—the present, where they are suspended together.

These are the things we will never do together,
you who have hidden so long
in death,
I who wrench you from my flesh
breathing or not.
No words. Pure sound.
Pain flooding my left eye.

—Margaret Randall

5 • Bearing (to) Witness:
The Erotics of Power in
Bastard Out of Carolina

The first time I read the Jewish lesbian Irena Klepfisz's poems, I experienced a frisson of recognition. It was not that my people had been
"burned off the map" or murdered as hers had. No, we had been
encouraged to destroy ourselves, made invisible because we did not
fit the myths of the noble poor generated by the middle class. Even
now, past forty and stubbornly proud of my family, I feel the draw of
that mythology, that romanticized edited version of the poor. I find
myself looking back and wondering what was real, what was true.
Within my family, so much was lied about, joked about, denied, or
told with deliberate indirection, an undercurrent of humiliation or a
brief pursed grimace that belied everything that had been said. What
was real?

—Dorothy Allison, *Skin*

Pleasure and Danger: Exploring Female Sexuality, edited by Carole Vance in
1984, was one of the first feminist anthologies dedicated to investigating
the complex interactions of pleasure and danger in women's sexuality.
Dorothy Allison opens her contribution to this book with two citations:
Audre Lorde—"I urge each one of us to reach down into that deep place of
knowledge inside herself and touch that terror and loathing of any difference that lives there,"[1] and Cherríe Moraga—"the deepest political tragedy
I have experienced is how with such grace, such blind faith, the commitment to women in the feminist movement grew to be exclusive and reactionary."[2] Having endured abject poverty and years of repetitive sexual
abuse, Allison maintains that the trauma she may never survive is the pain
she experienced when her writing became the cause of her exclusion from
the feminist community. She was "destroyed, completely. [She] can only
now begin to acknowledge how much damage it did . . . and is more or less
deep into the process of recovering from it. . . . it just completely broke [her]
heart." Allison was called a "pimp for the pornographic-incest society," for
the very work that was saving her life.[3]

I began chapter 3 with the observation that analogies can be politically pernicious and intellectually bankrupt. Somewhat cautiously agreeing with Judith Roof about the way in which analogies level all differences, maintaining rather than making accessible the "space between the lines,"[4] my uneasiness over the *absolute* discrediting of analogies persists, first because it could imply that *no* similarities exist, and thereby lead to a kind of ahistorical relativism. S. P. Mohanty's critique, "Us and Them: On the Philosophical Bases of Political Criticism," offers a cautionary note in this regard. He argues that the "relativist thesis initially becomes a valuable political weapon," but then goes on to show how the "weapon" becomes untenable, even "rather dangerous [as] a philosophical ally for political criticism."[5] Citing Raymond Firth, the anthropologist who argues that "the logical *assessment* of an assertion, and the identification of its nearest equivalent in our language are intimately linked and inseparable,"[6] Mohanty points out how the relativist links rationality with translation, thus underscoring the imperialist tendency to presume that adjudication *requires* a fundamentally analogical method. At the same time, however, Mohanty wants to restore to political criticism the ability to "recover our commonality, not the ambiguous imperial-humanist myth of our shared human attributes . . . but, more significantly, the imbrication of our various pasts and presents, the ineluctable relationships of shared and contested meanings, values, material resources."[7] Mohanty's contribution to this project lies in formulating a different understanding of "rationalities" that is not consonant with reason, a conscious will to attribute to different cultures "different—and *competing*—rationalities."[8]

I would like to suggest that Allison's citations can also be regarded as a set of unconscious relations, affinities that might be understood, borrowing Raymond Williams's terminology, as a "structure of feeling" that recognizes differences but that nonetheless acknowledges similarities without enforcing a resolution inadequate to the task of representing the complex psychic and political negotiations among, between, and within feminists.

I return to this point now because it is curious, first, to notice that the two writers whom Allison selects to open her essay on sexuality and danger are women of color, unlike herself. Second, the quotation that opens this section, from Allison's essay "A Question of Class," cites a Jewish lesbian Holocaust survivor as her text of recognition. Notice, however, that after making her point that it was Klepfisz's poems that first engendered in her a way of thinking about her own survival as "poor white trash," she immediately elucidates the differences between them. Nonetheless it was that moment of *frisson* that preceded her thinking about differences. Indeed it was the emotional reaction that appears to have enabled her ability to think about differences. Affective identifications are, to a large extent, foundational moments in the contemporary women's movement. They are also, however, the point beyond which we must immediately move to intellectual and political analysis. Allison makes that move in her discussion of Klepfisz, if not in any sustained way at least by recognizing that the affinities she feels with a Jewish lesbian poet are severely limited by their differences.

One infers from Allison's citing of Lorde and Moraga that this *frisson* is also a motivating factor. However, here they serve as merely introductory citations that frame her essay in *Pleasure and Danger*, where the subject becomes primarily focused on sexuality and gender. The elision of race and class in this framing device might be sutured by Allison's status as "white trash." As a representative member of the class of the working white poor, Allison is one of the too few feminist writers who continually refers to class structures both experientially and intellectually in her work. What might then be easily implied in the references to two women of color is an affinity that could be summed up in Stuart Hall's readily bandied about statement that "Race is the modality in which class is lived."[9]

As handy as this phrase has become however, it is too easily lifted out of Hall's context to become a catchphrase for the coalition between working-class whites and people of color. Hall's famous observation was made in the context of a specific time—the 1970s and 1980s, a specific place—Britain, and a specific group of people—young black men caught in the gap between "first-generational" blacks who partially believed in the dream of assimilation and "second-generational" blacks who renounced that dream as an ideological, oppressive illusion but had not yet entered into a fully organized political consciousness that permitted them to organize against the social and economic structures that *reproduced* them *as a raced class*. Hall, in fact, is at pains to show that there is *not* a class affinity between working-class whites and blacks: "The white working class and its economic and political organizations . . . fundamentally mistakes itself and its position when it extends itself, out of fellow feeling or fraternal solidarity, to struggle against racism on the behalf of our 'black brothers'; just as black organizations misrecognize the nature of their own struggle when they debate whether or not to form tactical alliances with their white comrades. This is certainly *not* to be interpreted as a tactical call for a united struggle, a common front. . . . It is said fully confronting the impossibility of developing the struggle in this form *at this time*."[10]

This is *not* to say that there is no ground for Allison's affinity/identification with writers who are racially and ethnically different from her. But it is to raise the question of how such identifications *work*, without falling into the mistake of presuming that class alone can function as a site of coalition between different racial and ethnic groups. And as Allison herself has remarked, it is not enough to say that all of these writers are "lesbian." For lesbian, as we surely know by now but as some continue to imply, is *not* the efficient category that transcends all other differences. That mythic, magic, "lesbian" moment has all but passed, persisting, as I see it, only in the phantasmatic of white middle-class lesbians who stubbornly refuse to make distinctions and relinquish their ahistorical fantasies, *and*, perhaps more significantly, in the imaginary of a heteropatriarchal middle and upper white class that uses this "lesbian imaginary" as an empty site around which to shore up the "reality" of their own symbolic—the "impossible real" *as* lesbian that I have discussed in chapter 3.

What Moraga, Lorde, Klepfisz, and Allison do share is a common alienation *from* this allusive/illusive category. Despite the fact that such alienations operate and are caused differently, I want nonetheless to consider why Allison's novel, *Bastard Out of Carolina*, has become such an important text for contemporary feminist movements. In *no way* do I mean to suggest that the novel has articulated a universal theme that speaks to all women whatever their experience, race, class, ethnicity, or sexuality. Its contents are highly specific in all of those regards, but its form is one that I think allows for various points of entry and identifications for a readership whose experiences are quite alien to the landscape, history, and other particulars of the novel's contents.

Allison's *Bastard Out of Carolina* is one of the most courageous novels of our time, a time that Shoshana Felman has described as the "age of testimony, an age in which witnessing itself has undergone a major trauma."[11] Felman argues that the traumatic paradox of the age of testimony is that it is both necessary, inescapable, and impossible in an "age of prooflessness, the age of an event whose magnitude of reference is at once below and beyond proof."[12] The referent for Felman's "event" is the Holocaust. *Bastard Out of Carolina* is the daring, excruciatingly graphic narration of a girl growing up in Greenville County, South Carolina, in the 1950s. Her protagonist, Bone, survives the repeated sexual abuse of her stepfather and, perhaps more painfully, abandonment by her mother. Whereas the Holocaust is an historical event that stands out singularly as a rupture so violent as to be almost incomprehensible to "human" understanding (and is therefore *the* historical moment that marks the crisis of "humanism"), Allison's story is an all-too-common narrative, an everyday occurrence that is, in some ways, the most banal instance of the reproduction of "family," i.e., heteropatriarchal values in the United States. "What's a South Carolina virgin?" the men in *Bastard Out of Carolina* joke: "at's a ten-year-old can run fast."[13]

I begin with Felman, not because I want to make the too easy and often heinous comparison between the Holocaust and any or all other traumatic events,[14] but because the testimonial *as form* is often the complex, intimate medium for the expression of the incest survivor as well. And, indeed, the language of psychologists who have written about incest survivors and Felman's articulation of the testimonial converge in often unexpected but immensely illuminating ways.

First, there is an historical connection between the Nazi persecutions of the Jews and the general concept of trauma as Freud theorized it. Reviewing the historical circumstances in which Freud created the theory of trauma, Cathy Caruth returns to Freud's history of the Jews, *Moses and Monotheism*, a project, she argues, which is "clearly linked . . . to [Freud's] attempt to explain the Nazi persecution of the Jews."[15] Caruth locates a paradox central to Freud's text. Citing Freud's letter to Arnold Zweig in 1934, in which he puzzles over why the Jews attract such undying hatred and discovers the answer in the formula: "Moses created the Jews," Caruth argues that the puzzle of *Moses and Monotheism* lies in Freud's paradoxical link between Moses, who liberated the Jews by leading them out of Egypt, and the persecution of the Jews. That is, the paradox of the Jews' persecution is that it occurs in the mode of their very liberation.[16] Expanding this point, Caruth theorizes that the history of a culture is "inextricably bound up with the notion of departure."[17] In Caruth's reading of Freud, then, "the very possibility of history [is situated] in the nature of a traumatic departure," that is "the forgetting (and return) of the deeds of Moses."[18] Linking this history with Freud's famous example of an accident in which someone escapes, apparently unharmed, but later develops symptoms that indicate a "traumatic neurosis," Caruth points out the correspondence between Freud's account of the departure of the Jews—the forgetting and return— and the accident victim who, after an "incubation period," demonstrates symptoms that appear *as if* she did not escape unharmed. Here Freud theorizes the notion of *latency*—a psychic phenomenon that appears as a correspondence between these two otherwise disparate experiences. However, the idea of the "return of the repressed" is insufficient to explain the complexities of this link, for, as Caruth explains further, "the central enigma . . . is not so much the period of forgetting that occurs after the accident, but rather the fact that the victim of the crash was never fully conscious during the accident itself."[19] Thus Caruth argues that the latency experienced is not an aftereffect of the traumatic incident, but rather "an inherent latency *within the experience itself*."[20]

Caruth's argument resonates with Felman's description of the age of testimony in regard to the *referentiality* of the event. Caruth writes: "For history to be a history of trauma means that it is referential precisely to the extent that it is not fully perceived as it occurs; or to put it somewhat differently, that a history can be grasped only in the very inaccessibility of its occurrence."[21] It is this model of trauma that is generally diagnosed by physicians, psychologists, and psychiatrists as "post-traumatic stress disorder," a diagnosis that has been applied not only to survivors of war but also to survivors of rape and incest.

In his ten-year retrospective of research in post-traumatic states, Henry Krystal primarily addresses Holocaust survivors. In fact, he does not mention incest survivors at all, though he does say that he was surprised to find many of the same characteristics among substance-dependent individuals. Nonetheless, many of the characteristics he finds among the former group are well-known attributes of the latter group as well, including: the destruction of basic trust; the retroactive idealization of their childhood problems; survivor's "guilt" feelings; disturbances in body image; aggression; rigid, religiously oriented superegos; psychic closing off or "affective anaesthesia"; a pattern of surrender (freezing or "panic inaction"); and shame.[22]

Shame is perhaps the survivor's symptom most resistant to therapeutic intervention. For while *all these traits* are coping mechanisms for the survivor, despite the fact that they are also self-destructive repetitions inherited from a period of crisis in which they served the survivor *as safety devices*, shame is particularly resistant to intervention: in order to work through it, one must in a sense reexperience it. For the Holocaust survivor, Krystal argues, this would be perceived not as self-healing but as " 'granting Hitler a posthumous victory', and they therefore angrily reject it. To them, self-integration appears antithetical to the only justification of their survival; that they are obligated to be angry witnesses against the outrage of the Holocaust."[23] Herein would seemingly lie a significant difference between the Holocaust survivor and the incest survivor. For whereas the former feels obligated to bear perpetual witness to an historical, public, and communal event, the latter would seem to have every reason to relinquish her shame, working through a private event—a secret-ed personal history. It would appear, however, from all accounts I have read of the incest survivor, that she also resists relinquishing her "shame," for she also believes that her *individual* survival continues to depend upon preserving her anger against the perpetrator. Whereas consciously the incest survivor most often feels that her experience is unique and isolated (and the cure according to most psychologists lies often in her recognition, most effectively accomplished through group therapy, that others have had similar experiences), the literature, nevertheless, supports the impression that incest survivors also feel as if they are the representatives of a community. Incest survivors' "shame" contains within it two contradictory components: on the one hand the conviction that they are *alone*, on the other the knowledge that incest is not an isolated deviance but rather a widespread occurrence indicative of a patriarchal symbolic in which men are taught that access to female bodies is their entitlement.

Laura Brown remarks upon the Diagnostic and Statistical Manual of Mental Disorders III-R (DSM III-R) definition of a traumatic event as that which occurs *outside the range of human experience* , and notes that while incest is a private event that is often not known to anyone outside the perpetrator/victim dyad, it is nonetheless one of the most widespread "secrets" of women's lives.[24] Statistics vary, but most agree that somewhere between a third and a half of all women experience some form of sexual abuse prior to or during adolescence. Brown's point is that girls and women experience the "private, secret, insidious traumata to which a feminist analysis draws attention [as] more often than not those events in which dominant culture and its forms and institutions are expressed and perpetuated."[25] Thus the "official" definition of trauma as that which occurs outside the range of human experience corroborates the status to which girls and women are always already assigned by the dominant culture. Taking this reading to its somewhat improbable but nonetheless "logical" conclusion, the girl who *escapes* sexual abuse is the exception rather than the rule. Again, the men in Allison's *Bastard Out of Carolina* who jokingly refer to a virgin as a ten-year old who can run fast reveal, as jokes will, the unconscious, unspeakable truth of the culture.

Much has been made, by both Allison and her commentators, of the generic status of *Bastard Out of Carolina*. Is it fiction or autobiography? A recent *New York Times Magazine* feature on Allison refers to the novel as "semi-autobiographical,"[26] and Jewelle Gomez comments: " 'Scare me,' [Allison] . . . tells her students in her writing courses. 'Tell me the forbidden story.' But even she can't always tell where the truth ends and the story begins."[27] While many of the events that occur in the novel are true to Allison's own history, the time and events of the novel are not strictly historical. Rather, the time of *Bastard Out of Carolina* is memorial, a remembrance, constructed in retrospect, and, as such, a hybrid of fiction and autobiography that could more accurately be described as pseudotestimonial. It thus partakes of the paradoxical and problematic mode that Felman attributes to the necessary but impossible task of undertaking the narration of "a historically ungraspable *primal scene* which both erases its witness and witnessing . . . explor[ing] the very boundaries of testimony by exploring, at the same time, the historical impossibility of *escaping* the predicament of being—and having to become—a witness." Like the film *Shoah*, Felman's text under discussion, *Bastard Out of Carolina* engages in "a relentless struggle for *remembrance*, but for the self-negating, contradictory, conflictual remembrance of—precisely—an *amnesia.*"[28] Allison speaks frequently of the struggle she undergoes not to lie in her fiction; she remembers her first creative writing teacher insisting that the only way to write is to "tell the truth" of one's experience. And yet, this is a challenge that Allison always fails to meet. It is the particular paradox of the survivor of a trauma to be in the position of needing to narrate the "truth," but just as Bone cannot find a way "to tell," Allison carries with her the particular mark of the incest survivor.

However, Allison's novel differs in some crucial aspects from other incest survivors' testimonies, as well as from the testimonial as it has been generically articulated. In regard to the form of *Bastard Out of Carolina*, it is curious at first why this text would not simply be recognized as a novel. In part, the slide perceived from fiction to autobiography still carries the historical presumption that "women writers" write from their personal experiences, whereas male writers are capable of the distance necessary from themselves to create true fiction. I think, however, that what is really at stake in this concern over the novel's genre is the content, for it is presumed that one who writes about incest *must* have experienced it, given that it is such a personal experience that is not accessible through dominant codes or conventions. In other words, since incest is the dominant culture's *secret*, then anyone who knows enough about it, must have been the "victim" in order to be capable of knowing about it from the *inside*. Readers are further confused, however, by the fact that Allison does write overtly marked autobiography, and details in work such as *Two or Three Things I Know for Sure* sometimes confirm, sometimes conflict with the events in *Bastard Out of Carolina*.

Doris Sommer's distinction between autobiography and testimony leaves Allison's work somewhere in between the two genres. For Sommer [who is writing about Latin American women's writing], autobiography "is precisely the genre which insists on singularity." The autobiographer desires to distinguish herself from others who write in the mode of the heroic "I" more common to masculine narratives. The writer of the testimonial, on the other hand, "does not invite us to identify," and makes "no pretense . . . of universal or essential human experience."[29] These differences have political implications that Sommer elucidates by distinguishing between the *metaphorical* trope of autobiography, "which assumes an identity by substituting one (superior) signifier for another," and the *metonymic* structure of the testimonial, which accomplishes "a lateral identification through relationship, which acknowledges the possible differences among 'us' as components of the whole."[30] The testimonial's strategy then is to "pry open the process of subject formation, to rehearse it with the reader in a way that invites her to hook into the lateral network of relationships that assumes a community of particular shared objectives rather than interchangeability among its members."[31] Thus it would seem that autobiography invites identifications that are accomplished through *translation*—or analogy. It is a substitutive form that posits a universalism through which any reader can presumably key in her/his own experience and put him/herself in the place of the narrator.

Testimonial, however, because it is "strikingly impersonal," insists upon the literalness of its content and thereby obstructs identifications, demanding instead a more complex relationship between the readers and the writer that is dialogic, communal. Whereas autobiography partakes in the humanist tradition that reifies individuality and privacy, testimonial, according to Sommer, "is always a public event."[32] It is perhaps in this sense that Allison's novel can be read as a form of testimony, for although it uses the conventions of mainstream realistic narrative and certainly, through Bone, posits a singular, individualistic "I," it nevertheless takes as its subject a topic that is presumably "private" and makes it public. Formally, there is no reason to doubt *Bastard Out of Carolina*'s status as a novel. The fact, however, that it *is* doubted and even much debated I attribute to the novel's subject matter, as opposed to its strategic conventions of inventing a communal *subjectivity*. The questions raised about its autobiographical bent are, I suggest, a confusion of the distinctions between autobiography and testimony. For what these readers are actually suggesting is that Allison's work *must* be *referential*. Sommer says that "to doubt referentiality in testimonials would be an irresponsible luxury, given the urgency of the call to action."[33]

Claude Lanzmann, in his seminar on the making of the film *Shoah*, reacts with horror and dismay when one of the interviewers asks him if he was ever tempted to "drop the minimalist esthetic and to go towards conventional illustrations." At first Lanzmann cannot even comprehend what is being asked. When the interviewer begins to repeat his question, Lanzmann replies angrily: "You say esthetic? How dare you. How do you dare to talk about esthetic? I am just telling you that it was with a hidden camera in a bag and that the esthetic was really the last of my . . . But one can see on the screen, it's horrible what's seen on the screen in this precise scene, it is not esthetical at all."[34] This insistence on the literalness of the referent is seconded by Sommer who claims that "Testimonials . . . never put the referentiality of language into question."[35] Thus they do not succumb to a kind of "sublime unrepresentability" or a "journalistic-touristic" reporting.[36]

For the postmodern theorist, of course, the referentiality of language is always already put into question. Fredric Jameson's point, that "the problem of reference has been singularly displaced and stigmatized in the hegemony of various poststructuralist discourses which characterizes the current moment" is pertinent here. Jameson argues for "the presence and existence of . . . a palpable referent—namely death and historical fact, which are ultimately not textualizable and tear through the tissues of textual elaboration, of combination, and free play."[37] He quickly adds, however, that this is not an unambiguous victory or a repudiation of the new theoretical problems:

> For the assertion of a buried referent . . . is a two-way street whose antithetical directions might emblematically be named "repression" . . . or "sublation": the picture has no way of telling us whether we are looking at a rising or setting sun. Does our discovery document the persistence and stubborn, all-informing gravitational charge of reference, or, on the contrary, does it show the tendential historical process whereby reference is systematically processed, dismantled, textualized, and volatized, leaving little more than some indigestible remnant?[38]

Caught up in a similar set of theoretical issues, testimonials, as political *acts*, insist upon the possibility of the signifier's ability to *refer*, but not in a way that suggests a simple or unmediated access to truth. While "truth" is the object of the testimonial's quest, Dori Laub argues that what the one who testifies speaks *is* the truth, regardless of discrepancies that might be found in historical "evidence." He describes the testimony of a woman who narrated her experience at Auschwitz for the video archive at Yale University. At one moment in her testimony her usually laconic, monotonous, self-effacing tone suddenly became passionate and vibrant as she said: "All of a sudden we saw four chimneys going up in flames, exploding. The flames shot into the sky, people were running. It was unbelievable."[39] Historians claimed that the woman's testimony had to be discounted, since there was evidence to show that only one chimney was blown up. Laub argued that it was "not the number of chimneys blown up, but . . . something else, more radical, more crucial: the reality of an unimaginable occurrence. . . . The woman testified to an event that broke the all compelling frame of Auschwitz, where Jewish armed revolts just did not happen, and had no place. She testified to the breakage of a framework. That was historical truth."[40] Laub's point, that "knowledge in the testimony is . . . not simply a factual given that is reproduced and replicated by the testifier, but a genuine advent, an event in its own right,"[41] insists upon the "truth" of an historical present tense independent of its relationship to an historical past.

Jameson also describes such experiences in which "the breakdown of temporality suddenly releases this present of time from all the activities and intentionalities that might focus it and make it a space of praxis; thereby isolated, that present suddenly engulfs the subject with undescribable vividness, a materiality of perception properly overwhelming, which effectively dramatizes the power of the material—or better still, the literal—signifier in isolation."[42] Such a breakdown in the chain of signifiers is often understood as a primary symptom of schizophrenia. Theorists of the testimonial, however, concur with Jameson's analysis in their insistence that this "breakdown," this release into the present, *is a space of praxis.*

I would add to this that competing claims about the testimonies of incest survivors, who are at risk for what some have dubbed the "false memory syndrome," concocted by groups organized to discountenance their testimony on the basis that there is no evidence, are like the historians who doubt the credibility of the woman who "saw" four chimneys explode at Auschwitz. For them, memories are either "fact" or "fiction," and the space in between these two borders on the psychotic. E. Sue Blume points out that incest survivors exist in a psychic space in which the holding of two seemingly mutually exclusive ideas is the very condition of their existence. While their "reality" is often "sharply divided into absolutes of good and evil" (how could "he" both love me and hurt me?), it is imperative to remember Lacan's famous formula that "reality is a fantasy-construction which enables us to mask the Real of our desire."[43] For of course this sharply divided reality for the survivor is generated and maintained by its *reference* to an ideological system that insists upon choosing between these two; whereas the person who inhabits both spaces simultaneously—or worse yet perhaps—balances perpetually on the border *between them,* is rendered psychotic. Blume points out that these "mutually opposite absolutes coexist in the real-life experience of the child" and thus produce in her, since she must find a way to function within the "reality" of the dominant order, a feeling "as if she is unreal and everyone else real, or *vice versa*" (my emphasis).[44] What is crucial to understand, however, is that this feeling of "unreality" is *not* merely the effect of the incest survivor's *history.* That is, it is not the "return of the repressed"; rather, it is also an artful reconstruction of the survivor's *present,* a set of coping mechanisms or survival strategies however "psychotic" they may appear and however self-destructive they may seem, which are actually clever ways of surviving within a dominant order that produces the incest survivor as an impossibility.

Not only is incest marked as a founding taboo and therefore presumed not to happen if the culture is to retain its illusion of coherency, but also, then, the survivor is *not meant to survive*. The fact that she does is due to her ability to create her own system, her own symbolic if you will, that is necessarily discordant with the dominant order's symbolic. In other words, the incest survivor *knows* that reality is a ruse that masks the Real, but she is forced to articulate this knowledge through a conceptual system that cannot be interpreted by dominant codes as other than pathological. Hence I would agree with Linda Alcoff and Laura Gray that the system of the incest survivor is closer to Foucault's discourse of madness than to the discourse of the confessional.[45] Or, perhaps more exactly, her "witnessing" is a specialized discourse that is other to that of the historical confessional, and this "otherness" is misrepresented, necessarily and conveniently, *as madness*. As Blume writes:

> the isolated, disbelieved, threatened child rallies her resources to protect herself from a reality that she cannot tolerate. Early in life, she develops a variety of cognitive adaptations. Many outsiders . . . view these adaptations as "pathological," or as mental disorders, although actually they are creative—even admirable—survival techniques. . . . By attaching the concept of "disorder" to these consequences, we damn the incest survivor to weakness instead of attributing to her the strength of spirit, creativity, and endurance that she deserves—that she has *earned.*[46]

While even mental health professionals, indeed *especially* some mental health professionals, continue to classify the incest survivor's adaptations as pathological, the fantasy identities, alter egos, hypnogogic episodes, auditory hallucinations, and other survival mechanisms are, according to Blume and other feminist therapists, not the symptoms of mental illness or signs of a loss of reality; rather, they are "*active manipulations of reality*" of which the "child or adolescent is conscious and aware."[47]

Allison's *Bastard Out of Carolina* is a hybridity of forms that partakes of the conventions of a traumatic narrative. While it does not adhere exactly to the specifics of the testimonial as elucidated by critics such as Beverley, Carr, and Sommer, it does attest to the paradoxical modes characteristic of the testimonial as a genre that speaks its "truths" in the belated historicity of the trauma. And it does so, not only in its narration of incest but also in its depiction of a sexuality that is formed through and fantasized within the traumatic memories. It is, perhaps, in this difference that the real courage of her novel lies. For Allison not only asks her readers to bear witness to Daddy Glen's spiraling violence as the cuddles progress to shakings, whippings, beatings, and, in the final climactic scene, the brutal rape of his twelve-year-old stepdaughter, Bone; not only does she resist sentimentalizing her ending with Anney Boatwright's heroic rescue of her daughter from her husband's evil grasp; she shows us instead the more common narrative of a wife's choice to "stand by her man," leaving her daughter to make her own way in the world profoundly wounded, consumed with rage, and destined, probably, to reenact the trauma that we, as readers, are called upon to witness. *Bastard Out of Carolina* does all this and more. And it is bold and brave.

But such a story is, sadly, horribly, a story that is part of the normative violence that subtends the gender configurations of our dominant culture. As Vikki Bell points out in her summary chapter of *Interrogating Incest*, "Familiar Stories": "Sociologists and anthropologists have traditionally regarded incest as disruptive of the family and therefore disruptive of the social order. By contrast, feminism has suggested that, paradoxical as it may seem, incest is actually produced and maintained by social order: the order of a male-dominated society."[48]

The extraordinary power and danger of *Bastard Out of Carolina* lies in the links that Allison dares to make, challenging us to witness both Bone's sexual fantasies and the ways they are shaped by the sexual abuse. She dares to say that her twelve-year-old protagonist's sexuality is then, and probably forever, a hybrid of pain and pleasure. And more: that these fantasies are Bone's own transformations, her own narrative—her "salvation" if you will. These fantasies seem distinctly theatrical in that they require a spectator and, as such, they inhabit a borderline between fantasy and reality. As she masturbates, Bone

> imagined people watching while Daddy Glen beat me, though only when it was not happening. When he beat me, I screamed and kicked and cried like the baby I was. But sometimes when I was safe and alone, I would imagine the ones who watched. Someone had to watch—some girl I admired who barely knew I existed, some girl from church or down the street, or one of my cousins, or even somebody I had seen on television. Sometimes a whole group of them would be trapped into watching. In my imagination I was proud and defiant. I'd stare back at him with my teeth set, making no sound at all, no shameful scream, no begging. Those who watched admired me and hated him. I pictured it that way and put my hands between my legs. It was

scary, but it was thrilling too. Those who watched me, loved me. It was as if I was being beaten for them. I was wonderful in their eyes.[49]

As Daddy Glen's beatings become more regular and increasingly brutal, Bone develops a fetish for the belts that hang, smooth, supple, and well-oiled behind the door of the closet where she helps her Mama put away the clothes. Sometimes she hides in the closet to smell the belts, reach up and touch them, wrap her fingers around them. She is more ashamed of masturbating than she is of the beatings. For though she hides the bruises "as if they were evidence of crimes [she] had committed,"[50] she cannot explain how she could hate being beaten but still masturbate to the story she told herself about it. But Allison does understand how both of these narratives can be true, how Bone can despise herself for being beaten *and* take illicit pleasure in the fantasies she constructs from their raw material:

> It was only in my fantasies with people watching me that I was able to defy Daddy Glen. Only there that I had any pride. I loved those fantasies, even though I was sure they were a terrible thing. They had to be; they were self-centered and they made me have shuddering orgasms. In them, I was very special. I was triumphant, important. I was not ashamed. There was no heroism possible in the real beatings. There was just being beaten until I was covered with snot and misery.[51]

In her consciousness, Bone desperately seeks escape from the sexualized violence of her daily life. She dreams of shooting Daddy Glen with her uncle's rifle; she works to build her hands so that one day they will be as threatening and powerful as her stepfather's and she can retaliate; she wants the hideous secret to be discovered but she has no access to a language for reporting it. But in her sexual fantasies, Bone *does not dream of being rescued.* On the contrary, her sexual fantasies repeat, magnify, and modify the actual abuse, often transforming it into brilliant scenarios that bear little if any resemblance to her actual experiences, such as her fantasy about masturbating in a burning haystack, where the sexual thrill is ambiguously located somewhere between the fire consuming her before she climaxes, just as she climaxes, or narrowly escaping it. These are indeed artful reconstructions. Her sexual pleasure is much more complicated than Allison describes it in an interview given after writing the novel. Bone has more imagination than to fantasize simply about enduring the pain.

Allison describes Bone's fantasies as survival techniques "whereby she retains a sense of power in a situation where she has none. And comfort, just sheer physical comfort of retelling herself the story in which she is not the victim. . . . She becomes the heroine. Even when she's the martyred heroine, she's still the heroine and they love her fiercely."[52] What the scene requires, however, in order to be both pleasurable and therapeutic, is someone who watches. These fantasies are not monologues that *narrate* the history of her abuse. They are dreams of a performance that take place in psychoanalytic time—the future anterior—the past that *will have been*. As Catherine Clément explains, the future anterior is a locution in which one finds the future retroactively, "a memory curious about its own future . . . which refuses simply to repeat the old saw 'once upon a time' over and over again . . . as if nothing had happened, the future anterior alters history: it is the miraculous tense, the tense of healing."[53] Jameson identifies the future anterior as the tense that "offers a very different machine for producing historicity . . . what one might in the strong sense call a trope of . . . the estrangement and renewal of our own reading present . . . history by way of the apprehension of [the] present as the past of a specific future."[54] Jameson cites the narration that occurs in the future anterior as a "brutal transformation . . . into a memory and reconstruction [in which] reification ceases to be a baleful and alienating process . . . and is transferred to the side of human energies and human possibilities."[55] Situated between dreams and events, this is the time of Bone's sexual fantasies, as it is indeed the time of Allison's novel. Written in a temporality that fluctuates between the present of Bone's narration and the retrospection of Allison as witness to her history, *Bastard out of Carolina* formally captures the double-bind of the traumatic voice.

For the paradox of the incest survivor is that the *survivor* is also at once, indeed by definition, the one who endured the abuse. How does one cease to be, or become other than the *survivor and still survive?* As Dori Laub has explained, the difficulty of working with survivors of trauma is that they resist voicing their pasts for fear that witnessing the event will mean losing their status *as survivors*. That is, they may not, and sometimes indeed do not, survive the witnessing.[56] Narrating the trauma entails a second becoming, an ironic resurrection that could equal death for the survivor.[57] Allison says that she writes to "save the dead . . . to save the people I have lost, some of whose bodies are still walking around."[58] She was very nearly one of those people herself, and still lives with the guilt of having left them behind. Allison's keynote address at the OutWrite conference in 1992 was called "Survival is the Least of My Desires." Having been asked to speak about survival to her gay and lesbian audience, she cautions them: "we must aim much higher than just staying alive if we are to begin to approach our true potential."[59]

If, as Felman argues, "testifying from the inside . . . would mean testifying from inside the death, the deadness and very suicide of the witness,"[60] then the voice that witnesses a trauma, such as incest, must literally be a voice from beyond the experience of the survivor—yet only the survivor can narrate her own experience. What we are faced with, then, in a narrative such as *Bastard Out of Carolina* is a story that theoretically cannot be told. It is no wonder that Freud reached the conclusion that his clients who repeatedly narrated stories of incest were engaged in oedipal fantasies. Feminist theorists have vehemently denounced Freud's "seduction fantasy" as a cowardly retreat from the truth of his patients' experiences; and contemporary theorists, such as Slavoj Žižek, provoke a cry of outrage and protest when they make such statements as "incest is inherently impossible."[61] These arguments, however, are stalled around a naive distinction between fantasy and reality as discrete psychic phenomena. Trapped in the logic of the classical Freudian talking cure, where Lacan also located himself in his early period, "the final moment of the analysis is reached when the subject is able to narrate to the Other his own history in its continuity; when his desire is integrated, recognized in 'full speech.'"[62] In this phase, articulating the events produces a language that negates the "things themselves." The signifiers annihilate the signifieds. Despite the distance from and disdain for psychoanalytic, particularly Freudian, theory that many feminists espouse, the fundamental methods of feminist praxis—consciousness-raising groups, speaking the unspeakable, self-nomination, identity politics, breaking the silences—accord with the "talking cure." Such methods are dialogical, communal. When Laub writes of the dialogic relationship between the listener and the one who has experienced the trauma, he says that: "for the testimonial process to take place there needs to be a bonding, the intimate and total presence of an *other*—in the position of the one who hears. Testimonies are not monologues; they cannot take place in solitude. The witnesses are talking to *somebody*, to somebody they have been waiting for a long time."[63] Most feminists would find resonances of their own experiences and theories in his words.

The issues that feminist practitioners and theorists have been addressing for centuries largely entail trauma survivors—rape, sexual harassment, incest, child abuse. Indeed many feminists would argue that the heteropatriarchal system as such is an ideological institution that interpellates and produces "women" *as* a traumatic category. If, as Felman has argued, the traumatic event is a special category that paradoxically is caught in the logic of a story that, at once, is impossible and necessary to witness and narrate, then we must seek an understanding of the cure that takes us beyond the limitations of language, whether we understand it as reproducing or anni-hilating the "thing itself." What becomes necessary is a third way, beyond the simplistic binary fantasy/reality.

Returning to Allison's novel, we see that her protagonist, Bone, deeply troubled by her sexual fantasies that reenact the abuse scenarios while embellishing them with the addition of spectators, hence creating a performative series of scenes, becomes fascinated with the idea of being saved. She turns to the discourse that is most evidently available to her for redemption, for she wants not only to be delivered from the scene of the crimes in which she is the victim but also to be redeemed for what she believes to be her own complicity with these acts and the desires they produce in her imaginary. She lies in bed at night and weeps as she listens to gospel music on the radio. She begins to attend the Baptist church, and she hovers on the edge as the pastor calls those who want to be saved to come forward and testify. She throbs to the swelling of the organ as it begins to hum the first notes of "Softly and Tenderly, Jesus is Calling." She sees something inexplicable in the eyes of the women in the pews who crane their necks backward to look down the aisles, waiting for the procession of repentant sinners. She remembers Uncle Earle telling her that "if you were not saved, not part of the congregation, you were all anyone could see at the invocation."[64] But Bone is ambivalent about being saved. She is fascinated with being the one who is *all that can be seen*, rather than a member of the congregation. Her desire for community draws her toward the church; but the need to hold onto her singularity and the "secret" she keeps of her differences from those who can be saved make this kind of witnessing impossible.

This Christian concept of witnessing is historically linked to juridical discourse as well as to the discourse of martyrdom. As Robert V. Moss Jr. points out: "the term 'witness' has been borrowed from the language of the lawcourt by the teachers and writers of ancient Israel and the early church. The term of course appears in its legal sense in both the Old Testament and the New Testament, where witnesses are called to appear for testimony in a court of law . . . the term 'witness' retains something of its original juridical meaning and Israel and the church are regarded as God's witnesses."[65]

Allison A. Trites, in her thorough historical and etymological analysis of the Christian concept of witnessing, shows that Christian witnessing was also related to the idea of martyrdom: "This latter approach has arisen partly from the fact that the English word 'martyr' comes from the Greek word *martyrs*, and partly from the close relation that developed in the early church between the two ideas."[66] Trites cites R. P. Casey, who argues that the movement from the juridical discourse of witnessing to the discourse of the witness as martyr "represents only one development of meaning" among many others, but that nonetheless "all of these developments begin with a metaphorical application of the legal term."[67]

This is of course the sense of "witnessing" that Foucault has extensively critiqued in the form of the Christian *confessional.* Most feminists are aware of the problematic status of the testimonial in light of Foucault's reading of the confessional as a form that has historically occurred in the context of unequal power relationships, in which the one who "witnesses" is coerced into disclosing sexual acts and fantasies that are then adjudicated by the listener. Furthermore, Foucault's argument sees this as a structural mechanism of discursive regimes that extend outside the strict form of the Christian pastoral. To speak one's sexual "secrets" thus becomes an opportunity for the dominant discourse to speak one's sexuality and to erect categories that contain, limit, and normalize a set of practices into sexual identities. He writes:

> The confession is a ritual of discourse in which the speaking subject is also the subject of the statement; it is also a ritual that unfolds within a power relationship, for one does not confess without the presence (or virtual presence) of a partner who is not simply the interlocutor but the authority who requires the confession, prescribes and appreciates it, and intervenes in order to judge, punish, forgive, console, and reconcile; a ritual in which the truth is corroborated by the obstacles and resistances it has had to surmount in order to be formulated; and finally, a ritual in which the expression alone, independently of its external consequences, produces intrinsic modifications in the person who articulates it: it exonerates, redeems, and purifies him; it unburdens him of his wrongs, liberates him, and promises him salvation.[68]

This is indeed a powerful argument against which feminists have had to work in order to maintain some of the movement's basic principles. Across disciplines, feminist theories and practices have heavily relied on concepts that could be easily subsumed under the mode of the confessional—"naming the violence," "speaking the unspeakable," "narrating the truth of women's experiences." Linda Alcoff and Laura Gray have taken on the most sustained and convincing discussion of this problem. As survivors, active practitioners in the feminist movement, and theorists who use and sometimes oppose postmodernist theories, Alcoff and Gray write an article that is an "attempt to rethink and repair this dissonance."[69] They argue that survivor discourse is

> closer to the discourse of the mad, as Foucault discusses it, than to the discourse of the repressed. Survivor speech is positioned . . . not in an

oppositional but still harmonious complementarity with the dominant discourse but rather in violent confrontation with it: its expression requires not a simple negation but a transformation of the dominant formulation. The point of contention between dominant and
survivor discourses is not over the determination of truth but over the
determination of the statable.[70]

In psychoanalytic terms, what Alcoff and Gray are arguing is that survivor
discourse is distinguishable as *foreclosure* rather than the return of the
repressed. As such, it is much more threatening to the dominant discourse;
indeed, it challenges the very constitution of the Symbolic Order rather
than rendering it stable by dis-covering what was necessarily "covered" in
the Imaginary in order to render the Symbolic its illusion of coherency and
wholeness. This is at once both the power of survivor's speech and the enormous *risk* that the speech entails to the speaker. It is also what we must
understand about survivor's speech in order to comprehend the fundamental paradox at its center.

Christian witnessing, in both its associations with the law and with martyrdom, would seem to converge around the notion of a trial. In the juridical sense, a trial is what ostensibly produces evidence—all that there is to
be seen—a public display of the "truth." Bone's Uncle Earle, the family
member who most resists the church and its doctrines, tells Bone that,
paradoxically, it was by *not* becoming a witness that one became "all that
there is to be seen." Bone tries to save Earle during her obsession with the
church, but finally he is the character whom she also most desires to emulate. Allison depicts Earle as the most "criminalistic" of all her characters.
Bone both fears and admires his stubborn resistance to the law, and it is his
"way of being seen" that she endorses. Significantly, it is Earle who takes
the lead in punishing Bone's stepfather when Raylene discovers the abuse.
Earle beats Glen nearly to death, fulfilling the fantasies that Bone has cher-
ished as survival tactics for a long time. The reality, however, does not satisfy her when it is accomplished. Imagining Glen's violence turned upon
himself sustains her through her ordeal, but when it becomes real she finds
that her desire is no longer constituted by her rage. The Christian concept
of witnessing is finally wholly inadequate to the complexities of Bone's psychic dilemma, one characterized by the conflicting desires to be known and
to keep her "secrets" concealed.

This state of irreconcilable oppositions is paradigmatic to the survivor
of sexual abuse. And it is not simply a matter of making one difficult choice
over another, thereby resolving the opposition between the desire to conceal and the desire to display. Rather, the incest survivor is trapped in the

absolute necessity for *both* of these opposites to be realized simultaneously—at once to keep her secret and to have it (her) be known. What the child who is abused and the adult survivor of incest must accomplish is not to *become a witness* but to *have a witness.* Hence when Raylene discovers Bone's bruises and guesses the truth of Daddy Glen's abuse, and Bone's uncles beat Daddy Glen, Bone's "secret" becomes known through her body. But Bone, whose relationship to this "body" is dissociative, still does not feel that she has been known. She has neither articulated her own story nor, more important, has she found a listener who can become her witness. This is what Bone wants from her mother, whose abandonment of her is arguably more psychically traumatizing than the sexual abuse itself. As a child victim of sexual abuse, Bone inhabits a psychic contradiction that simply cannot be resolved within the simplistic binary of concealment and display. One of the places that Bone can go to seek some kind of resolution, however, is into sexual fantasies. That these fantasies tend toward a sadomasochistic quality is not surprising, for as I have argued, s/m works toward unbinding the associations between traumatic sexual experience and the vestiges of it still present in the desire. Whereas the sexual abuse survivor is most clearly recognizable to others through *dissociative* symptomologies, the s/m practitioner acts out these scenes in ways that repeat, reorganize, and integrate them into her present. Dissociation is replaced by *consciousness* of associations. Such "acting out," however, is by no means a simple theatrical "trick." The fantasy location where such scenes take place balances precariously on the edge of a psychic space between the real and the performative. It requires very delicate and complex negotiation. And it sometimes fails to hold onto the line between.

In Allison's novel we see this psychic maneuvering acted out by Bone in the displaced space of her relationship to redemption. Somewhere in between the tantalizing clarity of the righteous who can clearly demarcate the struggle between salvation and damnation, good and evil, life and death, Bone holds precariously onto a borderline place. She comes close to being saved fourteen times, but each time as the preacher turns his gaze upon her, she is awash with indecision: "it was not actually baptism I wanted, or welcome to the congregation, or even the breathless concentration of the preacher. It was that moment of sitting on the line between salvation and damnation with the preacher and the old women pulling bodily at my poor darkened soul. I wanted that moment to go on forever."[71]

Bone weeps and sings and prays and contemplates the magic of grace. She is baptized beneath the painting of Jesus at the Jordan. But she cannot be saved. She retreats to her room and takes comfort in the book of Revelations.

Waiting for the apocalypse, loving the Whore of Babylon, cherishing the images of rivers of blood and fire, Bone is "mourning the loss of something [she] had never really had."[72] We cannot speak of an innocence that is lost before it is experienced as loss. Nor can we presume to know what is "right" or "wrong" about sexual desires without making nostalgic appeals to a time before . . . a time when . . . an authentic or natural moment to which we have no access. Excoriated for not "curing herself," like Bone, who resists the cure, Allison compares this self-righteousness to "the same old thing they told me in Sunday school: don't jerk off and don't think about it."[73]

Allison's insistence on claiming a feminist identity while celebrating her sexuality as one imbued with the erotics of power has made of her an outcast. But she has survived this second death: "I have to tell you," she says her in her keynote address, "that it is a miracle I did not kill myself out of sheer despair when I was told I was too lesbian for feminism, too reformist for radical feminism, too sexually perverse for respectable lesbianism, and too stubborn for the women's, gay and queer revolutions."[74] Allison's sexual "perversity" is intimately bound up with her creativity. Her desire to "write in such a way as to literally remake the world,"[75] what some people see as her obscenity and others regard as her divinity, is an evidently irreconcilable opposition. Her editor, Carole DeSanti at Dutton, says "people come to her to be healed."[76] And Allison herself refers to learning how to speak the words *rape, child, relentless* "as a sacrament, a blessing, a prayer. Not a curse."

The psychoanalytic theorist Janine Chasseguet-Smirgel's re-examination of Freud's theory of perversion sheds some light on this contradiction. Her hypothesis is that "perversion represents a . . . reconstitution of Chaos, out of which there arises a new kind or reality."[77] Citing examples of alchemical conceptions of the universe, passed down in myths, philosophies, and ideologies throughout the ages, she mentions Dionysian rites that "involved intersexual disguises," and the Gnostic gospel of Thomas in which Christ purportedly said: "When you make two human beings into one, and when you make the inside as the outside, and the outside as the inside and the top as the bottom! And if you make the male and the female into one so that the male is no longer male and the female no longer female, then you will enter into the Kingdom."[78] This, Chasséquet-Smirgel argues, is clearly a conception "contrary in every detail to the one described in that text on which our Judaeo-Christian civilization is based."[79] Rather than a universe based on separation and division, the alchemical commingling of all binary opposites into a chaotic whole is a world that is most thoroughly represented by Sade, a "catalogue of perversions" in which the only law is the "*absolute mixture.*"[80] Sade's world is one in which, at once, all differences are allowed as well as all mingling, whereas the Judaeo-Christian worldview is one in which differences must at all costs be isolated into seamless categories. And the founding law of the culture is the prohibition against incest. This separation is not only external but also intrapsychic, and its aim "is to prevent the breaking down of the barriers which ensure that the essential nature of things is preserved."[81] If the prohibition on incest is the founding law of this culture, the incest survivor finds herself in a strange location indeed. Somewhere on the border between these two worldviews, inhabiting them both simultaneously, carrying with her the mark of abjection from the dominant culture and a terrifying desire that is, at once, liberatory and indelibly *marked by the departure*, the incest survivor, like Allison's protagonist, Bone, is "sitting on the line between salvation and damnation." Such a location may well produce a sexuality that accords with Luce Irigaray's vision: "Our whole body is moved. No surface holds. No figure, line or point remains. No ground subsists. But no abyss, either. Depth, for us, is not a chasm. Without a solid crust, there is no precipice. Our depth is the thickness of our body, our all touching itself. Where top and bottom, inside and outside, in front and behind, above and below are not separated, remote, out of touch. Our all intermingled. Without breaks or gaps."[82]

Collapsing *all* differences into a unitary whole, however, produces the same boundary confusions as disciplinary categories. Chasseguet-Smirgel contends that the sexual abuse of incest is about the abolition of generational differences. Again she refers to Sade:

> It is clear that for Sade, incest is in no way connected with assuaging a deep longing for the Oedipal object, but it is linked with the abolition of "children" as a category and "parents" as a category. . . . the pleasure connected with transgression is sustained by the fantasy that—in breaking down the barriers which separate man from woman, child from adult, mother from son, daughter from father, brother from sister, the erotogenic zones from each other . . . —it has destroyed reality, thereby creating a new one . . . where all differences are abolished.[83]

Such breaking down of distinctions is often characteristic of the incest survivor's epistemology. For, one of the effects of incest for the abused child is that she is unable to tell her "secret," not only because she has no language, as a child, to articulate a sexual experience that surpasses her linguistic command but also because the "experience" itself surpasses the lexicon of "reality." The child is also often threatened, overtly or tacitly, by the abuser who tells her that further harm will befall her, or her mother, or both of them, if she reveals the secret. Thus in bearing the secret the child becomes an accomplice of sorts with the abuser, and more often than not the protector of the mother. Bone is "more terrified of hurting [her mother] than of anything that might happen to [her]," and she resolves to "work as hard as he did to make sure she never knew."[84] Anney does not notice how haggard, angry, and terrified her daughter is, but when she holds her it is as if Bone "*was her mother now* [my emphasis], holding her safe, and she was my child, happy to lean on my strong, straight, back."[85] Even when she finally gets the nerve to try to tell her Aunt Ruth, she is again treated as if she were an adult. While she is staying with Ruth, who is dying of cancer, she finally blurts out: "Daddy Glen hates me." Thinking that these words have revealed the whole story to her aunt, Bone waits expectantly for her reaction, expecting her to deny it perhaps so that she can elaborate, or hoping that these words alone will be enough for her Aunt to surmise the truth. But Aunt Ruth responds: "Tell me Bone . . . You think I'm dying?"[86] Ruth *does* recognize that Bone has spoken the unspeakable, but rather than responding to the child's demand she sees it as her own opportunity to ask the unspeakable question that has hovered around her illness. A few pages later Uncle Earle tells Bone about Teresa, a woman he "wanted to pour over like a river of love."[87] Repetitively the adults in her life treat Bone as if she were an adult, an equal, or even a parent to them. At the same time all the women, except Raylene, constantly tolerate the violence and neglect of the men with the excuse that they are all "just hurt little boys." This kind of reversal points to the wider parameters of incest; it is a "family affair," not simply a one-on-one encounter. Allison says that she speaks so openly about her sexual practices because the hardest thing for an incest survivor to do is to learn how to allow herself to experience her sexuality with pleasure.[88] Having been subjected to forcible rape for many years, an incest survivor may find that each sexual encounter brings up memories and that it is extremely difficult to place herself in the position of the subject, to find her own agency in the sexual act. Ironically, it may be in *actively choosing* to relinquish control that the incest survivor finds a way to manipulate the traumatic history into pleasurable activity.

In the introduction to her anthology, subversively entitled *Doing It For Daddy*, Pat Califia anticipates objections to the book. While the New Christian Right is picketing libraries that carry *Heather Has Two Mommies*, and Canadian Customs are confiscating copies of *Hot, Hotter, Hottest*, a cookbook about the tantric joys of jalapeño peppers, and United States legislators are resolved to censor "smut" on the Internet, Califia knows that some people will say: "Aren't we playing right into their hands. Can't we just . . . lay low about this stuff for a while? . . . Isn't *Doing It For Daddy* romanticizing incest? How can anybody find this material arousing when real incest is so traumatic, damaging its victims psychologically for life?"[89] Califia's answer is, as she herself says, obvious—that such work does not advocate incest or child abuse, but rather is "about sexual fantasies and erotic games played between consenting adults."[90] While I am completely in agreement with Califia in principle, her appeal to "free choice" and the autonomy of the ego is a construction that simply does not do justice to the complexities of subjectivity and sexual desire. Violence and sexuality are insufficiently historicized and theorized in these debates. In order to break past this impasse, each of them must be released from their stabilizing functions as the ground on which the controversies take place. As we are faced with an increasing onslaught of erotophobic forces, our counter-rhetoric and actions must take more subtle account of our differences. When the Australian writer Anna Munster, one of the most articulate thinkers about the erotics of power, announces that she is not a "horrified on-looker,"[91] the emphasis is on "horrified," for those who persist in imagining themselves as naive spectators who are positioned *outside* the spectacle are "looking" as well, even if they are looking away. We are all *participants* in this spectacle. Rather than fleeing from the scene while shouting fire in this crowded theater, we had better attend to the uncanniness of our own homes. The distinction between "inside and outside" *sustains* a politics of difference that has lead to facile and ultimately reproductive categories—litanies of "identities," institutionalized "multiculturalisms," system-driven "diversities"— that are as discrete, binding, and panoptical as the categories they espouse to explode.

"Most of all," Allison has written, "I have tried to understand the politics of 'they,' why human beings fear and stigmatize the different while secretly dreading that they might be one of the different themselves. Class, race, sexuality, gender—and all the other categories by which we categorize and dismiss each other need to be excavated from the *inside*."[92]

In her novel, Allison makes Aunt Raylene, the working-class, white trash, butch lesbian, the spokesperson for understanding differences. Bone goes out onto the landing to watch the cars pass by, and sees the bus from the housing development full of "flat-faced children staring at me hatefully." She glares back at them, hating them for what she imagines they have, hating them for hating her,—"Anger was like a steady drop of poison in [her soul." She tells Aunt Raylene that she hates them because they are "looking at us like we're something nasty." Aunt Raylene reaches down and slaps Bone's shoulder, then lectures her about making assumptions about people whom she knows nothing about: "You're making up stories about those people," she says, "Make up a story where you have to live in their house, be one of their family, and pass by this road. Look at it from the other side for a while. Maybe you won't be glaring at people so much."[93]

Ann Cvetkovich has suggested that Aunt Raylene serves as a "displaced marker of Bone's queer sexuality."[94] She also serves as the voice in the novel that understands how differences *between* people must be excavated from the *inside.* In response to Raylene's lecture about class differences, Bone turns to her and immediately asks her to reveal the story of her sexual history, the "secret" of Raylene's lesbianism that the novel has been withholding up until this point. This is not a casual juxtaposition. Rather, Bone's unconscious association serves to remind us that the shaping of one's sexuality is also a matter of class. Allison recalls how she lived a secret life while she was involved in the feminist movement as a political activist in the 1970s and 1980s. By day she was editing newsletters, stuffing envelopes, walking in protest marches; at night she would sneak out to the working-class bars where butch/femme role-playing was the standard scene of seduction. While not necessarily consonant with a subculture of women who acted out the erotics of power in their sexual practices, butch/femme nevertheless carried with it the connotation of imitating heteropatriarchal gender configurations. A predominantly white, heterosexual, middle-class women's movement was for some time unable to comprehend that class race and sexual orientation produced *interpsychical* differences that were incomprehensible from the reading of outward appearances. Women like Bone's Aunt Raylene were not "cross-dressers," for example. They were working-class women who wore clothes that were practical for their lifestyles. Despite the fact that feminist theory has been keenly aware of the limitations of the field of visuality, it has nonetheless fallen too often into a "looks like/is like" trap in which the *performative* is collapsed into the *ontological.* Allison is one of our most articulate speakers on the imbrication of differences, particularly the intersection of sexuality and class, the term in the litany of categories that is the most occluded in academic discourse, which is written primarily by women and men who are de facto in a privileged rank of the social hierarchy. In her collection of essays *Skin,* Allison speaks powerfully to this issue from her own experience:

> Traditional feminist theory has had a limited understanding of class differences and of how sexuality and self are shaped by both desire and denial. The ideology implies that we are all sisters who should only turn our anger and suspicion on the world outside the lesbian community. It is easy to say that the patriarchy did it, that poverty

and social contempt are products of the world of the fathers, and often I feel a need to collapse my sexual history into what I was willing to share of my class background, to pretend that my life both as a lesbian and as a working-class escapee was constructed by the patriarchy. Or conversely, to ignore how much my life was shaped by growing up poor and talk only about what incest did to my identity as a woman and as a lesbian. The difficulty is that I can't ascribe everything that has been problematic about my life simply and easily to the patriarchy, or to incest, or even to the invisible and much-denied class structure of our society.[95]

What Allison recognizes in this description of her own experience is the inability of *any* categorization to address fully the complex ways in which the "self" is constructed both externally and internally. Indeed that is still an insufficient locution, a false binary that cannot lead us past the impasse of oppositional, analogical, identitarian thinking. As long as the opposition between fantasy and reality, or in psychoanalytic terms, the Symbolic and the Imaginary, appears as discrete, there are only two possibilities open to the cure. As I have already indicated, the first constitutes the ability to achieve "full speech," or to constitute one's history in a coherent, linear narrative; and the limitations of this method for the trauma victim are severe—in effect, a kind of psychic suicide, if not a real one.

Midway in his career, Lacan sought to evade this impasse by formulating a theory in which he recognized, as do most feminists, that the Symbolic Order exacts a penalty, a lack or loss for the subject that must be accepted in order for her desire to be activated. This "castration theory" has been the subject of vigorous analysis and arguments between feminist theorists. It is the third phase, however, that addresses most adequately the situation in which the incest survivor or survivors of other traumatic events find themselves. Here Lacan posits his third term, the "Real," an impossible "traumatic kernel" that lies at, indeed is constitutive of, the very center of the Symbolic. John Beverley has suggested that the testimonial's "truth effect" is not simply the difference between any text and reality, rather, it "produces if not the real as such (in the Lacanian sense of that which resists symbolization absolutely), then certainly a sensation of *experiencing the real* that, for example, even news reports do not."[96] René Jara writes: "More than an interpretation of reality, the testimonio is '*a trace of the real,*' of that history which, as such, is inexpressible."[97]

This formulation should be of interest to feminist theoreticians, for notice that the "trauma" is no longer attributed to the very production of

the category *women*. Rather, the "Real" gives us a concept that acknowledges what many feminists have been claiming in a number of discourses:
that the symbolic order itself is what is "lacking," indeed it constructs itself
as the illusion of a coherent system that nonetheless depends upon dis-
guising the void in its center by displacing the "lack" onto an element that
is posited as "outside" when it always already *necessarily inside*. Lacan coins
the term *ex-timate*—the external intimacy—to describe this ideological
formation. It is much like the notion of the "proximate" that Jonathan
Dollimore articulates as the element inside a system that is made to appear
as if it were outside. Dollimore uses this term to discuss the ways in which
homophobia works to abject homosexuals.[98]

I would like to use Dollimore's term to further my discussion of the
ways in which women who practice a sexuality that is directly, often ritu-
alistically, formally engaged in an erotics of power can be understood in
their differences from the feminist "public policy" on sexual practices that
abhors any engagement in what is often described as the reinstatement, or
mimesis, of heteropatriarchal power structures that are abusive to women.
After years of apologizing for "unacceptable" sexual practices and fantasies,
more lesbians have begun to challenge this feminist party line and are now
defiantly asserting that controlling their desires produces neither pleasure
nor power. In her introduction to *The Persistent Desire*, Joan Nestle
announces the end of "defensive disclaimers."[99] New "truth" claims about
lesbian sexuality are being made, among them the pleasure in relinquishing control—the "lust to see how close we can get to the edge."[100] Allison
was herself one of the first lesbians to break this silence: "Two or three
things I know, but this is the one I'm not suppose to talk about, how it
comes together—sex and violence, love and hatred. I'm not ever supposed
to put together the two halves of my life—the man who walked across my
childhood and the life I have made for myself. I am not supposed to talk
about that man when I grew up to be a lesbian . . . stubborn, competitive,
and perversely lustful."[101]

In the early days of these arguments, I would describe the tension as a
contest between possession and self-possession. Lesbians interested in the
erotics of power and who desired to be "overtaken" were in need of consciousness-raising. Some lesbian feminists, fearing that they might somehow become possessed with unwanted desires, considered their qualifica-
tions as interventionists. Claudia Card asks "whether outsiders to consensual sadomasochism . . . can have good reason to intervene to stop, prevent,
or limit consensual sadomasochism."[102] Ellis Stanley ended her letter to
Off Our Backs protesting Califia's anti-antiporn commentary with this sen-

timent: "it is sad that Califia has been so duped by her conditioning that not only does she ape male misogynist practices but positively enjoys doing it. She has made a cage for herself with her own body and by doing so continues to *imprison all women*."[103] How this "contagion" spread to infect "all women" was never articulated. It was as if the idea of women as a communal group had grown so strong as to erase all boundaries between and among women. The combination of panic and fascination in these responses produces an *arresting* discourse, a juridical tone that plays in multiple registers: Authorization—seizing or taking into custody; Contagion—stopping or checking the motion of something that threatens to spread; Fascination—catching and keeping one's attention. Captured in their own logic, the interventionists not only do not confront the differences between women, they also fail to catch the traces of their own desire as "inside" rather than outside where they presumably need not go. Characteristic attitudes such as Andrena Zawinski's's concern with the "arduous task of reshaping culture and reducing violence *within ourselves*" (my emphasis),[104] and Tacie Dejanikus's comment that "the point is to get rid of power roles as much as possible. It's going to be hard. I don't think the Samois women are making it easier,"[105] were perhaps not so much displacements of their own fear onto other women as they were testimonies to the degree in which "woman" had become a category so bonded by feminist rhetoric that the permeable boundaries between self and other, the conscious and the unconscious had become manifestly impermeable.

Feminists like Susan Griffin went right to the contradictory logic at the heart of pro-sex testimonials. She noticed that on the one hand we are told that playing "games of power" leads to their transcendence; while on the other hand they are a source of ecstasy to be valued in and of themselves. Griffin joined other feminists who believed that the erotics of power damages all women by arguing that the games of power are "meant to conceal," existing in order to "create an illusion," and that this is no harmless illusion but one that not only services the "idea of the other" but indeed "creates the other," which is moreover the *originary* other, the model from which all others are copied.[106] Such infectious rhetoric has been toned down considerably over the course of the "sex wars" of the last two decades. Nonetheless, the resistance to and bias against s/m sexuality remains prevalent in recent and infinitely more subtle feminist analyses.

While Sheila Jeffreys continues her diatribe against sexuality by arguing that "orgasm politics," has hijacked the women's movement,[107] Ann Cvetkovich has recently written about the ongoing controversies about s/m performances at the Michigan Women's Festival. In 1994 the performance of Tribe 8, a dyke punk band, instigated the familiar protest that the performance promoted violence against women. It was the performance itself that was at issue, for surely Tribe 8's self-nomination as "gang-castrating, patriarchy-smashing snatchlickers"[108] could scarcely be interpreted as promoting violence *against* women. Cvetkovich builds a nuanced argument supporting the cathartic power of the performance. What is interesting in this case is that the controversy overtly centered on the issue of *memory*. Whereas the protesters warned that the performance could trigger "flashbacks" for sexual abuse survivors, Cvetkovich argues that it is possible to interpret flashbacks as therapeutic, "conversion experiences" for the spectators who realized that the performance "addressed" rather than "promoted" violence. Cvetkovich makes the daring move of suggesting that, despite the elision or avoidance of the connections between sexual abuse survivors and lesbianism in the literature and testimonials of sexual abuse survivors, it may be nonetheless more productive for the connection to be made openly, positing the possibility that sexual abuse *is* intimately connected to, perhaps even productive of, lesbianism. Why might we not say, Cvetkovich suggests, that lesbianism is a brilliant solution to the problem of sexual abuse?[109]

While I think this is a daring move that is predicated on beginning with the assumption that lesbianism is a source of pride rather than shame, and a choice rather than a genetic predisposition, I disagree with Cvetkovich's argument on the grounds that it posits a fairly simple notion of agency and causality. It seems much more likely to me that lesbians are the people who most frequently speak out about sexual abuse because they have already chosen social positions that require courageous enunciations. As members of an abjected category, the risks are in some sense greater for lesbians to speak about yet another "sexual secret." However, lesbians also are intimately aware of being positioned in a foreclosed relation to the dominant culture's symbolic order. If incest, in particular, is the founding law of a culture that forecloses a particular act so as to make it omnipresent and invisible, widely available to an entitled class, race, and gender while forbidden to be spoken at the speaker's risk of being labeled psychotic, then surely this is a situation in which lesbians have found themselves similarly located through their identity-formations alone.

It is worth noting that in the truce between the antiporn feminists and the s/m lesbians at Michigan, one of the compromises made was to permit s/m activities but assign them to a separate space dubbed "The Twilight Zone."[110] Cvetkovich does not say whether this name was chosen by s/m participants or the protesters. But besides its obvious allusion to the famous television program that could be generically labeled as horror, it also quite aptly situates s/m in the space between dreams and events, between consciousness and the unconscious, that borderline space of profound ambiguity that is nearly intolerable for the anti-s/m feminists.[111] It is also highly significant that s/m workshops at the festival are prohibited from *enacting* s/m, "to prevent women who have been sexually abused from accidentally or involuntarily witnessing this behavior and being painfully reminded of their own traumatic experiences."[112]

In an earlier chapter I argued that s/m "acts out the word as bond," that it is about "doing" not "talking," and that it insists upon the distinction. This prohibition against enactment clearly indicates that for all the postmodernist discourse theory many of us have absorbed, there remains that small particle of difference between speech and action. In speech-act theories, the "performative" may end up being an all-consuming category that persistently devours any search for the constative, the latter becoming little more than a "straw man" set up to permit performative proliferations. Nevertheless, whether it is in the form of protests and prohibitions or excitements to action, there remains at the least the desire, perhaps even the need or necessity, for recourse to an illusion of the constative. And the literature of testimonials is one place where this desire is expressed and, for some theorists, realized. I am suggesting that s/m sexuality has become such a lightning rod for controversy precisely because it embodies this desire, however impossible it may be to realize. Indeed, precisely *because* it is impossible to realize.

The continuing objections to s/m sexuality have taken much more sophisticated forms, but on close examination they remain embedded in a conflict between sexual identities and sexual acts. For example, taking strong issue with Parveen Adams's contention that "the homosexuality of the lesbian sadomasochist . . . is quite differently organized from that of the lesbian who is not a pervert [who is] fundamentally similar to the traditional heterosexual woman," Teresa de Lauretis charges Adams with "psychoanalytic fundamentalism."[113] Seizing on Adams's unconscious heterosexual metaphor in asserting that sadomasochistic sexualities are "divorced from gender positions," Lauretis counters with the (conscious) metaphor that Adams is "wedded" to the "truth of the master's words."[114] As I pointed out in chapter 1, it seems quite problematic to me to determine whether a writer's choice of words is conscious or unconscious, but I also think that partly what is at stake in this argument is a defensiveness shared by many feminists who use psychoanalysis as a theoretical discourse. For, of course, we are always speaking within the terms of a discourse, however subversive and oppositional our use of it may be, which is condemned at large not only by mainstream feminisms but also by the majority of academic feminists. Freud, in particular, is *the* culprit who is almost always cited as responsible for a host of offenses against women of any and all sexual persuasions. As a consequence, feminists who work *with* psychoanalytic paradigms are constantly justifying our very use of the discourse. Among this group, therefore, there is a tendency to project onto the "other" psychoanalytically informed feminists one's own fear of being seduced by the rhetoric of psychoanalysis. For while Lauretis derides Adams for her psychoanalytic orthodoxy, she also claims for herself a superior position in regard to *mastery* of the discourse. Lauretis's footnote is revealing in this regard. Here she states that "to my knowledge, the proponents, practitioners, and/or theorists of lesbian s/m in the United States have not engaged with the abundant psychoanalytic literature on perversion and sadomasochism in particular."[115] Outside the United States she acknowledges only Julia Creet's and Monika Treut's work on s/m. Lauretis dismisses the abundance (see the bibliography) of work on s/m for not being psychoanalytic enough. This tension among feminists between embracing and recoiling from psychoanalytic discourse could stand a psychoanalytic reading itself. The place of aversion within the structure of desire is a Freudian commonplace. That tension, however, is swept aside (negated or displaced) onto the continuing battle between "lesbians" and "sadomasochistic lesbians."

Lauretis is admirably up-front about the structure of her own desire and how her argument is necessitated by it. She says in her introduction: "I shall endeavor to remind the reader, as discreetly as can be done without offense to critical and stylistic conventions, that my theoretical speculations and my reading of the texts follow the yellow brick road of my own fantasies, the less-than-royal road of my personal or experiential history."[116] The double gesture in this passage, in which Lauretis locates herself on the margins of an academic discourse that conventionally demands both the erasure of the writer's personal history and experience and at the same time the promise to remain *discreet* (a trait that is expected, even demanded, of "women writers") in her defiance of those conventions is a dynamic that, in my reading, continues to play in her argument with Adams. She mocks Adams and all the other (unnamed and unrecognizable) proponents of s/m for their failure to master the complexities of psychoanalysis, tossing the whole range of theories and practices of s/m desire aside as "the current vacation spot for Feminists of Sexual Indifference," who are implicitly more (while she is explicitly less) "interested in locating rare specimens of non-phallic sexual organization or new brands of sexuality than in figuring out a theory of sexuality non-heterosexual and non-normatively heterosexual, perhaps a theory of sexuality as perversion, that may account for [*her*] own sexual structuring and perverse desire."[117] Lauretis is to be applauded for being so candidly interested in validating her own sexual desire. Undoubtedly that is what we are all on about whether we admit it or not. However, I want to point out here that her attack on Adams and s/m in general takes some rather dubious turns. First, in her reference to s/m as "a current vacation spot," she evokes the notion of a trendy and trivial sexuality (perhaps a "phase" that adolescent theorists are merely passing through?) that is implicitly inferior to her own because it is undertheorized, which is to say that it is less dependent upon the "master's truths" as opposed to her own mastery of them. Second, her own desire to theorize a sexuality (her own) that is "non-heterosexual and non-normatively heterosexual" belies her own agenda of surpassing the "metaphoric" relationship to heterosexuality. For surely her "nons" evoke the reversal of the very discourse which she seeks to evade. Third, I glimpse in Lauretis's multiple dismissals of s/m against her own more "normative non-normative" lesbian sexuality an uncanny reemergence of that sly, wily, indefatigable ghost—the "*realesbian.*"

S/m sexuality is treated with opprobrium not only by academic theorists but also by feminists in the "healing professions." Defenses of s/m are often made solely on the basis of a quasilibertarianism that simply celebrates the free play of any and all libidinal economies. Lauretis is correct in saying that there are very few readings of s/m that theorize its practices. While I think that E. Sue Blume's book, *Secret Survivors*, is a very sophisticated reading of the complexities of the aftereffects of incest, when she comes to the topic of s/m, her otherwise superb subtle analyses of "cognitive adaptations" are set aside for simple, untheorized condemnations of s/m sexual practices. Here she claims that the incest survivor will inevitably sexualize the postincest experience, which will sometimes take the form of "the sexual subjugation of a child. Or worse. Many mass murderers were incest victims as children."[118] These acts, Blume claims, provide only temporary relief for the survivor, who is then "faced with feeling even more out of control than before the abuse."[119] While it is very rare, according to Blume's own account, for women to become incest perpetrators, it is even rarer for a woman to become a mass murderer. Since, however, it is "inevitable" that the incest survivor will sexualize her experience, what is more common is for the survivor to internalize the feeling that she deserves to be a "victim." This, according to Blume, "sets her up for sado-masochistic sexual activity."[120]

Blume reiterates the common point that some women claim s/m activity is a personal choice and that the masochist really dictates the scenario.

But her only rebuttal to this obviously already preconceived notion that s/m is the return of the repressed is that incest survivors testify that women who are involved in s/m almost always were molested as children. Blume, in fact, cites only one of these testimonies—a woman, Claudia, with whom she worked. She overlooks or is ignorant of the hundreds of testimonials by s/m practitioners who either discount any connection between their sexual proclivities and childhood sexual abuse or acknowledge the abuse but insist that the experience of s/m sexuality is therapeutic, or simply— pleasurable. Blume does not mean to "blame the victims," but she does insist on naming them *as* victims, which is tantamount to blaming them. Furthermore, she falls into an analogical trap by comparing the inability to make a free choice about one's sexual practices to the "Jews, gays, gypsies, and dissidents victimized by the Holocaust . . . [who] did not understand the horror that was creeping up on them until, one by one, their freedoms had been annihilated, and then it was too late for most to fight back."[121] At the risk of sounding irreverent, I must point out that the analogy is clearly faulty on the simple grounds that Holocaust survivors are not known to have created a subculture in which they "play at being Holocaust survivors." Furthermore, Blume refers to s/m and b & d (bondage and discipline) "with their themes of abuse, dominance, humiliation, perhaps even pain, as necessary ingredients for arousal, [as] perfect expressions for these distortions of Post-Incest Syndrome."[122] Once again it is curious to find in an argument like Blume's, which is otherwise so meticulously careful not to confuse the appearance (the "symptoms") of one kind of behavior with some underlying deep structure of similarity, such naive comparisons. Blume's otherwise thorough research is completely ignorant of theories of s/m sexuality. She takes it as simply a given that the "thematics" of s/m are consonant with the structure of the practices; and, moreover, that the structure of sexual abuse is parallel to the structure of s/m. Like Susan Griffin, Blume refers to s/m play as creating an "illusion" of power. And it is in this context that the sexual abuse survivors with whom she has worked, who supplied the basic data of her theory, become "true victims" of their histories. In her references to s/m only, Blume takes on a juridical tone that is totally uncharacteristic of the way in which she positions herself as listener/witness/therapist to her clients who in every other respect must be validated, even celebrated, for having devised a set of "cognitive adaptations" that, however they may appear to the dominant order, are coping mechanisms that demonstrate the ingenuity, creativity, and life-sustaining strategies of the incest survivor. In her entire book, she never mentions sexual practices per se; for example, she may discuss how an incest survivor who was forced to have oral sex may have difficulties accomplishing simple tasks such as brushing her teeth. She mentions that withholding defecation may be a sign of an incest survivor's desire to refuse to release control. But she does not then conclude that incest survivors who have had these experiences should avoid oral or anal sex. But when it comes to s/m, she is overtly dictatorial: "the incest survivor can redefine her inner connections. She must not masturbate for the wrong reason, from anger and self-abusive S & M fantasies."[123] The only justification Blume offers for such prescriptive opinions is that the survivor is bound to experience an additional burden of guilt after having participated in or fantasized about s/m sexuality. Such shocking biases can only be attributed to ignorance of s/m sexuality and the most unsophisticated analogical thinking. As well as, perhaps, a certain unconscious horror of one's own sexual fantasies that are ubiquitous in this culture whether one is or is not a sexual abuse survivor. While I think it is important not to avoid possible connections between sexually abusive histories and current sexual practices, it is just as likely that a sexual abuse survivor would recoil from and resist any participation in s/m sex as it is that she would embrace it. The issue is not one of causality; rather, the question that active or phantasmatic participation in s/m raises is one of the relationship between different parts of the psyche that are "split off."

All the theorists of incest trauma speak about the tendency for survivors to dissociate, deny, and fragment their subjectivities—so that often the incest survivor may even appear to have multiple personality disorders. If integration is the goal of recovery, it would seem to me that the survivor who brings together these various aspects of her self, and performs them in a sexual space in which they can all be present at once, has achieved a level of integration that is the purported goal—the movement from survivor status to "recovery." What, after all, is Allison, for example, to do with that "man who walked across her life?" Forget him? Deny him? Repress or sublimate him? When the incest survivor "does it for/with daddy," she acknowledges that this is part of her history, part of her. And she can replace the original "him" with someone who can follow her through the labyrinthine journey of her past and remain with her in the present in a relationship that requires an ultimate test of trust. It is not a utopian playing space. It is a risky practice that can and does fail. But it is also more, I think, than a "cognitive adaptation." It is an attempt break the frame, to achieve that moment of vividness, that startling quality that Laub and Jameson speak of, a breakdown in temporality, an event in its own right. Like the testimonial, s/m sexual practices are metonymic, not metaphorical. They are not merely substitutions or repetitions of the subject's historical past. And despite the fact that s/m rhetoric is saturated with theatrical terminology, it is not theater. Theater has a particular framework and sets of conventions that are agreed upon in advance by the audience and the actors. And so, of course, does s/m sexuality. But they are not the same conventions or frameworks, despite some of their seeming parallels. One crucial difference is the role of the spectator.

As I mentioned in the beginning of this chapter, Bone's fantasies seem distinctly theatrical in that they require the presence of someone who watches. But this one who watches, in her fantasies, cannot distinguish between the fantasy and the event; only the participant can make that distinction. She alone knows that her fantasy is not the real thing, both inside and outside the fantasy. The spectators whom she imagines, however, have no way of knowing whether they are watching a "play" or a "life event." This, of course, is not theater. In effect, then, Bone does not have a spectator per se, even inside her fantasies. Allison is then positing a fantasy scenario with a spectator who, linked to my earlier discussion of the "queer real" in chapter 4, is completely naive, an absolutely "innocent" watcher. We might speculate then that this spectator is the fantasy projection of the participant, whose own melancholy for a lost moment is realized in this figure. But because the spectator and the protagonist are split off in the "drama," they are no longer self-identical, and a space for distance is opened. What Bone's fantasies allow her is to become aware of herself as her own onlooker, something akin to the notion of the incest survivor's "inner guide" (Blume's term), the part of her that is split off to protect and sustain her through the abusive episodes and their memories.

While this onlooker/inner guide is a vital part of maintaining the child as a survivor, she still needs a witness outside herself. Someone who not only believes her story but can listen to her tell it without challenging its historical accuracy as "truth." Most important, this witness must perform the precarious act of balancing on a borderline between entering fully enough into the survivor's space to convince her that she has knowledge of the "contents" of what appears to be a black hole and remaining on the sidelines, close enough to the edge to hold the survivor in the present. This witness/survivor relationship, often carried out in a therapeutic scene between analyst and analysand, is a communal journey. In chapter 4 I stated that the top in the s/m scene does not merely wait on the sidelines but "comes and goes" into the abyss with the bottom, meeting at that moment when the little girl is neither fully submerged nor fully emerged— "like Alice in the pool of her of her own tears." This is a sexual encounter that is as difficult to achieve as the therapeutic relationship. Neither of them can make any guarantees, but they are both journeys that are performative—they are the "event themselves," not a means toward an end.

Unlike theater, this is the life of the survivor. In *Bastard Out of Carolina*, one notices that Bone's consciousness is not a consistent realistic representation of a twelve-year-old girl. Allison writes to "save her life," for she is Bone, and she is Bone's witness, the one who arrives to listen after the girl has been waiting for a long long time. In *Pictures of a Childhood* Alice Miller writes of her own journey toward recovery from sexual abuse. It is that moment when the survivor recognizes the child not as her(self)—but as hers—as belonging with and to her, that the process begins. Miller characteristically begins with an image of the child as a separate being outside herself:

> She approached very hesitantly, speaking to me in an inarticulate way, but she took me by the hand and led me into territory I had been avoiding all my life because it frightened me. Yet I had to go there; I could not keep on turning my back, for it was my territory, my very own. It was the place I had attempted to forget so many years ago, the same place I had abandoned the child I once was. There she had to stay, alone with her knowledge, waiting until someone would come at last to listen to her and believe her. Now I was standing at an open door, ill-prepared, filled with all an adult's fear of the darkness and menace of the past, but I could not bring myself to close the door and leave the child alone again until my death. Instead, I made a decision that was to change my life profoundly: to let the child lead me, to put my trust in this nearly autistic being who had survived the isolation of decades.[124]

Although it encompasses a wide range of practices, sexuality that embraces the erotics of power moves toward a precarious, delicate borderline that tests and transgresses the line between fantasy and reality. For those women whose "selves" have been constituted in large part by a traumatic history of sexual abuse, this borderline is often not a place to which they travel in order to risk the repetition of oppressive social structures; rather, it is the place where they find themselves located in order to repeat and transform their histories with a difference.

Being there, rather than transcending it, may well be "the cure." It is a journey not unlike—or, more precisely, "not quite not like" to borrow Homi Bhaba's subtle concept of similarities within differences—the one that Felman describes in relation to Jan Karski, the underground Polish messenger who accepted the mission to go into the Jewish ghettos to become an eyewitness and report to the Western allies. She describes this visit as "the retracing of a journey equal to an oath of love. In repeating his descent to hell . . . he makes a gift to his companion of his fear, of his attention, of his memory, of his emphatic suffering, of his discipleship in trauma, and of the *oath of faithfulness* precisely to his *witness*—of the pledged promise of his future testimony."[125]

Debates that focus on the divide between fantasy and reality might do well to recall Lacan's fundamental thesis that "reality" is produced and maintained over and against the exclusion of the Real, a traumatic category. It requires a brave traveler to approach that limit, for the price of getting too close is (symbolic) death. And as Žižek reminds us, the "beyond" of this limit is prohibited; whoever enters it cannot return. Such, he explains, is the "logic of the most fundamental of all prohibitions, incest," hence its "inherent impossibility" (foreclosure). But those survivors who take the risk of trespassing this limit, open up a new space of possibility. For when the limit is transgressed, what was once "impossible" is transmuted into a prohibition and thereby enters into the domain of the speakable, albeit negatively. Žižek explains the "second death" as the exact opposite of the Symbolic order—"the radical annihilation of the symbolic texture through which the so-called reality is constituted."[126] The "cure" in this conception is accomplished not through full speech or acceptance of lack. It accepts that there is nothing "outside" except for the abjected others who are in fact necessarily produced as outside(rs) in order to maintain the ruse of a reality that disguises the void of the Real. Acceptance of the fact that there is nothing to be seen (the opposite/same of Bone's "all that can be seen") leads to the final moments of an analysis that requires traversing the fantasy, rather than oedipally attempting to circumvent it. Women who speak the unspeakable truths of incest thus become witnesses not to private acts secret-ed by personal shame and guilt but to an entire symbolic system that erects itself on the foundation of the negation of their experience. Surely this is a journey that feminists must find ways to comprehend.

There is a cure for love. It is absence. There is a cure
for grief. (It is absence.) I cannot say,
you died, and I don't want to live today.

—Marilyn Hacker, "Geographer," *Separations*

I know what the present, that
difficult tense, is: a pure portion of anxiety. Absence persists—I must
endure it. Hence I will manipulate it: transform the distortion of time into
oscillation, produce rhythm, make an entrance onto the stage of language.

—Roland Barthes, *A Lover's Discourse*

The light seared the eyes that
dared to seek.
So why should I speak?
For the things I would say
Could not be of any use to you.

—Charlotte Delbo, *Who Will Carry the Word?*

Epilogue: Crows III

Intreat me not to leave thee . . .
for whither thou goest, I will go;
and where thou lodgest, I will lodge:
where thou diest, will I die.

—Ruth 1:16–17

Promises are made to be broken. "Testifying from the inside . . . would mean the death and very suicide of the witness."[1] The tense is the future anterior—the *past that will have been*. Still I cannot quite get this right. I want so much to write in the subjunctive—the past that *would* have been—the mood/mode of subordination. That is why I am a top.

But I am a writer only when I surrender. For her, it is, I think, the other way around. She tops when she writes, she surrenders only for love. The writing does not heal, it merely smears balm on the savage wounds. She disagrees. We disagree.

Once upon a time we agreed to disagree about this, and we made up rituals where our conflicts could take full aim in the open air, under the trees where the crows sat on their perches and glared at us with their hot white eyes. They came every day, except when there was an abundance of rain that wet their feathers shiny black and weighed them to the ground. On those days, there was something missing, but we persevered and waited for the clouds to creep away from our sacred skies. For we had our memories and our hope. And we had found a way to make them one. Flesh of my flesh, bone of my bone.

We kept the secret of our unholy rites. We believed that there was redemption possible in the repetition. The splitting and mending, tearing and suturing. We did not give a damn about the eyes that might have watched in horror our plunderings, our penetrations, our ravaged bodies calling to each other silently, holding, waiting, trusting that these ministrations could rip through the barriers of our past and keep us suspended together, forever, in the present.

A time without end. And the crows watched. First just one, then another lighted on the branch to partner the witnessing and watch the watcher. Now, there are three of them. The third one watches the other two watching, and marvels at their fixation on the empty space where two girls once lay naked, not nude, but bare and baring all. We risked everything. And lost. For there came a time when she began to retreat. Slowly she withdrew; I could see that her desire was curling up inside her chest, stagnating, festering. She had lost her ability to believe in the ways I had shown her to go deep into the wounds to scour them. I watched our fear growing until I began to be frightened of and for her. I dreamed that she spoke in a tongue I could not decipher. I took her in my arms and pleaded with her to let us work together to release the pain. One must go deeply into oneself in order to escape from oneself. I dreamed that I took her in my arms and screamed at her to come back, come back. Her eyes had become onyx. One bright day when mountains of snow from the blizzard were still piled high on the streets, refracting an even brighter light than the rays of the sun, I saw her from a distance and did not recognize her. Until afterward.

I began trying to record. I wanted documentation, to leave a trace of where we had once been and no one knew.

One night as we walked home linked arm and arm through the cold streets of the Village, she felt my terror and asked me what I was thinking. "They are coming," I said, "they are coming to wreck our pretty house. How will we keep them out?" She pretended to be brave, and laughed her uncertain sounds: "I will not let them in," she promised. But I knew that they were already there. I wandered the rooms at night while she slept her sleep that she had learned to survive. The sleep I coveted because I could not own it for myself. I stood in the moonlight that came slipping through the blinds, and turned one eye on her motionless form and the other on the orange glowing "guardian light" sign that beamed its neon into our bedroom.

I wondered if I would die in this bed staring at that orange glow as its words grew fainter and my eyesight dimmed. Perhaps I hoped that I would, but I knew, in fact, that it would not be many more nights that I would look out this window across the city. For I could feel them all around us in the house, sliding under door frames, nestled in the folded towels, buried deep in the pockets of our jackets hanging on the pegs, perched on the leaves of the plants I brought in from the terrace to save from the encroaching cold. Some of them did not get in when I slammed the terrace door and locked it tight. But I could see them out there, lurking, their hands cupped around their eyes peering in through the glass, waiting for my attention to wane so they could scurry in. I prayed that if I kept the house neat enough, the counters wiped and the green things that lived wet, the doors and windows locked tight, but most of all, if I watched all night while she slept, I could be our sentry. The beacon who could burn bright white light onto their beckonings.

I would record them, make images of them where they would be framed. I set up the easel that she carried home, a/cross, on her back and began to paint them through the long hours of the night, hoping against hope that the paintings would catch and hold them on the canvases. I was delighted when she said that we could frame them and hang them high on the bedroom walls. Maybe then, they would guard the entrance to our gates.

I painted the owl from whose beak dangled a piece of my flesh. I painted myself as a purple buddha who did not know what sugarplums were dancing in the head of my sleeping girl. I painted the prodigal who left the barn where the bats hung from the rafters while the little pigs lay nestled in their beds. I painted the lake where the moon shone gold and green over the peaceful waters that held the floating form of a girl who had always been overboard. I painted the house that we built on fire with a hundred pathways all blocked by snarling blue dogs and spotted leopards. I painted the shed that read "vacancy" and the girl running toward it with her hair flying in the wind who did not notice that the vacant shed was inhabited by two blue-green legs jutting out from under its frame. I painted two girls with faces like dogs, two girls who might have been sisters or twins, or lookalike lovers, framed. Two girls who always picked out their own shoes. I called it "not you two?" And I prayed, "not her too, god, not her too, let it be just me and Clara, we will hold the pain."

I painted an air balloon in which she stood with elongated arms holding tight to the sides while the blue girl dove in and out headfirst, losing her shoes. I called it "would you like to ride?" I painted my dream of a woman who preached, her arms extended to the heavens, a white dove spreading its wings across her blue-gowned torso, a black crow sitting beside a tombstone where someone was buried, marked R.I.P. A gold cross swept across the canvas of the preacher with tiny figures marching across its sides. I inscribed it: "Suffer the little children to come unto me."

Each morning there was a new canvas and I would lie in bed pretending to sleep, waiting to hear her exclaim over it and come jumping into bed with me to tell me what it meant and why it was good. Then I could sleep for a few hours until it all started all over again and I would need to tear off another blank page and fill it with colors. For there was paper all over the house, much of it full of words and images, but too many that were empty where they could find a place to put their marks. And the walls of the house were tall and white and wide and uncovered. She would not help me fill them. I grew afraid that they would know that there was blank space on which to land their evil. I dared not paint on the walls, though many nights I stood for hours with wet brushes in my hands and struggled, wrestling with my angels. Of all my paintings there was one that I liked the most. I did not know why. I did not ask myself. A house, like the ones that children draw in grade schools, and inside a girl standing, smiling with her hair aflame. Making no effort to move. It was the only one that had no name.

But finally it was no good. I could not do it alone anymore, so I ask her to make a painting with me on a last night when we were pretending that it was all still possible. We sat on the green sofa in front of the easel and she went first, painting a yellow taxicab in which Dr. Seuss would have loved to take a ride. Then she handed me the brush and told me to "finish it." I painted fast, not letting my consciousness interfere. I put her in the driver's seat in profile and myself in the passenger seat with both my arms raised high.

(did you ever notice, she asked, that all your painted people have their arms extended toward the sky?)

But hers were on the wheel.

Then I painted a blue ocean in which the car floated and two palm trees, one with a cockatoo clinging to a limb. And two green roads that led off in opposite directions. She got angry with me because one of the roads led into the car, covering part of her yellow door. I showed her that the joy of colors was the ability to paint over such mistakes. This painting, in particular, came out fine. It gave us one last glimpse of hope. It would be all that I left behind when the day came that I would have to leave because they had taken every corner of the house. And as the space grew smaller and smaller, taken up by these Hungry Ghosts, my purple Buddha spoke to me from the canvas and showed me how to draw them vividly on the Wheel of Life. Like Tantalus, the hungry ghosts, with their withered limbs, long thin necks, bloated bellies, and insatiable cravings, had sucked up all our rage and desire, fusing them, "searching for gratification for old unfulfilled needs whose time had passed."[2] And they were eating us.

I sat for days before I got up to go and thought about joining them there in their deaths—"where you go, there will I go also; where you die, I will die." The canvas stood empty on its frame. I sat for hours on end starting at the paintbrushes, unable to move to pick them up, thinking only red, red, red. Finally I was able to dip one brush in water and plunge it into the dried pool of red paint on my palette. My hand made two bold red stripes, then dropped the brush onto the floor. I returned to primary colors—blue, then one small spot of yellow. This is all I will ever say again, I thought. And no one will know what it has meant, how close we were to finding the way that led out through the increasingly transparent flesh of our flesh. Her bones were showing, and then mine. I tried to lift my arm to point to the passageway, but it fell limply to my side. Staring, mutely into space, three days and nights passed through eternity.

But then I realized something extraordinary. In the painting we had made together, the two roads led off in opposite directions, and her gaze that I thought I had painted fixed on me was actually fixed on the cockatoo in the palm tree. She was looking elsewhere. And cockatoos do not live in palm trees. And then I knew something so astounding that had I been in that yellow taxi cab I would have veered right off the road and plunged into the sky blue ocean.

I was drowning in this recognition: that the girl, whom she named "Clara," was *not my witness.* For all these years I had believed that Clara, who would come and go, sometimes with her own will, sometimes because I would summon her when I was too frightened to face the world, was not, as I had always believed, the *one who watched.* I had mistaken her indifference, her aloofness, her cold, sensible, above and beyond it all bearing, her inimitable ability to move through the world *as if* she were merely a dispassionate onlooker who could appreciate the beauty of some things but could never allow herself to be *inside them.* Clara, who could accomplish anything but not *feel anything,* was *not* my protector, was *not* the one of me that split off and watched to make sure that someone was there to be an eyewitness, someone there to tell when the day might come that words became possible again. No. No. It was so obvious now.

Clara was the girl *who was there.*

She was the one who lay beneath him; she was the one who bit her lips until they bled so as not to cry out her shameful secret to the unyielding ones; she was the one who counted the cracks in the ceiling to occupy her mind until it was over; she was the one who had no body left; she was the one . . . she was the one. And no wonder she had named her: "Who is that girl?" she had asked me casually after forty years of feeling sure that no one could ever know or tell. No wonder she recognized her so easily, for she was Clara too, and in her way she knew something I had never known—the difference between the watcher and the watched. And I then, who was I?

When they went to the ocean together and I was driving the car, it was *Clara* who imagined my body floating ashore to be found by boys playing on the beach who would read the note pinned to my chest with wonder— "Clara was sleeping." It was Clara *who could sleep*; Clara who had been waiting for such a long long time for ME to say out loud that *I* was *her* witness. Waiting for me to listen to her, waiting for me to get to a place where I could go far enough inside the black hole of her forgetting and help her pull out the memories in little pieces and make them into something half-whole. It was Clara who was walking through the earth without her spirit; Clara who did not know how to find her soul before she died. Clara who was begging me in her expressionless eyes to join her and tell her that I would help her pull through.

But I could only go halfway there with her. The vortex into which she was pulled was only half-mine. I would hold out my hand to her and help her pull herself up to the edge. The edge, though, was as far as I could risk going. For if I fell in with her, we would both be lost. Or so I thought. But once again it was Clara who gripped my arm and pulled me down into the well with her to show me that I could see in the darkness. Ah, little Clara you are not so small and you know so much. In the deepest darkness of the pit she whispered in my ear: "You must doubt deeply, again and again, asking yourself *what the subject of hearing could be.* . . . only doubt more and more deeply."[3] And we began to awaken from our long long sleep, and I began to watch her and listen intently for her whisperings. For it was I who was *her witness, and she knew the way.* "Dark is a Way: Light is a Place." Clara was the preacher in my dream. Clara was the one who saved me *then*; it was my turn to save her *now*.

And then there was an abundance of rain made from my salt tears for all the years that I had left Clara to her own devices, not even knowing that she was the one who was suffering. And the rain poured and poured and it was cleansing though it burned my face. But I did not care any longer who saw it. I cried on buses, and trains, and planes, and in the waiting rooms. I cried wherever the floods came. I told myself that should someone ask, and some did, that I would say someone I loved very much and whom I thought had died was coming back to life. And these were tears of joy and sorrow without contradiction. The tears that only a miracle could make.

But you see, when it rained for more than forty days and forty nights, the crows did not come. And after awhile they gave up even the thought of coming. And they dried their wings as best they could with the last leaves of autumn—

> *Whoever has no house now, will never have one.*
> *Whoever is alone will stay alone*[4]

—and clumsily they flew away to search for a new apple tree in which to light.

> *And then we thought, no one is watching at all*
> *And we were naked and alone, even as we were together.*

With the crows gone from the trees there was no one to ward off the lightning. It struck again, just as it did that night when I stood on the back porch in my yellow pajamas with padded feet and watched it fall to split the apple tree right down the middle. Its limbs hung like a body crucified. My body. His body. Two parts that I dreamed of splitting. Two parts wedded together in the most unholy of unions. All my life I would look for someone to come and take his place beside me. Someone whose frame hung as loose and broken as my own. Someone whose touch could mend my splintered woodened parts.

Then I found her, one day as she casually said: "Who is this girl?" And I knew that she recognized me for what I was. But we fell apart. For all our bloodied rituals, for all the times we fought to mend our tangled limbs and sew them back into a cloth we both could wear. She said: "What we must hope is that we survive each other." But survival was not my desire. I had spent all those years surviving too well. She was distressed when I told her that I had "nothing to lose." She did not understand that this was the beginning, the only way to find the million broken pieces all scattered across the decades, lying about here and there like a child's puzzle that is too obvious to compose. I wanted the pain to stop. I believed that I would not miss it. But that is not entirely true.

I dreamed about her for thirteen nights in a row. The same dream. I was afraid that I would go mad, that I would wake up and never know again whether I was sleeping or waking. I had not seen her for almost three months, when hours that once passed without a word seemed an eternity. And there was no grave to visit. And though others had seen her they said,

I knew that the girl I had lost was nowhere to be found. I was mourning the loss of something I had never had.

I dreamed that many years had passed and I had found her again on the streets. We went walking through the market together on a crisp day. Picking through the goods on the merchants' tables, trying not to remember that we had once done this before in another time and place. A time and place that had not really been. It was not the past nor the present nor the future. It was somewhere else. A dream space. My dream was about dreaming.

Then suddenly I spied a large bunch of blueberries nesting in a bowl of green leaves. And the sight of them propelled me into the present—the impossible moment had actually come. I darted toward them with an exclamation of childlike joy, and plunged my nose into the basket. They were made of yarn. Knitted to look blue by an old woman with delicate bony hands. I turned to look at her and she was smiling, that half-smile, slightly crooked grin that I knew so well. I was humiliated. Both because I had openly expressed such childlike pleasure and because I had mistaken the blueberries for real. My shame was manifest. And she was aroused by it. Aroused by the little girl who had humiliated herself in public, displayed her anticipation and desire, then was crushed by its loss. She said, "I want you. Would you consider coming home with me?" I paused, and in my dream I struggled for an answer, for I too was aroused by my shame and her desire for it. Then I said, "No, I wouldn't even consider it." But I knew that I would. Knew that I was. Knew that considering was something I would always do.

When the dream would not stop following me, I was terrified that I would lose all memory. I was tangled up in the twisted blue yarns of my dream. So I went to the only other person who had ever seen the girl in my dreams. She said: "Your psyche is not unkind. It is painful, but it is trying to show you something that you must know. There is something missing in the dream. What is missing? You have to find it and make it readily available to you like your slippers at the side of your bed in the mornings." I laughed and said: "My slippers are not at the side of my bed in the mornings. My slippers are not even my slippers. They are hers. I stole them. I am a thief. Everywhere I go I steal something. I have stolen things from you and you have never known. I take something everywhere I go: surgical gloves from the doctor's box, pens and pads from the secretaries' desks, ashtrays and forks and spoons from restaurants, magazines from waiting rooms. I still have the first thing I ever stole: a plastic flower from a box of candy at the drugstore. I keep these things. I like knowing that they could be missed and will never be found."

"There," she said, "there is your answer then. What is it in the dream that was stolen?" I began to sleep with my slippers on. I thought the answer might be found in the heel or toe of her shoes. Stuffed away by some one like the tooth fairy who hides things under children's pillows when they sleep. I had forgotten that you had to leave something for the fairy in exchange. I would wake from the dream and find that the slippers had fallen off in the night, and scramble under the covers to retrieve them, shaking them out over the side of the bed as if a grain of sand that wore through them in the night might fall. Cinderella's feet were not too big. The princess could not stack enough mattresses to bury over the pea.

So I went back to the one who was supposed to know. She asked me three questions:

Who called the Crows? [she did]

Who named Clara? [she did]

What do blueberries mean?

Blueberries mean nothing to me. I am indifferent to blueberries.

I dreamed the dream one more time. I woke from it screaming my own name out loud. Who was calling for me?

Why should you believe those stories of ghosts

Ghosts who came back and who are not able to explain how?[5]

Outback, behind the shed Grandma let vines of blueberries grow wild. It was tangled and dark and prickly there. One had to be small as a bird to wind one's way through the thickets to get to the blueberries. She wanted to make cobblers with her made-from-scratch crust and six cups of white sugar. She rolled the dough onto the cutting board and pushed her sleeves back over her dusty elbows. When the fresh pie crust was round and smooth and white as a young girl's flat belly, she called to me to go and squirm through the thickets to pick the blueberries for the pie.

There was another way into the tangled vines though. A way around the side of the shed that no one knew. A way that only he knew. I would be gone too long. She would think I was never coming back. After a while, when she remembered that I had not returned, after the oven was warmed to receive the crust, and the white flour was wiped from the counters, and her hands were clean again. She would open up the back screen door and call to me: "Hurry with those blueberries now. You want to get them before the crows come to eat them." Two girls came from behind the shed; two girls whose hands were stained bright blue, an indelible dye that will never wash.

There are things of which we will never speak. But there are many more of which we have spoken that no one else will ever hear. There are things we know. Even now when she is gone and I am mourning the loss of something I never had, I know she knows. She left me clues, bread crumbs on the forest trail. I ate them all. They are part of me now. So carefully. She took such care to leave

> *. . . the page of the book carelessly open,*
> *something unsaid, the phone off the hook*
> *and the love, whatever it was, an infection*[6]

If not now, then next time. Together we promised each other that we would be the "two girls who knew" (they always picked out their own shoes). And one day we would tell what we had found when we opened the attic window and crawled through the tiny space together. But as my legs were slipping through that space, the trap fell shut behind me, and I realized that I was on the inside and she had not followed me. I planned to die in there. I could not hear her voice calling me from the other side. And that is where I have stayed, though the light grows gradually, nearly imperceptibly clearer, and Clara's murmurings are persistent in my ears. I do not know where the girl has gone. Perhaps she is still standing at that porthole numb and frozen. Perhaps she is pounding on the door and I cannot hear her. Perhaps she has simply gone back into the worlds she invents to pretend that the opening is not there and has forgotten me. I wonder if this is where we will remain forever, separated by a wall that all the love and trust and desire in the world could not penetrate. We have met before, and we will meet again.

> *Death's a sad bone; bruised, you'd say,*
> *and yet she waits for me, year after year,*
> *to so delicately undo an old wound,*
> *to empty my breath from its bad prison.*7

The crust was rolled, the sugar poured, the oven warmed to receive the food of her love. Grandma paused only for a second to wonder, then burned her finger on the flame and forgot. Two girls came through the swinging back gate, hands cupped, filled with blueberries to pour into the pie. One could barely tell them apart—"not you too?" Yes, you too, we two, both of us. The blueberries stained our flesh, a deep purple glow that could only be seen when the night was dark and the lightning lit up the room where we were buried under the sheets. We hid these crushed blueberry marks from the light of our days. We showed our hands only to each other under the sheets. All the blueberries were smashed into our flesh. All but one. Clara put one blueberry deep in the pocket of her coat where the lining was torn. She carried it around with her for forty years, slipping her hand casually into her pocket to feel it still intact. She would not eat it. Even when she was famished. And when she vanished she took it with her. She kept it safe. It would prove one day that she was the one who was there in the thickets.

AND ONE SHALL SAY UNTO HER WHAT ARE THESE WOUNDS IN THINE HANDS? THEN SHE SHALL ANSWER, THOSE WITH WHICH I WAS WOUNDED IN THE HOUSE OF MY FRIEND. (Zechariah 13:16)

But then perhaps I am both wrong and wronged. Maybe Clara has not yet spoken loudly enough to tell me how to see my way in this darkness. I asked her once to try, if she died before me, to keep speaking with me from the other side. She has. We do.

Notes

Introduction
1. Califia and Sweeney, *Second Coming*, p. xvi.
2. This position on identities is psychoanalytic. For a brilliant discussion of this issue that does not depend on psychoanalysis to defend his position, see Jonathan Dollimore, "Bisexuality, Heterosexuality, and Wishful Theory." *Textual Practice* 10 (3) (1996): 523–539.
3. Irigaray, *This Sex*, pp. 206–207.
4. Deleuze, *Masochism*, p. 60.
5. Ibid., p. 125.
6. Felman, *What Does a Woman Want?*, p. 15.
7. Ibid., p. 16.
8. Sacher-Masoch, *Venus in Furs*, p. 186.
9. Ibid., p. 159.
10. Nietzsche, *Genealogy of Morals*, p. 227.
11. Ibid., p. 226.
12. Schleifer, "Space and Dialogue of Desire," p. 873.
13. Hartman, *Criticism in The Wilderness*, p. 90.
14. Fineman, "Structure of Allegorical Desire," p. 41.
15. Nietzsche, *Genealogy of Morals*, p. 189.
16. Sacher-Masoch, *Venus in Furs*, p. 160.
17. Ibid., p. 169.
18. Hacker, p. 58.

1. Knights in Shining Armor and Other Relations
1. Murphy, *On Our Backs Interview*, p. 23.
2. Califia, *Forbidden Passages*, p. 11.
3. Steiner, p. 7.
4. Allison, "Private Rituals," in Scholder and Silverberg, eds., *High Risk*, p. 177.
5. Ibid., p. 173.
6. Strangely enough, one of the initial, anonymous readers of this manuscript was very disturbed by the book's title—*Between the Body and the Flesh*. She/he thought it

sounded too much like the title of a romance novel. I thank this anonymous reader for the association that led me down this provocative path.

7. Douglas, "Soft-Porn Culture," p. 28. Cited in Radway, p. 4.

8. Radway, pp. 5–6.

9. Ibid., p. 212.

10. Grosz, *Volatile Bodies*, p. 6. Although Grosz's book is wonderfully thorough and philosophically rigorous in its analysis, here she formulates the question of the relationship between fantasy (mind) and matter (body) in terms of the nonspatial and the spatial. In other words, she does not seem to question the idea that fantasy is nonspatial, whereas theorists led by Laplanche and Pontalis *begin* with the assumption that fantasy is a *location*, precisely a scene or space. Of course the space of the body and the space of fantasy are differently *felt*, but that is not to say that they are not both spatial. As Grosz continues in her analysis, particularly in her discussion of the "bodily" or "skin" ego in psychoanalysis, she makes some extremely important points about the ways in which the space of fantasy is located on the body, not as depth to surface but as intersecting and merging surfaces.

11. Mulvey, "Visual Pleasure and Narrative Cinema." This article has been cited more frequently than any other as a starting point for the profusion of feminist film theory. It has been applauded and variously critiqued in more ways and by more people than I can begin to mention here. I mention it in this context because Mulvey's theory of cinematic narrative, which she finds both pleasurable and ultimately "sadistic," a pleasure that women spectators must therefore be willing to relinquish for a greater social good, is the starting point for a over decade of discussion about narrative as a gendered form. This will become more pertinent to my discussion as I move into Anna Freud's essay and her case study of a fifteen-year-old girl's beating fantasies.

12. Allison, "Private Rituals," p. 173.

13. Ibid., p. 185.

14. Ibid.

15. Thompson, in *Sadomasochism*, cites an article by Spencer Woodcock (*Fetish Times* 3 [1994]) that compares standard women's romantic fiction to s/m, the former "pulling no punches when it comes to violence, and sexual violence in particular" (252). A great deal of Thompson's book is given over to a defense of s/m on the basis of comparing it to other cultural practices—like sporting events—that are not only not censored but state-supported. Finally, although I find his book immensely useful historically, it is a plea for tolerance directed at a liberal audience, a position I do not share. See my review of Thompson's book in *Journal of the History of Sexuality*. Another interesting response to the correspondences between s/m and the romance novel is Wardrop's article, "The Heroine is Being Beaten." Using Judith Butler's idea of the performative in relation to identity and identifications, Wardrop proposes a reading strategy that would defend the experience of Radway's Smithton community. She argues, in effect, that the "sadist" and "masochist" can oscillate between identities through identifications that are psychically mobile, and that we see this enacted in such novels as Linda Howard's *McKenzie's Mission*. In this novel the hero, Joe, finds himself "unmanned" by his desire for the heroine, and his subsequent "loss of control" (he rapes her) "bespeaks Caroline's true power" (468–469). Wardrop relies on Lynn

Chancer's theory of the masochistic pleasure achieved through "neutralizing sexual guilt by fiat" (Chancer 51) and her ability to "acknowledge dependence [which] is only possible in someone for whom such an admission does not equate with death of the self . . . " (59). Depending, further, on Chancer's argument that the sadist's loss of control puts an end to the s/m dialectic, Wardrop then concludes that romance novels signal a culture going through a process in which "a view of society and heterosexuality as rigidly hierarchized and antagonistic [is transforming] toward a view of love as based on mutual respect, power and regard" (470–471). Wardrop not only misreads Butler's idea of the performative, she also bases her reading on clinical notions of sadism and masochism, which are far removed from the s/m dynamic of the subcultures who have radically reinvented them. The notion that a woman's power is in making a man surrender to her reinstates a conventional idea of a heterosexual dynamic that is retrograde. The "sadomasochistic" dialectic that she speaks of in this article is Freudianism at its worst (and most misunderstood).

16. Anna Freud, "Beating Fantasies and Daydreams," p. 286.
17. Ibid., p. 288.
18. Ibid., p. 291.
19. Ibid., p. 293.
20. Ibid., p. 294.
21. Ibid., p. 295.
22. Ibid.
23. Ibid., my emphasis.
24. Ibid., p. 296.
25. See Bersani, *Freudian Body*, also see his "Theory and Violence," chap. 1, passim.
26. Califia, "Personal View," in Samois, ed., *Coming to Power*, p. 255.
27. Anna Freud, "Beating Fantasies," p. 296.
28. Ibid., p. 297.
29. Ibid.
30. Ibid.
31. Ibid., p. 298.
32. Ibid.
33. Ibid., pp. 298–299, my emphasis.
34. Ibid., p. 299.
35. Lauretis, *Practice of Love*, pp. 37–39.
36. Merkin, "Unlikely Obsession," p. 98.
37. Ibid., p. 99.
38. Ibid., p. 100.
39. Ibid.
40. Ibid., p. 102.
41. Ibid.
42. Ibid., p. 111.
43. Ibid., p. 112.
44. Chancer, *Sadomasochism in Everyday Life*. Although Chancer does acknowledge that the s/m dynamic she is discussing is not necessarily equated with gay or lesbian s/m, this qualification fails to obviate the argument that s/m is intrinsic to the social

structure of our everyday lives. Because Chancer finds "s/m" nearly everywhere, it loses any distinctiveness in this analysis and thus threatens or accomplishes a permeation of any and all exchanges of power—sexual or nonsexual.

45. Merkin, p. 115.

46. Ibid.

2. To Each Her Other: Performing Lesbian Sadomasochism

1. Cartoon by Andrea Natalie, "Stonewall Riots," *Bad Attitude*, 1991.

2. Sterling, "Sex Wars Rage On," p. 2.

See this issue for other letters detailing the controversies at the Michigan Womyn's Festival.

3. Foucault, "Sexual Choice," p. 14.

4. As Califia and Sweeney point out in their introduction to *Second Coming*: "Since the early '80s, there has been tremendous change in the community of leatherdykes and the people we love. Almost every major city has a women's S/M support group. . . Several national magazines have been devoted to women who do S/M with other women. We're on the Internet and are invited to speak to college classes." However, as they remind us, "our community is still deeply divided along lines of gender and sexual orientation." And, as the essays in this collection and others constantly point out, women's s/m spaces are consistently under threat of erasure. Even major cities like London and New York depend upon single-night, "women-only" spaces borrowed from gay or mixed clubs, and lesbian magazines and journals go out of business on a regular basis. They are almost always, however, replaced by a new group of women who are willing to take on the work of resuscitating them in another form.

5. I have made every effort to locate the precise origin of the term *vanilla*. It appears in italics in a 1985 issue of *Outrageous Women*, one of the first magazines devoted to lesbian s/m. The italics here may signify that it was a fairly new term among lesbians at the time, or it may simply refer to the particular writer's desire to signal that she means it in a special sense, though what that special sense is is not possible for me to verify. In *Different Loving*, the term is glossed as "conventional relations, or any intimate relations that do not include D&S or S/M sexuality" (49). This definition marks the term as an absolute "other," while obviously there are elements of "vanilla" in s/m and vice versa. Such definitions erect a very rigid binary, a dualism that is bound to lead to tension and sometimes hostility.

Larry Townsend uses the term as early as 1972: "Knowing the scene as I do, I feel it is important not to deflate someone else's bag, simply because it isn't mine. For this reason, you will find a good many comments wherein I will preface my remarks by saying, 'It's my opinion that . . . .' I do not feel that there is any mutually agreeable activity, regardless of the number of people involved, that is intrinsically 'bad' or 'wrong' or 'evil.' I don't happen to like vanilla ice cream, but it is not for me to tell someone else he won't enjoy it. It is a matter of taste, and the way a thing tastes is sometimes difficult to describe. In an attempt to overcome this hurdle, I have included a number of vignettes to depict the particular action I am discussing. If some of these grab you, even just a little, I will have enabled you to sample the flavor" (*The Leatherman's Handbook*, 1st ed. (New York: Affiliated with Olympia Press and Traveler's Companion, 1972). (I wish to thank Gayle Rubin for providing me with this citation).

I cannot establish that this was the first use of the term, but it does establish the referential context as existing at that time. The question of the origin of the term is not, in my view, as significant as the way in which it came to take on a rigid oppositional connotation during the sex wars of the 1980s between lesbian feminists who were antiporn, anti-s/m and pro-sex, pro-s/m lesbians and their supporters. Obviously in the context in which Townsend is using it, he means to signify a *range of possible* sexual practices (a variety of "flavors"), none of which are subjected to judgment or censure in his mind. Sexual practices, as he states quite clearly, are a matter of "taste"— hence the analogy with ice cream. While on the one hand the ice cream analogy is an obvious one—signifying bland, ordinary, and pure—it also strikes me as interesting that *vanilla* would be lifted out of this context and come to signify *non*-s/m sexualities. It seems quite likely that the term began in the gay leather community, since Townsend uses it here as vanilla ice cream (my inference being that had it been current at the time he would simply have said "vanilla," *not* that Townsend was the originator of the term).

Risking that this is the worst sort of overreading, the kind that literary critics and theorists are often accused of performing like the sending up of hot air balloons, I can nonetheless not resist wondering how or if *vanilla* signifies *white* in the Western collective unconscious? Freud's depiction of women's sexuality as the "dark continent" has been picked up by a number of writers and discussed as a racialized term (see Doane and Kofman). Both outside and within various s/m communities, sexual practices that deviate even slightly from normative, reproductive, heterosexuality are often referred to as the "darker side" of one's desires. In *Fatal Women*, I pointed out that Havelock Ellis relegates the women who *really do it* primarily to his footnotes (the underside of the text). And that there we find that it is the women of color in other ("othered") countries who are the ones that hold the place of the "real" in Ellis's representation.

To go back to the cartoon in *Bad Attitude*, it is interesting that the s/m couple is depicted as interracial, while the other two couples are white. What was once called "miscegenation" was threatening for all sorts of reasons, but basic to the fear of interracial mixing was the threat to white supremacy and simply (or not so simply) the basic idea of "mixing" (of any kind) in and of itself. That is, "mixing" as a confusion or recombination of categories, the breaking down of boundaries. S/m communities have achieved this kind of mixing not only in terms of making affiliations between and among people who are otherwise kept separate by identity categories (bisexual, transsexual, lesbian, etc., etc.) but also along racial, ethnic, and class categories. These communities are held together, however sometimes uneasily, *not* by identity categories but by theoretical and political affiliations. As Gayle Rubin has written: "There is a lot of separation between the straight, gay, and lesbian S/M communities. But there is also pan-S/M consciousness. As one wise woman who has been doing this for years has said, 'Leather is thicker than blood' " ("Leather Menace," 218–219). That is *not*, by any means, the way in which racial categories are held together by the dominant culture. The "white" race holds onto its "purity" and psychic coherence by trying to guarantee the *exclusion* of all others. As James Baldwin put it in "The Price of the Ticket,": "white people are not white: part of the price of the white ticket is to delude themselves into believing that they are" (xiv).

I am not saying that vanilla = white, but I am suggesting that it is an interesting choice of words that conjures certain racial associations. For I think that part of the threat to the dominant culture of s/m communities is that they *have achieved* an intellectual, spiritual, and political bonding in ways that precisely contradict the dominant culture's notion of maintaining order through disciplining categories. It is the dominant culture that is really "into discipline." The "discipline" within s/m is *inclusive and heterogeneous*, though certainly not without its tensions and fears arising from racial, ethnic, gender, and sexual practice/preference differences. If *white* is the term that oversees the discipline and regulation of Western cultural orders, then it is a clever and apt (if unconscious) political move for s/m cultures to *disidentify* themselves from this particular "flavor."

The etymologies of the word *vanilla* complicate this term further. The *Oxford English Dictionary* gives us entries that tell us "Vanilla" was an "Indian Nectar" (1662), which was "mingle[d] with Cacao to make Chocolate" (1673); it is of the "climbing orchid variety . . . which, like the ivy, grows to the trees it meets with" (1783); the pod-like capsules of the plant produce an "aromatic substance [which] is the succulent fruit of a climbing West Indian plant of the order [Orchid]" (1830). If vanilla has come to signify plain or old-fashioned in the latter half of the twentieth century ("go to Schrafft's for a plain vanilla" [1955] and "old-fashioned vanilla sundae" [1984]), in the seventeenth, eighteenth, and nineteenth centuries it was an exotic import from Panama, Brazil, Jamaica, and Granada.

Furthermore, bizarrely enough, its etymology is linked to the word *vagina*: "Vanilla . . . dim. of vaina (:-L. *vagina*) sheath." The vanilloes are "long flattish pods, containing a reddish pulp, with small shining black seeds" (1812); hence, I presume, its association with vagina—from the Latin *sheath*.

6. For the most recent and thorough historical information on this debate, see Duggan and Hunter, *Sex Wars.*

7. National Organization for Women, in *Heresies*, p. 92.

8. Ibid. The full text of the NOW resolution on Lesbian and Gay Rights reads: "*Whereas*, the National Organization for Women's commitment to equality, freedom, justice, and dignity for all women is singularly affirmed in NOW's advocacy of Lesbian rights; and *Whereas* NOW defines Lesbian rights issues to be those in which the issue is discrimination based on affectional/sexual preference/orientation; and *Whereas*, There are other issues (i.e., pederasty, pornography, sadomasochism and public sex) which have been mistakenly correlated with Lesbian/Gay rights by some gay organizations and by opponents of Lesbian/Gay rights who seek to confuse the issue, and *Whereas*, Pederasty is an issue of exploitation or violence, not affectional/sexual preference/orientation; and *Whereas*, Pornography is an issue of exploitation and violence, not affectional/sexual preference/orientation; and *Whereas*, Sadomasochism is an issue of violence, not affectional/sexual preference/orientation; and *Whereas*, Public Sex, when practiced by heterosexuals or homosexuals, is an issue of violation of the privacy rights of non-participants, not an issue of affectional/sexual preference/orientation; and *Whereas*, NOW does not support the inclusion of pederasty, pornography, sadomasochism and public sex as Lesbian rights issues, since to do so would violate the feminist principles upon which this organization was founded; now therefore, *Be it*

resolved, that the National Organization for Women adopt the preceding delineation of Lesbian Rights issues and non-Lesbian rights issues as the official position of NOW; and *Be it further resolved* that NOW disseminate this resolution and the resolution concept paper on Lesbian rights issues 1980 attached hereto throughout the National, State, and Local levels of the organization; and *Be it further resolved* that NOW will work in cooperation with groups and organizations which advocate Lesbian rights as issues as defined above."

9. Compare this resolution to the Jesse Helms amendment, in which NEA support was to have been withdrawn from any artist whose work depicted "obscene or indecent materials, including but not limited to depictions of sadomasochism, homoeroticism, the exploitation of children, or individuals engaged in sex acts; or material which denigrates the objects or beliefs of the adherents of a particular religion or non-religion; or material which denigrates, debases, or reviles a group, or class of citizens on the basis of race, creed, sex, handicap, age, or national origin," and one can readily see how "feminist" rhetoric has been appropriated by the New Right.

10. This letter was published in *Heresies,* "The Sex Issue," and was signed by Rosalyn Baxandall, Bonnie Bellow, Cynthia Carr, Karen Durban, Brett Harvey, M. Mark, Alix Kates Shulman, Ann Snitow, Katy Taylor, and Ellen Willis.

11. Brame, et al., p. 32. The National News Council later censured CBS for making such unsubstantiated claims. But the damage had already been done.

12. Hunter, pp. 23–24.

13. Steiner, *Scandal of Pleasure.*

14. Cited by Steiner, p. 22.

15. The tyranny inherent in that principle began to become evident when it started to extend its reach to behaviors, clothing, styles, etc. I am thinking of the restrictions that some feminists felt compelled to institute in the name of protecting everyone from "harmful" behavior—the wearing of scented perfumes, the use of certain cosmetics, the monitoring of language, and so on. The term *politically correct* entered the left's lexicon and has subsequently been appropriated by the "New Right" in a widespread, insidious censorship campaign.

16. Rubin, "Leather Menace," in *Coming to Power,* p. 207.

17. In an interesting choice of words, and in a different context, Judith Butler argues that "it is important to *risk losing control* of the ways in which the categories of women and homosexuality are represented, even in legal terms, to *safeguard* the uncontrollability of the signified" ("Force of Fantasy," 121, my emphases). This is a political gesture that is aligned with the bottom's paradoxical situation, in which she lets go of control in one area in order to attain "safety" in another.

18. Cocks, *Augustine,* p. 145.

19. Cited in Cocks, p. 151.

20. Ibid., p. 153.

21. Ibid., p. 154.

22. Ibid., p. 149.

23. Ibid., p. 155.

24. Wendy Brown, p. 75.

25. Ibid., p. 76.

26. Ibid., p. 67.
27. Ibid., p. 75.
28. Rubin, in *Coming to Power*, p. 215.
29. Cruikshank, *Lesbian Path*, pp. 23, 26, 31–38.
30. Wolff, *Love Between Women*, p. 86.
31. Hammond, p. 44.
32. Ibid.
33. Ibid., p. 45.
34. Valverde, Letter to *The Body Politic* 62 (1980): 5.
35. Wittig, *Lesbian Body*, p. 27
36. Califia, "Secret Side of Lesbian Sexuality," p. 20.
37. Faderman, *Odd Girls and Twilight Lovers*, p. 54. This also reinforces my argument vis à vis the historical connection between race and sexuality. Ellis, too, argued that the women who "really did it" were "foreigners." That is, the *real* lesbians were women of color in Ellis's implicit analysis, although presumably all he was doing was gathering "data" from his sources.
38. See Faderman's *Odd Girls*, pp. 48–56.
39. Forel, *Sexual Question*, p. 244, and Moll, *Perversions of the Sex Instinct*, p. 89.
40. McClintock, "Maid to Order," pp. 208–210.
41. See Faderman's chapter 5 in *Odd Girls* and my *Fatal Women*, particularly chapter 1.
42. Bannon, *Women in the Shadows*.
43. Taylor, *Journey to Fulfillment*.
44. Samois, p. 7.
45. Rubin, "Leather Menace," p. 212.
46. King, p. 68.
47. See Schor's "This Essentialism Which Is Not One," and Fuss's *Essentially Speaking*, passim.
48. In an early article covering the emergence of the "lavender menace" into the National Organization for Women, Diana Davies and Judith Cartesian presented this moment as benign, even idealistic. While the NOW congress was planning their workshops, the lesbian group "took the first day of the Congress by surprise after dousing the auditorium lights and appearing among the throng resplendently attired in [their] Lavender Menace tee-shirts brandishing such signs as "Take a Lesbian to Lunch," "You're going to love the Lavender Menace," "The Women's Liberation Movement is a lesbian plot." According to this coverage, they were greeted with shock, joy, laughter, and applause, then met in a discussion group that "destroyed any derogatory illusions that any women had about their gay sisters" (*Everywoman*, 19 June, 1970, 8). Sue-Ellen Case, in her article, "Toward a Butch-Femme Aesthetic," has a very different take on this history. Case argues that the feminist movement, since the early 1970s, built its political platforms and its ideologies around the dismissal of lesbians, particularly lesbians from the "bar culture" and lesbians who were interested in butch-femme roles. She points out that the Daughters of Bilitis openly and proudly admitted to changing their identifications in ways that would appease the more mainstream feminist movement, one of the goals being to erase b/f role-playing and refashion the butch into a

lesbian feminist. Case points out that this alliance between heterosexual feminists and lesbians who "adopted the missionary position" in relation to them "led to an antipornography crusade and its alliance with the Right" (286).

49. Gay Liberation Front, p. 202.

50. Butler, *Gender Trouble*, p. 39.

51. See my *Fatal Women* for a fuller discussion of this point.

52. Žižek, *Sublime Object*, p. 163.

53. Freud, "Fetishism."

54. Butler also makes the perfectly credible claim that the focus on masochism could be accounted for through the fear of "acknowledging an identification with the one who debases [rather] than with the one who is debased or perhaps no longer to have a clear sense of the gender position of either." This "refusal to identify with aggression" ties in with Cocks's and Brown's theses. See Butler, "Force of Fantasy," p. 114.

55. Foucault, *History*, vol. 1, chapter 5, especially p. 153.

56. It is also interesting to note that two of the five readers of this manuscript put forward the view that the book was really about masochism, and even suggested that I drop the *sado* in sadomasochism, or that I call for another term. It may be that these readers identified more with the bottom's position than with the top's. While I recognize that I am theorizing women's masochism much more extensively than I am their sadism, there are certainly a number of "sadists" in these chapters. And though I do make a distinction between a "top" and a "sadist," I don't think that the top is acting out of purely altruistic desires. That is, though I say that she is facilitating and accompanying the bottom on a certain kind of psychic, emotional, and physical journey, I also think that tops thoroughly enjoy disciplining, binding, humiliating, and punishing bottoms, but in my experience *only* if the bottom wants that as well. Though there are some tops who disabuse their "service," they are generally ostracized from lesbian s/m communities. One can hold these two positions at once: to take pleasure in inflicting the above, and to want the bottom to take pleasure in it as well. The latter attitude does not distract the top from her pleasure in inflicting "pain," indeed it heightens it.

57. See Faderman's chapter 4 in *Odd Girls*.

58. Kofman, p. 66.

59. Bartky, pp. 55, 61.

60. *Unleashing Feminism* (1993); *On Our Backs*, the longest-standing and most readily available lesbian s/m magazine (very much on the "softer" side) has gone out of business. One of the first seizures under the Butler decision in Canada was *Bad Attitude* (my local gay and lesbian book store no longer displays it in the front); and the Helms amendment quite prominently focused on s/m; in fact, the other terms that remained in the clause after the Senate committee "cleaned it up," could easily be grouped under "s/m," given that the majority of people know little or nothing about it. See Califia's *Forbidden Passages*, Duggan's and Hunter's *Sex Wars*, Steiner's *Scandal of Pleasure*, Thompson's *Sadomasochism*, and Dubbin's *Arresting Images*, for recent and thorough accounts.

61. Mason, Sims, and Pagano, p. 100.

62. Valverde, *Body Politic* 43, (February 1980), n. p.

63. Dejanikus, "Our Legacy," p. 86.

64. Butler, *Excitable Speech*, p. 21.

65. Zawinski, p. 28.

66. Samois, eds., *Coming to Power*, p. 22.

67. Wayne, in Califia and Sweeney, eds., *Second Coming*, p. 248.

68. Califia, *Macho Sluts*, p. 152.

69. Baumeister, p. 41.

70. Wittig, "One Is Not Born a Woman," in *Straight Mind*, p. 20.

71. See p. 347 of *Second Coming*.

72. Rubin, "Outcasts," in *Second Coming*, pp. 340–41.

73. Butler, *Gender Trouble*, p. 117.

74. Ibid., p. 118.

75. Rubin, "Thinking Sex," pp. 267–319.

76. Adams, pp. 247–265.

77. Blau, p. 162.

78. Ibid., p. 182.

79. I do not mean to imply that identity formations *alone* limit our sexual imaginations. In the opening chapter of Sedgwick's *Epistemology of the Closet*, she makes this point powerfully. I do think, however, that identity formations further limit what we are able to imagine about bodies and pleasures. That is not to say that I am opposed to identity formations. I always and everywhere refer to myself as a lesbian; nevertheless, I think it is a good idea to remind myself that this is an historically constructed identity and that one cannot assume that others who self-nominate themselves as lesbians will necessarily have anything in common with me, except, perhaps, the occasion to begin a conversation about why we have chosen this name. And that's not an insignificant moment of affinity.

80. Anonymous, "Typical Week and a Half," p. 1.

81. But see Whisler, "Celibacy Letters," in *Heresies*, pp. 26–28.

82. Califia, *The Advocate*, p. 19.

83. Derrida, "Women in the Beehive," pp. 189–203.

84. Žižek, *Sublime Object*, pp. 165–166.

85. Ibid.

86. Ibid.

87. Beauvoir, "Must We Burn Sade?" p. 15.

88. Orlando, "Power Plays," p. 39.

89. Beauvoir, p. 32.

90. Deleuze, *Coldness and Cruelty*, p. 42.

91. Ibid., p. 45, my emphasis.

92. Ibid., p. 68.

93. Ibid., p. 77.

94. Ibid., p. 84.

95. Califia, *Macho Sluts*, pp. 15–16.

96. Bersani, "Rectum," p. 215.

97. Klossowski, cited in *Coldness and Cruelty*, p. 119.

98. Mulvey, *Visual and Other Pleasures*, p. 22.

99. See Lauretis, chapter 5 of *Alice Doesn't*, p. 103.

100. Deleuze, p. 130.
101. Ibid., pp. 55, 53.
102. Ibid., p. 93.
103. Rubin, "Traffic in Women," pp. 157–210.
104. This would account for a puzzle that I was unable to articulate at the heart of the fantasies about the infamous "murderers of Le Mans," the two sisters who, in 1933 brutally slaughtered their employer and her daughter. During the trial, which lasted for six months, even though the sisters had confessed immediately, the focus was on the sisters' sexual relationship, which was implied to be lesbian. The incest issue was displaced onto a "lesbianism" that had virtually no grounding in evidence. See my article, " 'They Don't Even Look Like Maids Anymore': Wendy Kesselman's *My Sister in This House,*" in Hart, ed., *Making a Spectacle.*
105. I have not been able to trace the origin of the "butch bottom" in lesbian subcultures. The concept seems to be fairly recent among lesbians. An anonymous reader of this manuscript suggested that the "butch bottom" is an import from the gay leather culture.
106. Irigaray, *Speculum,* section 1.
107. Lacan, *Encore,* cited in Irigaray, "Così Fan Tutti," in *This Sex,* p. 88.
108. Ibid., p. 102.
109. Ibid., p. 89.
110. Merck, pp. 247–248.
111. Ibid., p. 254.
112. Ibid., p. 236.
113. Brame, p. 19.
114. Merck, p. 237.
115. Kristeva, "About Chinese Women," p. 149.
116. Ibid.
117. Lauretis, "*Practice of Love,* pp. 109–110.
118. "Jessie," in Califia, *Macho Sluts,* pp. 61–62.
119. "The Surprise Party," in ibid., p. 242.
120. "The Hustler," in ibid., p. 210.
121. "Jessie," p. 62. Merck finds similar endings in three different lesbian s/m narratives.
122. Foucault, "Sexual Choice," p. 20.
123. See Doane, *Desire to Desire,* passim.
124. Foucault, "Sexual Choice," p. 20.
125. Cited by Žižek in *Flash Art* interview, p. 69.
126. Cited in Borch-Jacobsen, *Lacan,* p. 140. For a full discussion see Lacan, "Thou Art the One Who Will Follow Me," in Jacques-Alain Miller, ed., Russell Grigg, trans., *The Seminar of Jacques Lacan: Book 3, The Psychoses,* pp. 271–284 (New York: Norton, 1993).
127. Ibid.
128. Thompson, *Leatherfolk,* p. xvii.
129. Ibid. p. xix.
130. Ibid., p. 55.

131. Ibid., p. 63.
132. Ibid., p. xx.
133. Califia, *Macho Sluts*, p. 27.
134. Ibid.

3. Doing It Anyway: The Impossible-Real

1. Roof, *Lure of Knowledge*, p. 224.
2. Jeffreys, *Lesbian Heresy*, pp. 173–174.
3. Evans, "Rodney King," pp. 74–78. I am otherwise in agreement with Evans's critique of the Rodney King beating. It is her *analogy* with s/m that I find simplistic.
4. Bersani, "Is the Rectum a Grave?" p. 208.
5. Foucault, *Pipe*, p. 44.
6. Diamond, "Mimesis," p. 64.
7. Ibid.
8. Ibid.
9. Bhabha, "Of Mimicry and Man," p. 318.
10. Deleuze, "Plato and the Simulacrum," pp. 48–49.
11. Marcus, *Taste for Pain*, p. 181.
12. Dworkin, *Ms.* 4, no. 4 (January/February 1994): 39.
13. Bersani, *Freudian Body*, p. 39.
14. Bersani, *Homos*, p. 102.
15. Ibid., p. 103.
16. Ibid.
17. Bersani, *Freudian Body*, p. 39.
18. Ibid., p. 41.
19. Ibid., p. 45.
20. Bersani, "*Is the Rectum a Grave?*" pp. 211–212. This citation has so frequently been lifted out of context that I wanted to restore it here. Bersani is speaking of the historical fantasy of female sexuality as "intrinsically diseased," "the *sign of infection*" (Bersani's emphasis), and insatiable. He is suggesting, further, that, in the *unconscious of the dominant culture*, gay men are positioned as "women" when they assume the "passive" position in anal intercourse. More specifically, the context in which he places this "suicidal ecstasy" is in reference to the middle-class citizens of Arcadia, Florida, who chased a family with three HIV-infected hemophiliac children from their midst. His point is, then, that such behavior, one could speculate, is based on an unconscious displacement from the children with HIV to the anally receptive gay man. While this may seem like quite a stretch, I *agree* with Bersani's argument here. What I find disconcerting is the way in which the "woman's position" is critiqued for its homophobia only by this transference to the gay man. Once again, as Eve Sedgwick points out so forcefully, women's anal eroticism does not mean. It means *nothing*. Not to mention lesbians' anal eroticism. I want, further, to emphasize that I am not merely "complaining" that Bersani does not discuss lesbians. I see no reason whatsoever why he should. My question here concerns what must remain unspeakable (even *more* unspeakable than Bersani's "intolerable"—but not "unsayable"—description of a gay man being anally penetrated). What is omitted, erased, excluded, is the passive lesbian position. As Judith Butler points out in *Excitable Speech*, "such a constitutive exclusion

provides the condition of possibility for any act of speech" (139). Hence, my opportunity to speak.

21. Bersani, *Homos*, pp. 106–107.
22. Freud, "Economic Problem in Masochism," p. 162.
23. Austin, *How to Do Things With Words*. Austin's most famous example is the "I do" of the Christian marriage vow, which effectuates the bond in its enunciation: "in saying these words we are *doing* something—namely, marrying, rather than *reporting* something, namely that we are marrying" (12–13).
24. Silverman, "Masochism and Male Subjectivity," p. 52.
25. Brown, "Sex, Lies, and Penetration," p. 412.
26. Farr, "Art of Discipline," p. 185.
27. Derrida, "Theater of Cruelty" p. 234.
28. Bersani, "Is the Rectum a Grave?" pp. 206–208.
29. Clément, pp. 168–169.
30. Butler, "Force of Fantasy," p. 118.
31. *Oxford English Dictionary.*
32. See my discussion of Ellis's footnotes in Chapter 1 of *Fatal Women*. I elaborated there, but it is important to repeat here, that when Ellis discusses women who are "really" inverts, they almost all use dildos and, significantly, they are almost all women of color. Thus the "lesbian" gets constructed in Ellis's sexology as either white and nonexistent, or real and foreign.
33. Lane, "What's *Race* Got to Do With It," p. 21.
34. Smyth, "Crossing," pp. 43–45.
35. Those on the "left" have paid attention to this issue. Butler, for example, writes: "By focusing on the homoeroticism of [Mapplethorpe's] photographs, the anxiety over interracial homo- and hetero-sexual exchange is contained and permanently deferred. The naked Black men characterized by Mapplethorpe engage a certain racist romanticization of Black men's excessive physicality and sexual readiness, their photographic currency as a sign. Perhaps the most offensive dimension of Mapplethorpe's work, it is never that which is explicitly named as the offense by Helms; the fear of miscegenation operates tacitly here as well, disavowed, contained, and deferred by the stated spectre of 'homoeroticism' or the generalized possibility of 'individuals engaged in sex acts' " ("Force of Fantasy," 118–119). Butler's assurance that Mapplethorpe's photographs of black men is racist is contested, however. See, for example, Kobena Mercer, "Robert Mapplethorpe and Fantasies of Race," in Lynne Segal and Mary McIntosh, eds., *Sex Exposed: Sexuality and the Pornography Debate*, pp. 92–110. London: Verso, 1992.
36. Findlay, p. 329.
37. Ibid., p. 334.
38. Ibid.
39. Ibid., p. 329.
40. Cited in Steiner, *Scandal of Pleasure*, p. 9.
41. Best, *Race for Invention*, p. 209.
42. Ibid.
43. Cowie, "Fantasia," p. 159.
44. Ibid., p. 150.

45. Cited in Bersani, *Homos*, p. 102.

46. Ibid., p. 110.

47. Ibid., p. 112.

48. Ibid., p. 102.

49. Haraway, *Symians, Cyborgs, and Women*, pp. 152–153.

50. Stanley Aronowitz, "Technology and the Future of Work," in Gretchen Bender and Timothy Druckrey eds., *Culture on the Brink: Ideologies of Technology*, p. 5 (Seattle: Bay Press, 1994).

51. *Quim* 3 (Winter 1991): 10, 13.

52. Ibid., p. 36.

53. Bersani, "Is the Rectum a Grave?," p. 208.

54. Wittig, "Straight Mind," p. 32.

55. Ibid., pp. 27–28.

56. Ibid., p. 25.

57. MacKinnon, *Feminism Unmodified*, p. 172.

58. Butler makes a similar "paradoxical alliance with Dworkin," also calling for a proliferation of representations and discursive sites. Butler agrees with Dworkin to the extent that the Helms amendment is "violent and violating" but goes on to point out that Helms could not have written it without the help of the Dworkin/Mackinnon rhetoric. Butler positions herself in alignment with Dworkin in opposition to the violence of rhetoric and representation but argues that the very means of containing or controlling the violence, as Dworkin and Mackinnon would have it, instead works to produce and proliferate "precisely the kind of reductive and phantasmatic representations that it seeks to forestall" ("Force of Fantasy," 119). While I am very much in agreement with Butler's theory and its application to political strategies, I am not so convinced by the position that Dworkin and Mackinnon wrote legislation with "good intentions" that then mysteriously backfired on them. For long after they have seen how this legislation has actually worked in the social context, they have continued to push it, despite some rhetorical backtracking by Dworkin (see Duggan and Hunter for a thorough analysis of this). Why is it seemingly inconceivable to some feminists that Dworkin and Mackinnon's legislation is not, in fact, accomplishing precisely what they set out to do—to censor representations of homosexuality and sadomasochism, which they understand as "violence" toward women, i.e., white heterosexual women?

59. Bersani, "Is the Rectum a Grave?," p. 214.

60. Wittig, "Straight Mind," p. 28.

61. Lacan, "Meaning of the Phallus," pp. 79–85.

62. Butler, "Lesbian Phallus," p. 156.

63. Ibid., p. 157.

64. Foucault, *Pipe*, passim.

65. Butler, "Lesbian Phallus," p. 157.

66. Wittig, "Straight Mind," p. 26.

67. Silverman, *Male Subjectivity at the Margins*, p. 381.

68. Ibid., p. 383.

69. Lasher, "Hot Buttered Bum," p. 23.

70. Butler, "Force of Fantasy," p. 113.

71. Butler was one of the contributors to *Against Sadomasochism* in 1982. Her position on this matter has certainly changed significantly, but her more recent work still indicates an ambivalence about sadomasochism.

72. Butler, "Force of Fantasy," p. 117.

73. Bersani, "Is the Rectum a Grave?," p. 217.

74. Modleski, *Feminism Without Women*, p. 154.

75. Bersani, "Is the Rectum a Grave?" p. 216.

76. Miller, "Anal Rope," p. 135.

77. Sedgwick, "Poem," in *Tendencies*, p. 177.

78. Ibid., p. 209.

79. Barthes, *Lover's Discourse*, p. 14.

80. Ibid.

81. Sedgwick, "Poem," in *Tendencies*, p. 183.

82. Ibid.

83. Ibid., p. 209.

84. Blau, *Eye of Prey*, p. 162.

85. Sedgwick, "Poem," in *Tendencies*, p. 177.

86. Freud, "Child Is Being Beaten," p. 180.

87. Sedgwick, "Poem," p. 182.

88. Ibid., p. 191.

89. Ibid., pp. 197–198.

90. Ibid., p. 179.

91. Ibid., p. 180, my emphasis.

92. Cited in Fussell, *Poetic Meter*, p. 5.

93. Fussell, p. 12.

94. Sedgwick, "Poem," in *Tendencies*, p. 184.

95. Ibid.

96. Ibid.

97. Barthes, *Pleasure of the Text*, p. 57.

98. Ibid., p. 14.

99. Barthes, *Lover's Discourse*, p. 15.

100. Barthes, *Pleasure of the Text*, p. 14.

101. Sedgwick, "Poem," in *Tendencies*, p. 207.

102. Ibid., p. 209.

103. Foucault, "Sexual Choice," p. 19.

104. Ibid.

105. Ibid., p. 21.

106. Hegel, "Phenomenology of Spirit," p. 105.

107. DeLynn, *Don Juan*, pp. 146–147.

108. Ibid., p. 147.

109. Ibid., pp. 150–151.

110. Ibid., p. 151.

111. Ibid.

112. Ibid.

113. Ibid., p. 234.

114. Case, "Student and the Strap," pp. 38–46.

115. *Newsweek*, 21 June, 1993.

116. *Vanity Fair*, August 1993.

117. Califia, review of Camille Paglia's *Sex, Art, and American Culture*, in the *Philadelphia Inquirer*, Sunday, 4 October, 1992, pp. M1, M6.

118. Lamos, "Postmodern Lesbian Position," p. 88.

119. Ibid., p. 89.

120. Ibid.

121. Ibid.," p. 99.

122. Butler, "Lesbian Phallus," p. 138.

123. Ibid., p. 159.

4. Death and the Referent: The Queer Real

1. Munster, "Queer Operations," p. 35.

2. Ibid., p. 21.

3. Ibid., p. 24.

4. Jameson, *Postmodernism*, pp. 91–92.

5. Ibid, pp. 95–96.

6. See my chapter, "Lesbians in the Mainstream," in *Acting Out*, pp. 119–137.

7. Munster, "Queer Operations," unpublished ms.

8. Derrida, "Theater of Cruelty," p. 234.

9. Munster, "Queer Operations," unpublished ms.

10. Such anecdotes are rife in theatrical history. For the Garrick/Woffington one, see Donald Sinden, *The Everyman Book of Theatrical Anecdotes* (London and Melbourne: Dent, 1987), p. 32.

11. This is not to say that they do not, in some way, have a point. I too am often made very uncomfortable by enforced audience participation. I have even refused to participate and made a "scene" in the theater by doing so. I have also encouraged it, sitting on the front row and deliberately trying to catch Peggy Shaw's eye when she moves into the audience to sing "The Girl's I've Loved," in her performance piece *You're Just Like My Father*. Obviously there is an issue of consent that is often ignored when performers break the fourth wall in this way. However, the point I'm trying to explore here is about the relationship between speech acts and physical gestures on the stage. The body and its gestures are clearly being taken for the "real" in a way that language is not, indicating that the tenacious soldering of the "flesh" with the "real" is ongoing.

12. For a full discussion of Finley's part in the NEA controversies, see my article "Karen Finley's Dirty Work," pp. 1–15.

13. Cited by Carr in "Washed in the Blood," p. 16.

14. As part of the installation "Sanctuary" at the T'Z Art Gallery, 28 Wooster St. New York City, 21 July–26 August, 1994.

15. I am indebted to Cherry Smyth for reminding me that cutting has recently seemed to become the most controversial practice in s/m communities. It was Catherine Opie's photograph "Self-Portrait" (in Bright, Blank, and Posener, eds., *Nothing But the Girl*, 40) that awakened old debates about s/m. One reviewer wrote, "this photo repels me, it scares me, and it makes be think about why. It is one of the few photos in *Nothing But the Girl* that actually challenges my assumptions about the kinds of sexual practices

this 'pervert' is engaged in, because according to the status quo, hey, I'm a pervert too" (Judith Katz, *Lambda Book Report* 5 [August 1996]: 33–34). The photo in question is of Opie, naked from the waist up with the word *pervert* scarred across her chest. Her arms from shoulder to wrist are lined with neat rows of piercing needles. There is no blood visible on her body. The photograph has at once the history of cutting in the scar and the promise of more blood when the needles are removed. She is also wearing a black hood. While I think Smyth is right to point out that "cutting" and, less obviously, piercing have seemed to constitute a line that many people cannot cross in s/m practices, I find it interesting that weeks before I had this correspondence with Smyth, I was flipping through *Nothing But the Girl* with a friend who is also quite open to s/m sexuality, and she and I both paused at this photo and agreed that we found it terrifying and repelling. But then when Smyth pointed it out to me in the context of the issue of cutting, or blood-letting, I had to search the reference list to find the photo. When I realized that it was the same one that I found repelling, I also noticed the *needles for the first time*. What had given me such pause was the leather hood; I had not even gotten past seeing the hood to *see the needles*. Checking with my friend, it turns out the hood was her point of reference too. Still I don't think this obviates Smyth's point. Breaking the surface of the skin would logically be more upsetting for some people than various forms of penetration and markings on the body's surface. There are very few photographs of *lesbian* sadomasochism that even show the marks left on the body of the bottom, much less actual blood. Because objections to s/m, in practice and in performance, have so much to do with what some people see as a violation of the boundaries between the inside and the outside of the body, it would seem to follow logically that the more this boundary is broken, the more difficult it is for people to accept. Blood, of course, has all sorts of conscious and unconscious associations that I cannot elaborate here; one obvious one being its association with "women's impurities." For an interesting story on blood and the eroticization of the loss of exchanging bodily fluids, see "Bloody" by Lydia Swartz, in Califia and Sweeney, eds., *Second Coming.*

16. Croce, "Discussing the Undiscussable," p. 54.
17. Rich, "Dance of Death," p. 19.
18. Croce, p. 55.
19. Kushner, "Letter to the Editor," p. 11.
20. Rich, p. 19.
21. Dean, "Psychoanalysis of AIDS," pp. 84–85.
22. Ibid., p. 85.
23. Ibid., p. 86.
24. Croce, p. 54.
25. Dean, p. 87.
26. Ibid., p. 86.
27. Ibid., p. 88.
28. MacVey, "Who's the Victim ?" p. 13.
29. Ron Athey, cited in *LA Weekly* (8–14 July, 1994) p. 24.
30. Ibid.
31. Cited in Carr, p. 16.
32. Ibid.

33. Scarry, *Body in Pain*, passim.

34. Reich, cited in Marcus, *Taste for Pain*, p. 158, my emphasis.

35. Reik, *Masochism in Modern Man*, p. 27.

36. In a discussion with Rubin and Califia, Califia says that s/m has been "mythologized around the whole issue of pain and violence. The stereotype of s/m is that it is all whips and chains and blood—that it is mostly about pain," whereas in her experience it is really about power "in which the participants have agreed to act out a fantasy in which one of them controls the sex and the other is sexually submissive." See Wechsler, *Gay Community News*, pp. 6–8. I think the key word here is "mythologized," and I agree with Califia that s/m has been stereotyped in such ways. But I also think there is a certain defensiveness about receiving and administering pain that the s/m community has, understandably, attempted to downplay.

37. Munster, unpublished ms.

38. Ibid.

39. Bob Flanagan, *Supermasochist*, in Juno p. 12.

40. Ibid., p. 13.

41. Kauffman, "Bob Flanagan's Sadomedicine," p. 120.

42. Ibid., p. 114.

43. Ibid., p. 115.

44. Sedgwick and Frank, "Shame in the Cybernetic Fold," p. 500.

45. Ibid.

46. Ibid., pp. 520–521.

47. Bledsoe, "Old-Fashioned Way," in Elwin and Tulchinsky, eds., *Tangled Sheets*, pp. 143–150.

48. Ibid., p. 146.

49. Ibid., p. 148.

50. Ibid., p. 147.

51. Kauffman, p. 118.

52. Flanagan, p. 31.

53. Drier, "Rack Talk," p. 79.

54. Ibid., p. 80.

55. Sedgwick, "Queer Performativity," p. 2.

56. Pavis, "Production," p. 124.

57. Ibid., p. 132.

58. Ibid., p. 134.

59. Ibid.

60. Blau, *Eye of Prey*, p. 180.

61. Blau, p. 161.

62. Califia, "Calyx of Isis," in *Macho Sluts*, pp. 152–153.

63. Blau, p. 162.

64. Ibid., pp. 164–165.

65. Ibid., p. 179.

66. Felman, *Literary Speech Act*, p. 110.

67. Ibid., p. 111.

68. Califia, "Calyx" p. 97.

69. Lacan, "Seminar of 21 January, 1975," in Rose and Mitchell, eds., *Feminine Sexuality*, p. 170.
70. Califia, "Calyx," p. 97.
71. Ibid., p. 136.
72. Ibid., pp. 136–137.
73. Austin, *How to Do Things with Words*, pp. 16–17.
74. Felman, p. 84.
75. Lacan, Book 1, p. 174.
76. Ibid.
77. Califia, "Calyx," p. 172.
78. Ibid., p. 176.
79. Ibid., p. 147.
80. Irigaray, *This Sex*, p. 197.
81. Ibid.
82. Ibid., p. 209.
83. Califia, "Calyx," p. 141.
84. Blau, p. 173.
85. Rainer Maria Rilke, "8th Elegy."
86. Reik, p. 73.
87. Ibid., p. 78.
88. Ibid., p. 199.
89. Ibid., p. 203.
90. Ibid., p. 207.
91. Ibid., pp. 203–204.
92. Ibid., p. 90.
93. Such arguments are ubiquitous in antiporn, anti-s/m feminist rhetoric. Two anthologies represent these positions well: Robin Ruth Linden, et. al., eds., *Against Sadomasochism: A Radical Feminist Analysis* (East Palo Alto, Calif.: Frog in the Well Press, 1982) and Irene Reti, ed., *Unleashing Feminism: Critiquing Lesbian Sadomasochism in the Gay Nineties* (Santa Cruz, Calif.: HerBooks, 1993).
94. Blau, p. 166.
95. Derrida, "Theater of Cruelty," p. 249.
96. Blau, p. 163.
97. Ibid., pp. 163–164.
98. Nietzsche, *Genealogy of Morals*, p. 189.
99. Ibid., p. 189.
100. Clément, *Lives and Legends*, p. 122.
101. Ibid., p. 123.
102. Reik, p. 124.
103. Ibid., p. 118.
104. Ibid.
105. Reik, p. 121.
106. Ibid.
107. Ibid., p. 124.
108. Felman, p. 34.

109. Ibid., p. 35.

110. Ibid., p. 31.

111. Dollimore, "Sex and Death," p. 28.

112. Deleuze, pp. 335–336.

113. Ibid., p. 335.

114. In "The Truth of Self-Certainty," in *Phenomenology of Spirit*, Hegel writes: "As self-consciousness, it is movement; but since what it distinguishes from itself is *only itself* as itself, the difference, as an otherness, is *immediately superseded* for it; the difference is *not*, and *it* [self-consciousness] is only the motionless tautology of: 'I am I'; but since for it the difference does not have the form of *being*, it is *not* self-consciousness" (105).

115. Thompson, *Leatherfolk*, p. 1.

116. Deleuze, *Logic of Sense*, p. 93.

5. Bearing (to) Witness: The Erotics of Power in Bastard Out of Carolina

1. Cited by Allison, "Public Silence, Private Terror," in Vance, p. 103.

2. Ibid.

3. Allison, interview with Michael Rowe, *Harvard Gay and Lesbian Review*, p. 8.

4. Roof, *Lure of Knowledge*, p. 236.

5. Mohanty, "Us and Them," pp. 6–7.

6. Cited by Mohanty, p. 8, second emphasis mine.

7. Ibid., p. 13.

8. Ibid., p. 16.

9. Hall, *Policing the Crisis*, p. 394.

10. Ibid., p. 395.

11. Felman, in Felman and Laub, eds., *Testimony*, p. 206.

12. Ibid., p. 211.

13. Allison *Bastard*, p. 124.

14. As I point out in an earlier chapter, analogies between the Holocaust and "violent" sexual practices are rampant in radical feminist rhetoric. It is not the assault on sexuality that offends here but, rather, the unspeakably hideous trivialization of a global disaster that escapes historical comparisons. It is important to remember, however, that many Holocaust survivors *are also sexual abuse survivors*, as is well documented.

15. Caruth, *Trauma*, p. 182.

16. Ibid., p. 183.

17. Ibid.

18. Ibid., p. 185.

19. Ibid., pp. 186–187.

20. Ibid., p. 187, my emphasis.

21. Ibid.

22. Henry Krystal, "Integration and Self-Healing," p. 95 and passim.

23. Ibid., p. 103.

24. Laura Brown, "Not Outside the Range: One Feminist Perspective on Psychic Trauma." *American Imago* 48, no. 1 (1991): 119–133.

25. Ibid., p. 122.

26. Jetter, p. 54.

27. Ibid., p. 56.

28. Felman, *Testimony*, p. 224.
29. Sommer, "Not Just a Personal Story," p. 108.
30. Ibid.
31. Ibid., p. 109.
32. Ibid., p. 120.
33. Ibid.
34. Lanzmann, "Seminar," p. 97.
35. Sommer, p. 119.
36. Ibid.
37. Jameson, *Postmodernism*, pp. 93–94.
38. Ibid.
39. Laub, *Testimony*, p. 59.
40. Ibid., p. 60.
41. Ibid., p. 62.
42. Jameson, "Nostalgia," p. 27.
43. From Lacan, *Four Fundamental Concepts*, cited in Žižek, *Sublime*, p. 47.
44. Blume, *Secret Survivors*, p. 81.
45. Alcoff and Gray, "Survivor Discourse," passim.
46. Blume, p. 75.
47. Ibid., p. 85.
48. Bell, *Interrogating Incest*, p. 57.
49. Allison, *Bastard*, p. 112.
50. Ibid., p. 112.
51. Ibid., p. 113.
52. Allison, in Megan, "Moving Toward Truth," p. 72.
53. Clément, *Lives and Legends*, p. 123.
54. Jameson, "Nostalgia," p. 524.
55. Ibid.
56. See Laub, "An Event Without a Witness," in Felman and Laub, eds., *Testimony*.
57. It is interesting to note that after I had written this chapter, Califia and Sweeney's sequel to *Coming to Power* was published, entitled *The Second Coming*. This title's reference to the earlier volume is obvious. But it also strikes me that the theological connotation it carries of a "resurrection" is a concept that is deeply inscribed in s/m practice. Such a "redemptive" grammar, which is pervasive in the literature, could be perceived as pastoralizing in tone, and indeed must be in part. But it is also campy and ironic, parodic in one sense and, like all parody carrying with it a certain ambivalent reverence for the model that it both mocks and imitates.
58. Jetter, *New York Times Magazine*, p. 56.
59. Allison, *Skin*, p. 209.
60. Felman, *Testimony*, p. 228.
61. Žižek, *Tarrying With the Negative*, p. 116. To contextualize: Žižek is explaining the logic whereby the *impossible* is transmuted into the *prohibited*. As he explains: "the symbolic prohibition is nothing but an attempt to resolve this deadlock by a transmutation of impossibility into prohibition. *There is one* which is the prohibited object of incest (mother), and its prohibition renders accessible all other objects" (116).

62. Žižek, *Sublime*, p. 133.
63. Laub, pp. 70–71.
64. Allison, *Bastard*, p. 151.
65. Cited in Trites, *New Testament Concept*, p. 2.
66. Ibid.
67. Ibid., p. 3.
68. Foucault, *History*, 1:61–62.
69. Alcoff and Gray, p. 261.
70. Ibid., p. 269.
71. Allison, *Bastard*, p. 151.
72. Ibid., p. 152.
73. Allison, Rowe interview, *Harvard Gay and Lesbian Review*, p. 8.
74. Allison, *Skin*, p. 215.
75. Ibid., p. 212.
76. Jetter, p. 57.
77. Chasseguet-Smirgel, *Creativity and Perversion*, p. 11.
78. Ibid.
79. Ibid., p. 6.
80. Ibid.
81. Ibid., p. 7.
82. Irigaray, p. 213.
83. Chasseguet-Smirgel, p. 3.
84. Allison, *Bastard*, p. 118.
85. Ibid., p. 118.
86. Ibid., p. 122.
87. Ibid., p. 126.
88. Allison, in Jetter, p. 57.
89. Califia, introduction to Califia, ed., *Doing It For Daddy* pp. 9–11.
90. Ibid., p. 11.
91. Munster, p. 35.
92. Allison, *Skin*, p. 35, my emphasis.
93. Allison, *Bastard*, p. 262.
94. Cvetkovich, "Sexual Trauma," p. 371.
95. Allison, *Skin*, pp. 15–16.
96. Beverley, *Against Literature*, p. 82.
97. Cited by Beverley, p. 82.
98. Dollimore, *Sexual Dissidence*, passim.
99. Nestle, *Persistent Desire*, p. 18.
100. Ibid., p. 411.
101. Allison, *Two or Three Things*, p. 45.
102. Card, *Lesbian Choices*, p. 230.
103. Ellis Stanley, *Off Our Backs* (February 1981), p. 27.
104. Zawinski, "Letter to Editors," p. 28.
105. Dejanikus, "Our Legacy," p. 6.
106. Griffin, "Sadomasochism," p. 186.

107. Jeffreys, "Orgasm," pp. 18–21.
108. Cvetkovich, p. 351.
109. Ibid., p. 357.
110. Ibid., p. 352.
111. For more on the Michigan Womyn's Festival, see Rebecca Dawn Kaplan, "Sex, Lies, and Heteropatriarchy" in Califia and Sweeney, eds., *Second Coming*, pp. 123–130.
112. Cvetkovich, p. 226.
113. Lauretis, *Practice of Love*, p. 226.
114. Ibid.
115. Ibid., p. 226, fn. 11.
116. Ibid., p. xiv.
117. Ibid., pp. 226–227.
118. I certainly do not mean to perpetuate the notion of women's inherent "goodness." Violence within lesbian s/m communities does occur. It is only quite recently that it has begun to be spoken about more openly. See Califia's essay, "A House Divided," in *Second Coming*, pp. 262–274 for a bold discussion of these problems. There is also a tendency to say that women do not sexually abuse their own and others' children. This myth is also beginning to be debunked. In my opinion, not talking about these things is a just another way of preserving the myth of pure womanhood.
119. Blume, p. 56.
120. Ibid., p. 178.
121. Ibid.
122. Ibid., p. 219.
123. Ibid., p. 234.
124. Alice Miller, foreword to *Pictures of a Childhood*, p. 10
125. Felman, *Testimony*, p. 237.
126. Žižek, *Sublime*, p. 132.

Epilogue: Crows III
1. Felman, *Testimony*, p. 228.
2. Epstein, *Thoughts Without a Thinker*, p. 28.
3. Ibid., p. 56.
4. Rilke, "Autumn Leaves."
5. Delbo, p. 325.
6. Sexton, "Wanting to Die," in *Live or Die*, p. 59.
7. Ibid.

Bibliography

"Actual S & M Incidences." *Echo of Sappho* 1, no. 4 (1973): 19.

Adams, Parveen. "The Bald Truth." *Diacritics* 24, no. 2, special eds. Judith Butler and Biddy Martin (Summer/Fall 1994): 184–189.

———. "Of Female Bondage." In *Between Feminism and Psychoanalysis*, ed. Teresa Brennan, pp. 247–265. New York: Routledge, 1989.

Alcoff, Linda and Laura Gray. "Survivor Discourse: Transgression or Recuperation?" *Signs: Journal of Women in Culture and Society* 18, no. 2 (Winter 1993): 260–290.

Alexandre, Wayne. "Black Homosexual Masochist." In *Black Men/White Men: A Gay Anthology*, ed. Michael J. Smith, pp. 78–83. San Francisco: Gay Sunshine, 1983.

Allison, Dorothy. *Bastard Out of Carolina.* New York: Plume, 1993.

———. "Public Silence, Private Terror." In *Pleasure and Danger: Exploring Female Sexuality*, ed. Carole S. Vance, pp. 103–114. London: Pandora, 1992.

———. *Skin: Talking About Sex, Class, and Literature.* Ithaca, N.Y.: Firebrand, 1994.

———. *Trash.* Ithaca, N.Y.: Firebrand, 1988.

———. *Two or Three Things I Know For Sure.* New York: Dutton, 1995.

Anonymous. *Quim.* Issue 3 (Winter 1991): 36.

Anonymous. "Typical Week and a Half." *Heresies* 3, no. 4 (1981): 1.

Antoniou, Laura, ed. *Leather Women.* New York: A Rosebud Book, 1993.

Apter, Emily and William Pietz, eds. *Fetishism as Cultural Discourse.* Ithaca: Cornell University Press, 1993.

Ardill, Susan and Sue O'Sullivan. "Upsetting the Applecart: Difference, Desire, and Lesbian Sadomasochism." In *Out the Other Side*, ed. Christian McEwan and O'Sullivan, pp. 122–144. Freedom, Cal.: Crossing Press, 1989.

Artaud, Antonin. *The Theater and Its Double.* Trans. Mary Caroline Richards. New York: Grove, 1958.

Ashley, Barbara Renchkovsky and David Ashley. "Sex as Violence: The Body Against Intimacy." *International Journal of Women's Studies* 7, no. 4 (September/October 1984): pp. 352–371.

Atkinson, Ti-Grace. "Why I'm Against S/M Liberation." *Majority Report* (1976): 90–92.

Austin, J. L. *How to Do Things with Words.* Cambridge: Harvard University Press, 1962.

Bad Object-Choices, eds. *How Do I Look? Queer Film and Video.* Seattle: Bay Press, 1991.

Baldwin, James. *The Price of the Ticket: Collected Nonfiction, 1948–1985.* New York: St Martin's/Marek, 1985.

Bannon, Ann. *Women in the Shadows.* Tallahassee: Naiad, 1983.

Barcley, Clare and Elaine Carol. "Obscenity Chill: Artists in a Post-Butler Era." *Fuse* 16, no. 2 (Winter 1992/93): 18–28.

Barish, Jonas. *The Antitheatrical Prejudice.* Berkeley: University of California Press, 1981.

Barnard, Ian. "*Macho Sluts*: Genre-Fuck, S/M Fantasy, and the Reconfiguration of Political Action." In *Sexual Artifice,* ed. Ann Kibbey, Kayann Short, and Abouali Farmanfarmaian, pp. 265–291. New York: New York University Press, 1994.

Barry, Kathleen. "Sadomasochism: The New Backlash to Feminism." *Trivia* 1, no. 1 (1989): 79–92.

Barthes, Roland. *A Lover's Discourse.* Trans. Richard Howard. New York: Hill and Wang, 1978.

———. *The Pleasure of the Text.* Trans. Richard Miller. New York: Farrar, Straus and Giroux, 1975.

Bartky, Sandra. *Femininity and Domination.* New York: Routledge, 1990.

Bashford, Kerry, Jasper Laybutt, Anna Munster, and Kimberly O'Sullivan. *Kink.* Sydney, Australia: Wicked Women Publications, 1993.

Bassein, Beth Ann. *Women and Death: Linkages in Western Thought and Literature.* Westport, Conn.: Greenwood, 1984.

Bataille, Georges. *Erotism.* Trans. Mary Dalwood. San Francisco: City Lights, 1986.

Baumeister, Roy F. "Gender Differences in Masochistic Scripts." *Journal of Sex Research* 25 (November 1988): 478–499.

———. "Masochism as Escape from Self." *Journal of Sex Research* 25, no. 1 (February 1988): 28–59.

Baxter, Sarah. "Lesbian Sado-Masochism: Chain Reaction." *Timeout* 8 (September 1988). n.p.

Beauvoir, Simone de. "Must We Burn Sade?" In *The Marquis de Sade: The 120 Days of Sodom and Other Writings,* trans. and ed. Austryn Wainhouse and Richard Seaver, pp. 3–64. New York: Grove Weidenfeld, 1966.

Bell, Vikki. *Interrogating Incest: Feminism, Foucault, and the Law.* London and New York: Routledge, 1993.

Benjamin, Jessica. "The Bonds of Love: Rational Violence and Erotic Domination." *Feminist Studies* 6, no. 1 (Spring 1980): 144–174.

———. *The Bonds of Love: Psychoanalysis, Feminism, and the Problem of Domination.* New York: Pantheon, 1988.

Bennetts, Leslie. "k. d. lang Cuts It Close." *Vanity Fair* 56, no. 8 (August 1993): 94–98, 142–146.

Berlant, Lauren. *The Anatomy of National Fantasy: Hawthorne, Utopia, and Everyday Life.* Chicago: Chicago University Press, 1991.

Bernhard, Sandra. "Not Just Another Pretty Face." *Playboy* 39, no. 9, pp. 70–77.

Bersani, Leo. "Artists in Love." In *Literature and Psychoanalysis*, ed. Edith Kurzweil and William Phillips, pp. 347–352. Columbia University Press, 1983.

——. *Baudelaire and Freud.* Berkeley: University of California Press, 1977.

——. *The Freudian Body: Psychoanalysis and Art.* New York: Columbia University Press, 1986.

——. "The Gay Outlaw." Special eds. Judith Butler and Biddy Martin. *Diacritics* 24, no. 2 (Summer/Fall 1994): 5–18.

——. *Homos.* Cambridge: Harvard University Press, 1995.

——. "Is the Rectum a Grave?" In *AIDS: Cultural Analysis—Cultural Activism*, ed. Douglas Crimp, pp. 197–222. Cambridge: MIT Press, 1988.

Best, Stephen. "The Race for Invention: Blackness, Technology, and Turn-of-the-Century Modernity." Ph.D. diss., University of Pennsylvania, 1997.

Beverley, John. *Against Literature.* Minneapolis: University of Minnesota Press, 1993.

Bhabha, Homi. "Of Mimicry and Man: The Ambivalence of Colonial Discourse." In *October: The First Decade, 1976–1986*, ed. Annette Michelson et. al., pp. 317–325. Cambridge: MIT Press, 1987.

Blasius, Mark. *Gay and Lesbian Politics: Sexuality and the Emergence of a New Ethic.* Philadelphia: Temple University Press, 1994.

Blau, Herbert. *The Eye of Prey: Subversions of the Postmodern.* Bloomington: Indiana University Press, 1987.

Blume, E. Sue. *Secret Survivors: Uncovering Incest and Its Aftereffects in Women.* New York: Wiley, 1990.

Bolton, Richard, ed. *Culture Wars.* New York: New Press, 1992.

Bolton, Richard. "Denial Isn't Just a River in Egypt." *High Performance* 17, no. 3 (Fall 1994): 12–13.

Borch-Jacobsen, Mikkel. *Lacan: The Absolute Master.* Trans. Douglas Brick. Stanford, Cal: Stanford University Press, 1981.

Boyer, Edward. "Bob Flanagan; Artist's Works Explored Pain." *Los Angeles Times*, 9 January 1996. Home ed., p. B10.

Brame, Gloria G., William D. Brame, and Jon Jacobs, eds. *Different Loving: The World of Sexual Dominance.* New York: Villard, 1996.

Brennan, Teresa, ed. *Between Feminism and Psychoanalysis.* London and New York: Routledge, 1989.

Breslauer, Jan. "The Body Politics." *Los Angeles Times*, 2 July 1994, Home ed., p. F.1.

Bright, Susie and Joani Blank. *Herotica 2.* New York: Penguin, 1992.

Bright, Susie, Joani Blank, and Jill Posener. *Nothing But the Girl: The Blatant Lesbian Image.* New York: Freedom, 1996.

——. *Susie Bright's Sexual Reality: A Virtual Sex World Reader.* Pittsburgh: Cleis, 1992.

——. *Susie Sexpert's Lesbian Sex World.* Pittsburgh: Cleis, 1990.

Brigman, William E. "Pornography as Political Expression." *Journal of Popular Culture* 17, no. 2 (1983): 129–134.

Bronski, Michael. *Culture Clash: The Making of a Gay Sensibility.* Boston: South End, 1984.

Brown, Beverley. "A Feminist Interest in Pornography: Some Modest Proposals." *m/f,* no. 5/6 (1981): pp. 5–18.

Brown, Jan. "Sex, Lies, and Penetration: A Butch Finally 'Fesses Up.'" In *The Persistent Desire: A Femme/Butch Reader,* ed. Joan Nestle, pp. 410–415. Boston: Alyson, 1992.

Brown, Wendy. "Feminist Hesitations, Postmodern Exposures." *differences: A Journal of Feminist Cultural Studies* 3, no. 1 (1991): 63–84.

Browning, Frank. "Boys in the Barracks." *Mother Jones* (March/April 1993): 24–25.

Burana, Lily. "Sandra Bernhard: Acting Lesbian." *Advocate* (15 December 1992): 66–73.

Butler, Judith. *Bodies That Matter.* New York and London: Routledge, 1993.

——. *Excitable Speech: A Politics of the Performative.* New York and London: Routledge, 1997.

——. "The Force of Fantasy: Feminism, Mapplethorpe, and Discursive Excess." *differences: A Journal of Feminist Cultural Studies* 2, no. 2 (1990): 105–125.

——. *Gender Trouble: Feminism and the Subversion of Identity.* New York: Routledge, 1990.

——. "The Lesbian Phallus and the Morphological Imaginary." *differences: A Journal of Feminist Cultural Studies,* "The Phallus Issue" 4, no. 1 (Spring 1992): 133–171.

Califia, Pat. "Anti Anti-Porn." *Off Our Backs* (October 1980): 25.

——, ed. *Doing It for Daddy: Short and Sexy Fiction About a Very Forbidden Fantasy.* Boston: Alyson, 1994.

——. "Feminism vs. Sex: A New Conservative Wave?" *Advocate* (21 February 1980): 13–15.

——. "Gay Men, Lesbians and Sex: Doing it Together." *Advocate* (7 July 1983): 24–26.

——. *The Lesbian S/M Safety Manual.* Boston: Lace, 1988.

——. *Macho Sluts.* Boston: Alyson, 1988.

——. *Melting Point: Short Stories.* Boston: Alyson, 1993.

——. "Pleasure/Pain and Power: A Lesbian's View." *Variations,* no. 1, special issue 5 (1979): 56–65.

——. *Public Sex: The Culture of Radical Sex.* Pittsburgh: Cleis, 1994.

——. "Radical Assessment." *Philadelphia Inquirer.* 4 October 1992, pp. M1, 6.

——. *Sapphistry: The Book of Lesbian Sexuality.* Tallahassee, Fla.: Naiad, 1980.

——. *Sensuous Magic: A Guide for Adventurous Couples.* New York: A Richard Kasak Book, 1993.

——. "Unraveling the Sexual Fringe: A Secret Side of Lesbian Sexuality." *Advocate* (27 December 1979): 19–23.

—— and Janine Fuller, eds. *Forbidden Passages: Writings Banned in Canada.* Introduction by Pat Califia and Janine Fuller. Pittsburgh: Cleis, 1995.

—— and Robin Sweeney. *The Second Coming: A Leatherdyke Reader.* Los Angeles: Alyson, 1996.

Cameron, Deborah. "Discourses of Desire: Liberals, Feminists, and the Politics of Pornography in the 1980s." *American Literary History* 2, no. 4 (Winter 1990): 784–798.

Capone, Janet. "Developing a Perspective: Lesbian Sadomasochism." *Bay Area Women's News* (March/April 1988): 22.

Card, Claudia. *Lesbian Choices.* New York: Columbia University Press, 1995.

Carr, C. "Washed in the Blood." *Village Voice,* 5 July 1994, p. 16.

Carter, Angela. *The Sadeian Woman and the Ideology of Pornography.* New York: Pantheon, 1978.

Caruth, Cathy. *Trauma: Explorations in Memory.* Baltimore and London: Johns Hopkins Press, 1995.

Case, Sue-Ellen. "The Student and the Strap: Authority and Seduction in the Class(room)." In *Professions of Desire,* ed. George E. Haggerty and Bonnie Zimmerman, pp. 39–46. New York: The Modern Language Association of America, 1995.

——. "Toward a Butch-Femme Aesthetic." In *Making a Spectacle,* Lynda Hart, ed., pp. 282–299. Ann Arbor: University of Michigan Press, 1989.

Chancer, Lynn S. *Sadomasochism in Everyday Life: The Dynamics of Power and Powerlessness.* New Brunswick, N.J.: Rutgers University Press, 1992.

Chasseguet-Smirgel, Janine. *Creativity and Perversion.* New York: Norton, 1984.

Clément, Catherine. *The Lives and Legends of Jacques Lacan.* Trans. Arthur Goldhammer. New York: Columbia University Press, 1983.

Cocks, Joan. "Augustine, Nietzsche, and Contemporary Body Politics." *differences: A Journal of Feminist Cultural Studies* 3, no. 1 (1991): 144–158.

Cooper, Dennis, ed. *Discontents: New Queer Writers.* New York: Amethyst, 1992.

Cooper, Dennis. "Flanagan's Wake." *Artforum* 24, no. 8 (April 1996): 74–77.

Cooper, Marc. "Queer Baiting in the Culture War." *Village Voice,* 13 October 1992, pp. 29–36.

Coover, Robert. *Spanking the Maid.* New York: Grove, 1982.

Cordova, Jeanne, ed. "Toward a Feminist Expression of Sado-Masochism." *Lesbian Tide* (November/December 1976): 14–17.

Cowie, Elizabeth. "Fantasia." In *The Woman in Question: M/f,* ed. Parveen Adams and Elizabeth Cowie, pp. 140–196. Cambridge: MIT Press, 1990.

Creet, Julia. "Daughter of the Movement: The Psychodynamics of Lesbian S/M Fantasy." *differences: A Journal of Feminist Cultural Studies* 3, no. 2 (Summer 1991): 135–159.

Crimp, Douglas. "Mourning and Militancy," OCTOBER 51 (Winter 1989): 3–18.

Croce, Arlene. "Discussing the Undiscussable." *New Yorker,* 26 December 1994, pp. 54–60.

——. Responses to Croce's "Discussing the Undiscussable": "Who's the Victim." *New Yorker,* 30 January 1995, pp. 10–13.

Cruikshank, Margaret, ed. *The Lesbian Path.* Monterey, Calif.: Angel, 1985.

Cubilié, Anne. "The Limits of Culture: Testimonial Literature and the Constraints of Human Rights Discourse." Ph.D. diss., University of Pennsylvania, 1995.

Cvetkovich, Ann. "Sexual Trauma/Queer Memory: Incest, Lesbianism, and Therapeutic Culture." *GLQ: A Journal of Lesbian and Gay Studies* 2 (20 October 1995): 351–377.

Davis, Katherine, for the Ministry of Truth. "What We Fear We Try to Keep Contained." Introduction to *Coming to Power: Writings and Graphics on Lesbian S/M*, ed. Samois, pp. 7–13. Boston: Alyson, 1982.

Davis, Robert Con, ed. *Lacan and Narration: The Psychoanalytic Difference in Narrative Theory.* Baltimore and London: Johns Hopkins University Press, 1983.

Dean, Tim. "The Psychoanalysis of AIDS." *OCTOBER* 63 (Winter 1993): 83–116.

Dejanikus, Tacie. "Our Legacy." *Off Our Backs* (November 1980): 6–8.

Delbo, Charlotte. *Who Will Carry the Word?* In *The Theater of the Holocaust*, ed. Robert Skloot, pp. 273–325. Madison: University of Wisconsin Press, 1982.

Deleuze, Gilles. *The Logic of Sense.* Trans. Mark Lester. New York: Columbia University Press, 1990.

——. *Masochism: Coldness and Cruelty.* New York: Zone, 1989.

——. "Plato and the Simulacrum." *OCTOBER* 27 (Winter 1983): 45–56.

——. "The Schizophrenic and Language: Surface and Depth in Lewis Carroll and Antonin Artaud." In *Literature and Psychoanalysis*, ed. Edith Kurzweil and William Phillips, pp. 324–339. New York: Columbia University Press, 1983.

DeLynn, Jane. *Don Juan in the Village.* New York: Pantheon, 1990.

De Lauretis, Teresa. *Alice Doesn't.* Bloomington: Indiana University Press, 1984.

——. *The Practice of Love: Lesbian Sexuality and Perverse Desire.* Bloomington: Indiana University Press, 1994.

Derrida, Jacques. "The Theater of Cruelty and the Closure of Representation." In *Writing and Difference*, trans. Alan Bass, pp. 234. Chicago: University of Chicago Press, 1978.

——. "Women in the Beehive: A Seminar." *Men in Feminism*, ed. Alice Jardine and Paul Smith, pp. 189–203. New York: Methuen, 1987.

Dhairyam, Sagri. "Racing the Lesbian, Dodging White Critics." In *The Lesbian Postmodern*, ed. Laura Doan, pp. 25–46. New York: Columbia University Press, 1994.

Diamond, Elin. "Mimesis, Mimicry, and the 'True-Real.' " *Modern Drama* 32, no. 1 (March 1989): 58–72. Reprinted in *Acting Out: Feminist Performances*, ed. Lynda Hart and Peggy Phelan, pp. 363–382. Ann Arbor: University of Michigan Press, 1993.

Doan, Laura. *The Lesbian Postmodern.* New York: Columbia University Press, 1994.

Doane, Mary Ann. *The Desire to Desire: The Woman's Film of the 1940s.* Bloomington: Indiana University Press, 1987.

Dollimore, Jonathan. "Sex and Death." *Textual Practice* 9, no. 1 (Spring 1995): 27–54.

——. *Sexual Dissidence: Augustine to Wilde, Freud to Foucault.* Oxford: Clarendon, 1991.

Douglas, Ann. "Soft Porn Culture." *New Republic* 30 (August 1980): 25–29.

Douglas, Carol Anne. *Love and Politics: Radical Feminist and Lesbian Theories.* San Francisco: Ism Press, 1990.

Drier, Deborah. "Rack Talk." *Artforum* 24, no. 8 (April 1996): 78–81.

Duberman, Martin Bauml. " 'I Am Not Contented': Female Masochism and Lesbianism in Early Twentieth-Century England." In *Women, Sex, and Sexuality*, ed. Catherine Stimpson and Ethel Spector Person, pp. 308–324. Chicago: University of Chicago Press, 1980.

Dubin, Steven. *Arresting Images: Impolitic Art and Uncivil Actions*. London and New York: Routledge, 1992.

Duggan, Lisa, and Nan Hunter. *Sex Wars: Sexual Dissent and Political Culture*. New York: Routledge, 1995.

Durell, Anna. "Uproar over Violent Images." *New Statesman* 109 (14 June 1985): 16–17.

Dworkin, Andrea. *Intercourse*. New York: Free Press, 1987.

Echols, Alice. *Daring to Be Bad: Radical Feminism in America 1967–1975*. Minneapolis: University of Minnesota Press, 1989.

Edwards, Tim. "Sado-Masochism, Masculinity, and the Problem of Pornography." In *Erotics and Politics: Gay Male Sexuality, Masculinity and Feminism*, ed. Tim Edwards, pp. 74–89. New York: Routledge, 1994.

Ellis, Havelock. *Studies in the Psychology of Sex*. Vol. 2, *Sexual Inversion*. Philadelphia: F. A. Davis, 1904.

Elwin, Rosamund and Karen Tulchinsky, eds. *Tangled Sheets: Stories and Poems of Lesbian Lust*. Toronto: Women's Press, 1995.

English, Deirdre, Amber Hollibaugh, and Gayle Rubin. "Talking Sex." *Socialist Review* 11 (4) (July/August 1981): 43–62.

Epstein, Mark. *Thoughts Without a Thinker*. New York: Basic Books, 1995.

Escoffier, Jeffrey. "Inside The Ivory Closet: The Challenges Facing Lesbian and Gay Studies." *Out/look* 10 (Fall 1990): 40–48.

Esterberg, Kristing Gay. "From Illness to Action: Conceptions of Homosexuality in *The-Ladder*, 1956–1965." *Journal of Sex Research* 2, no. 1 (February 1990): 65–80.

Evans, Jamie Lee. "Rodney King, Racism, and the S/M Culture of America." In *Unleashing Feminism: Critiquing Lesbian Sadomasochism in the Gay Nineties*, ed. Irene Reti, pp. 74–78. Santa Cruz: Her Books, 1993.

Everywoman 1, no. 3 (19 June 1970): 8.

Faderman, Lillian. *Odd Girls and Twilight Lovers: A History of Lesbian Life in Twentieth-Century America*. New York: Columbia University Press, 1991.

Farr, Susan. "The Art of Discipline: Creating Erotic Dramas of Play and Power." In *Coming to Power: Writings and Graphics on Lesbian S/M*, ed. Samois, pp. 181–189. Boston: Alyson, 1982.

Felman, Shoshana. *The Literary Speech Act*. Trans. Catherine Porter. Ithaca: Cornell University Press, 1983.

——. *What Does a Woman Want?: Reading and Sexual Difference*. Baltimore: Johns Hopkins University Press, 1993.

——. and Dori Laub. *Testimony: Crises of Witnessing in Literature, Psychoanalysis, and History*. New York: Routledge, 1992.

Findlay, Heather. "Freud's 'Fetishism' and the Lesbian Dildo Debates." In *Out in Culture: Gay, Lesbian, and Queer Essays on Popular Culture*, ed. Corey K. Creekmur and Alexander Doty, pp. 328–342. Durham and London: Duke University Press, 1995.

Fineman, Joel. "The Structure of Allegorical Desire." In *Allegory and Representation*, ed. Stephen J. Greenblatt, pp. 26–60. Baltimore: Johns Hopkins University Press, 1981.

Flanagan, Bob. *Fuck Journal*. New York: Hanuman Books, 1987.

Flanagan, Bob. "Pain Journal [excerpts]." *Artforum* 34, no. 8 (April 1996): pp. 74–81.

Foucault, Michel. *Foucault Live: Interviews, 1961–1984)*. Trans. Lysa Hochroth and John Johnston, ed. Sylvère Lotringer. New York: Semiotext(e), 1966.

——. *The History of Sexuality: An Introduction*. Vol. 1. New York: Vintage, 1980.

——. "Sexual Choice, Sexual Act: An Interview." *Salmagundi* 58/59 (Fall 1982/Winter 1983): 10–24.

——. "Theatrum Philosophicum." In *Language, Counter-Memory, Practice: Selected Essays and Interviews*, trans. Donald F. Bouchord and Sherry Simon, ed. Donald F. Bouchord, pp. 165–196. Ithaca: Cornell University Press, 1977.

——. *This Is Not a Pipe*. Trans. and ed. James Harkness. Berkeley: University of California Press, 1982.

Franklin, Deborah. "The Politics of Masochism." *Psychology Today* 21 (January 1987): 53–57.

Freedman, Estelle, Barbra Gelpi, Susan Johnson, and Kathleen Weston, eds. *The Lesbian Issue: Essays from Signs*. Chicago and London: The University of Chicago Press, 1985.

Freud, Anna. "Beating Fantasies and Daydreams." In *Essential Papers on Masochism*, ed. Margaret Ann Fitzpatrick Hanly, pp. 286–299. New York: New York University Press, 1995.

Freud, Sigmund. "A Child is Being Beaten." *The Standard Edition of the Complete Psychological Works of Sigmund Freud*. Trans. and ed. James Strachey, 17:175–204. London: Hogarth, 1955. (Hereafter referenced as *SE*.)

——. "Civilization and Its Discontents." *SE* 21:57–145.

——. "Economic Problem in Masochism." *SE* 19:155–172.

——. "Instincts and Their Vicissitudes." *SE* 14:109–140.

——. "On Fetishism." *SE* 21:149–157.

Frye, Marilyn. *The Politics of Reality: Essays in Feminist Theory*. New York: Crossing Press, 1983.

Fuss, Diana. *Essentially Speaking*. New York: Routledge, 1989.

——. "Fashion and the Homo-Spectatorial Look." *Critical Inquiry* 18 (Summer 1992): 713–737.

——. *Inside/Out: Lesbian Theories, Gay Theories*. New York: Routledge, 1991.

Fussell, Paul. *Poetic Meter and Poetic Form*. New York: Random House, 1979.

Gallop, Jane. *Around 1981*. New York: Routledge, 1992.

Gibbs, Liz, ed. *Daring to Dissent: Lesbian Culture from Margin to Mainstream*. London and New York: Cassell, 1994.

Girard, René. "Narcissism: The Freudian Myth Demythified by Proust." In *Literature and Psychoanalysis*, ed. Edith Kurzweil and William Philips, pp. 363–377. New York: Columbia University Press, 1983.

Gibson, Pamela Church and Roma Gibson, eds. *Dirty Looks: Women, Pornography, Power*. London: BFI, 1993.

Goffman, Erving. *Frame Analysis: An Essay on the Organization of Experience*. Cambridge: Harvard University Press, 1974.

Goldsby, Jackie. "What It Means To Be Colored Me." *Out/Look* 9 (Summer 1990): 9–17.

Greene, Gerald and Caroline. *S/M: The Last Taboo*. New York: Grove, 1974.

Grewal, Inderpal and Caren Kaplan, eds,. *Scattered Hegemonies: Postmodernity and Transitional Feminist Practices*. Minneapolis: University of Minnesota Press, 1994.

Griffin, Gabriele. *Heavenly Love?: Lesbian Images in Twentieth-Century Women's Writing*. New York: St. Martin's, 1993.

Griffin, Susan. "Sadomasochism and the Erosion of Self: A Critical Reading of *Story of O*." In *Against Sadomasochism: A Radical Feminist Analysis*, ed. Robin Linden, Darlene Pagano, Diana Russell, and Susan Star, pp. 184–201. East Palo Alto: Frog In the Well, 1982.

Grosz, Elizabeth. *Jacques Lacan: A Feminist Introduction*. London: Routledge, 1990.

Grosz, Elizabeth A., and Elspeth Probyn, eds. *Sexy Bodies: The Strange Carnalities of Feminism*. London and New York: Routledge, 1995.

Grosz, Elizabeth A. *Space, Time, and Perversion: Essays on the Politics of Bodies*. New York: Routledge, 1995.

——. *Volatile Bodies*. Bloomington: Indiana University Press, 1994.

Groves, Amy, Judith Zutz, Terry Kolb, and Ian Young. "Lesbian S&M: Valverde Roasted." *The Body Politic* (April 1980): 4–5.

Gubar, Susan. "Representing Pornography: Feminism, Criticism, and Depictions of Female Violation." *Critical Inquiry* 13, no. 4 (Summer 1987): 712–741.

Gundermann, Christina. "Orientalism, Homophobia, Masochism: Transfers between Pierre Loti's *Aziyade* and Gilles Deleuze's 'Coldness and Cruelty.' " *Diacritics* 24, no. 32, special eds. Judith Butler and Biddy Martin (Summer/Fall 1994): 151–168.

Hacker, Marilyn. *Selected Poems: 1965–1990*. New York: Norton, 1994.

Haggerty, George E. and Bonnie Zimmerman, eds. *Professions of Desire*. New York: Modern Language Association of America, 1995.

Halberstam, Judith. "Imagined Violence/Queer Violence: Representation, Rage, and Resistance." *Social Text* 37 (Winter 1993): 187–201.

Hall, Stuart, et al. *Policing the Crisis: Mugging, the State, and Law and Order*. London: MacMillan, 1978.

Hamer, Diane and Belinda Budge, eds. *The Good, the Bad, and the Gorgeous: Popular Culture's Romance with Lesbianism*. London: Pandora, 1994.

Hammond, Harmony. "A Sense of Touch." *Heresies* 3, no. 4 (1981): 44.

Hanly, Margaret Ann Fitzpatrick, ed. *Essential Papers on Masochism*. New York and London: New York University Press, 1995.

Haraway, Donna. *Simians, Cyborgs, and Women: The Reinvention of Nature*. New York: Routledge, 1991.

Hart, Jeffrey. "Reflections on Pornography." *Partisan Review* 52, no. 4 (1985): 414–420.

Hart, Lynda, and Peggy Phelan, eds. *Acting Out: Feminist Performances*. Ann Arbor: University of Michigan Press, 1993.

——. *Fatal Women: Lesbian Sexuality and the Mark of Aggression*. Princeton: Princeton University and London: Routledge, 1994.

——. "Karen Finley's Dirty Work: Censorship, Homophobia, and the NEA." GEN-DERS 14 (Fall 1992): 1–15.

——. *Making a Spectacle: Feminist Essays on Contemporary Women's Theater*. Ann Arbor: University of Michigan Press, 1989.

——. Review of Bill Thompson, *Sadomasochism: Painful Perversion or Pleasurable Play?* [London: Cassell, 1994] in *Journal of the History of Sexuality*, vol. 6 (October 1995): 336–338.

Hartman, Geoffrey. *Criticism in the Wilderness*. New Haven:Yale University Press, 1981.

Harvey, Penelope, and Peter Gow, eds. *Sex and Violence: Issues in Representation and Experience*. London: Routledge, 1994.

Haug, Frigga. *Beyond Female Masochism*. London and New York: Verso, 1992.

Hegel, G. W. F. *Phenomenology of Spirit*. Trans. A. V. Miller. Oxford: Oxford University Press, 1977.

Henderson, Lisa. "Lesbian Pornography: Cultural Transgression and Sexual Demystification." In *New Lesbian Criticism*, ed. Sally Munt, pp. 173–192. New York: Columbia University Press, 1992.

Hite, Shere. *The Hite Report on the Family: Growing Up Under Patriarchy*. New York: Grove, 1994.

Hollibaugh, Amber, and Cherríe Moraga. "What We're Rolling Around in Bed With." *Heresies*, no. 12, "Sex Issue" (1981): 58–62.

Hopkins, Patrick D. "Rethinking Sadomasochism: Feminism, Interpretation, and Simulation." *Hypatia* 9, no. 1 (Winter 1994): 116–139.

hooks, bell. *Black Looks: Race and Representation*. Boston: South End, 1992.

Houlberg, Rick. "The Magazine of a Sadomasochism Club: The Tie that Binds." *Journal of Homosexuality* 21, no. 1–2 (1991): 167–183.

Hunt, Margaret, "The De-Eroticization of Women's Liberation: Social Purity Movements and the Revolutionary Feminism of Sheila Jeffreys." *Feminist Review*, no. 34 (Spring 1990): 23–46.

Irigaray, Luce. *Sexes and Genealogies*. Trans. Gillian C. Gill. New York: Columbia University Press, 1993.

——. *Speculum of the Other Woman*. Trans. Gillian C. Gill. Ithaca: Cornell University Press, 1985.

——. *This Sex Which Is Not One*. Trans. Catherine Porter. Ithaca: Cornell University Press, 1985.

Jagose, Annamarie. *Lesbian Utopics*. New York: Routledge, 1994.

Jameson, Fredric. "Nostalgia for the Present." *South Atlantic Quarterly* 88, no. 2 (Spring 1989): 517–537.

——. *Postmodernism; or, the Cultural Logic of Late Capitalism*. Durham: Duke University Press, 1991.

Jardine, Alice, and Paul Smith. *Men In Feminism*. New York and London: Methuen, 1987.

Jay, Karla, ed. *Lesbian Erotics*. New York and London: New York University Press, 1995.

Jeffreys, Sheila. "How Orgasm Politics has Hijacked the Women's Movement." *On the Issues: The Progressive Woman's Quarterly* 5, no. 2 (Spring 1996): 18–21.

———. *The Lesbian Heresy: A Feminist Perspective On the Lesbian Sexual Revolution.* North Melbourne, Australia: Spinifex: 1993.

Jetter, Alexis. "The Roseanne of Literature." *New York Times Magazine*, December 17, 1995, pp. 54–57.

Juno, Andrea and V. Vale. *RE/Search People Series.* Vol. 1, "Bob Flanagan, Super-Masochist." San Francisco: RE/Search Publications, 1993.

Kaplan, Caren. "Resisting Autobiography: Out-Law Genres and Transitional Feminist Subjects." In *De/Colonizing the Subject: The Politics of Gender in Women's Auto-biography,* ed. Sidonie Smith and Julia Watson, pp. 115–138. Minneapolis: University of Minnesota Press, 1992.

Kasindorf, Jeanie Russell. "Lesbian Chic: The Bold, Brave New World Of Gay Women." *New York* 26 (10 May 1993): 30–37.

Kauffman, Linda S. "Bob Flanagan's Sadomedicine." In *Obscenity/Divinity: Two Girls Review* 1, no. 2 (1995/96): 112–121.

Katz, Jonathan Ned. *Gay American History: Lesbians and Gay Men in the United States.* New York: Meridian, 1992.

Kaye, Elizabeth. "What Women Think of Other Women." *Esquire* 118, no. 2 (August 1992): 94–105.

Kennedy, Elizabeth, and Madeline Davis. *Boots of Leather, Slippers of Gold: The History of the Lesbian Community.* New York and London: Routledge, 1993.

Kerr, Barbara T. "Too Much S/M-Hating." *Off Our Backs* (February 1981): 27.

Kimmelman, Michael. "Tattoo Moves From Fingers To Fashion But Is It Art?" *New York Times*, 15 September 1995, p. C.1.

King, Katie. "The Situation of Lesbianism as Feminism's Magical Sign: Contests for Meaning and the U.S. Women's Movement, 1968–1972." *Communication* 9 (1986): 65–91.

———. *Theory in its Feminist Travels: Conversations in U.S. Women's Movements.* Bloomington: Indiana University Press, 1994.

Klossowski, Pierre. *Sade My Neighbor.* Trans. Alphonso Lingis. Evanston: Northwestern University Press, 1991.

Knight, Christopher. " 'Narcissistic': Art for Artist's Sake." *Los Angeles Times*, 14 February 1995, Home edition, part F., p. 1.

Kofman, Sarah. *The Enigma of Woman: Woman in Freud's Writings.* Trans. Catherine Porter. Ithaca: Cornell University Press, 1985.

Kojeve, Alexandre. *Introduction to the Reading of Hegel: Lectures on the Phenomenology of Spirit.* Assembled by Raymond Queneau, trans. James H. Nichols, ed. Allan Bloom. New York: Basic Books, 1969.

Kristeva, Julia. "About Chinese Women." In *The Kristeva Reader,* ed. Toril Moi, pp. 139–159. New York: Columbia University Press, 1986.

Krystal, Henry. "Integration and Self-Healing in Post-Traumatic States: A Ten Year Retrospective." *American Imago: Studies in Psychoanalysis and Culture* 48, no. 1 (Spring 1991): 93–118.

Kushner, Tony. Letter to the Editor. *New Yorker*, 30 January 1995, p. 11.

Lacan, Jacques. "God and the *Jouissance* of The Woman: A Love Letter." In *Feminine Sexuality: Jacques Lacan and the école freudienne*, trans. Jacqueline Rose, ed. Jacqueline Rose and Juliet Mitchell, pp. 137–161. New York: Norton, 1985.

——. "The Meaning of the Phallus." In *Feminine Sexuality: Jacques Lacan and the école freudienne*, trans. Jacqueline Rose, ed. Jacqueline Rose and Juliet Mitchell, pp. 74–85. New York: Norton, 1985.

——. *Le Seminaire III: Les Psychoses*. Paris: Seuil, 1981.

——. *Seminar VII: The Ethics of Psychoanalysis 1959–1960*. Trans. Dennis Porter, ed. Jacques-Alain Miller. New York and London: Norton, 1986.

——. *The Seminar of Jacques Lacan Book II: The Ego in Freud's Theory and in the Technique of Psychoanalysis 1954–1955*. Trans. Sylvana Tomaselli, ed. Jacques-Alain Miller. New York: Norton, 1988.

Lady Winston, ed. *The Leading Edge*. Denver: Lace, 1987.

Lamos, Colleen. "The Postmodern Lesbian Position: 'On Our Backs.'" In *The Lesbian Postmodern*, ed. Laura Doan, pp. 85–103. New York: Columbia University Press, 1994.

Lane, Alycee J. "What's Race Got to Do with It?" In *Black Lace* 2 (Summer 1991): 21.

Lanzmann, Claude. "Seminar with Claude Lanzmann, 11 April, 1990." *Yale French Studies* 79 *Literature and the Ethical Question*, ed. Claire Nouvet (1991): 82–99.

Laplanche, Jean. *Life & Death in Psychoanalysis*. Trans. Jeffrey Mehlman. Baltimore and London: Johns Hopkins University Press, 1970.

——. and Jean-Bertrand Pontalis. "Fantasy and the Origins of Sexuality." In *Formations of Fantasy*, ed. Victor Burgin, James Donald, and Cora Kaplan, pp. 5–34. New York: Metheun, 1986.

Lasher, Liz. "Hot Buttered Bum." *Bad Attitude* 7, no. 4 (1991): 21–23.

Leidholdt, Dorchen. "Lesbian S/M: Sexual Radicalism or Reaction." *New Women's Times* (July/August 1982): 95.

Lewis, Reina and Karen Adler. "Come To Me Baby; Or, What's Wrong with Lesbian S/M." *Women Studies International Forum* 17, no. 4 (1994): 433–441.

Linden, Robin Ruth, et. al. *Against Sadomasochism: A Radical Feminist Analysis*. East Palo Alto: Frog in the Well, 1982.

Lingis, Alphonso. *Abuses*. Berkeley: University of California Press, 1994.

——. *Deathbound Subjectivity*. Bloomington: Indiana University Press, 1989.

——. *Excesses: Eros and Culture*. Albany: State University of New York Press, 1983.

Los Angeles Times. "HIV-Infected Artist's Show Draws Anger of 2 Senators." 21 June 1994, Home Ed., part A, p.7.

MacKinnon, Catherine A. *Feminism Unmodified: Discourses on Life and Law*. Cambridge: Harvard University Press, 1987.

Macvey, Carol. "Who's the Victim?" *New Yorker*, 30 January 1995, p. 13.

Maggiore, Dolores J. *Lesbianism: An Annotated Bibliography and Guide to the Literature, 1976–1986*. Metuchen, N.J.: Scarecrow, 1988.

Mains, Geoff. *Urban Aboriginals*. Gay Sunshine, 1984.

Marcus, Maria. *A Taste for Pain: On Masochism and Female Sexuality*. Trans. Joan Tate. New York: St. Martin's, 1981.

Marissa. "S/M Relationships." *Out and About* (December 1981), n.p.

Marks, Elaine, and Isabelle de Courtivron. "Introduction I: Discourses of Anti-Feminism and Feminism." In *New French Feminisms*, ed. Marks and Courtivron, pp. 3–8. New York: Schoken, 1981.

Martin, Biddy. "Sexualities without Genders and Other Queer Utopias." *Diacritics* 24, no. 2, special eds. Judith Butler and Biddy Martin (Summer/Fall 1994): 104–121.

Mason, Rose, Karen Simms and Darlene R. Pagano. "Racism and Sadomasochism: A Conversation with Two Black Lesbians." In *Against Sadomasochism: A Radical Feminist Analysis*, ed. Robin Ruth Linden, et al., pp.99–106. East Palo Alto: Frog in the Well, 1982.

Mass, Lawrence. *Dialogues of the Revolution*, New York: Haworth, 1990.

McClintock, Anne. "Maid to Order: Commercial S/M and Gender Power." In *Dirty Looks: Women, Pornography, Power*, ed. Pamela Church Gibson and Roma Gibson, pp. 207–231. London: British Film Institute, 1993.

McCormack, Thelma. "Keeping Our Sex 'Safe': Anti-Censorship Strategies vs. the Politics of Protection." *Fireweed, Sex, and Sexuality* 1 (Winter 1993): 25–34.

Megan, Carolyn E. "Moving Toward Truth: An Interview with Dorothy Allison." *Kenyon Review*, no. 16 (Fall 1994): 71–83.

Merck, Mandy. *Perversions: Deviant Readings*. New York: Routledge, 1993.

Merkin, Daphne. "Unlikely Obsession." *New Yorker*, "Special Women's Issue," 26 February and 4 March 1996, pp. 98–115.

Michelson, Peter. "Women and Pornorotica." *Another Chicago Magazine* 16 (1986): 131–176.

Miller, Alice. *Pictures of a Childhood: Sixty-Six Water Colors and an Essay*. Trans. Hildegarde Hannum. New York: Farrar, Straus and Giroux, 1986.

Miller, D. A. "Anal Rope." In *Inside/Out: Lesbian Theories, Gay Theories*, ed. Diana Fuss, pp. 119–141. New York: Routledge, 1991,

Miller, Jacques-Alain, ed. *The Seminar of Jacques Lacan, Book 1: Freud's Papers on Technique 1953–1954*. Trans. John Forrester. Cambridge: Cambridge University Press, 1988.

Miller, Neil. *Out of the Past: Gay and Lesbian History from 1869 to the Present*. New York: Vintage, 1995.

Miller, Richard B. "Violent Pornography: Mimetic Nihlism and the Eclipse of Differences." *Soundings* 69 (1986): 326–346.

Modleski, Tania. *Feminism Without Women: Culture and Criticism in a "Postfeminist" Age*. New York: Routledge, 1991.

Mohanty, S. P. "Us and Them: On the Philosophical Bases of Political Criticism." *Yale Journal of Criticism* 2, no. 2 (Spring 1989): 1–31.

Moll, Dr. Albert. *Perversions of the Sex Instinct*. Trans. Maurice Popkin, Ph.D. Newark: Julian, 1931.

Montgomery, Jill D., and Ann C. Grief, eds. *Masochism: The Treatment of Self-Inflicted Suffering*. Madison, Conn.: International Universities Press, 1989.

Mood, John L. *Rilke on Love and Other Difficulties*. New York: Norton, 1975.

Moraga, Cherríe. *Loving in the War Years*. Boston: South End, 1983.

———. and Gloria Anzaldúa. *This Bridge Called My Back.* New York: Kitchen Table: Women of Color Press, 1981.

Ms. 4, no. 4 (January/February 1994).

Mulvey, Laura. *Visual and Other Pleasures.* Bloomington: Indiana University Press, 1989.

Munster, Anna. "Toward a Theater of Queer Operations." Paper presented at *Performing Sexualities,* The Performance Space, Sydney, Australia, 16 July 1994, p. 1. (A portion of this paper is published in *Kink* [Sydney, Australia: Wicked Women Publications, 1993].)

Murphy, Melissa. "The *On Our Backs* Interview: Dorothy Allison." *On Our Backs* (July/August 1993): 23–24, 40–43.

Natalie, Andrea, "The Stonewall Riots." Cartoon illustrating editorial by Jasmine Sterling. "The Sex Wars Rage On. . . ." *Bad Attitude* 7, no. 1, (January 1991): 2.

National Organization for Women. "Lesbian and Gay Rights," 1980 manifesto. Reprinted in *Heresies* 3, no. 4 (1981): 92.

Neisen, Joseph. "Heterosexism or Homophobia?: The Power of the Language We Use." *Outlook* 10 (Fall 1990): pp. 36–37.

Nietzsche, Friedrich. *The Genealogy of Morals.* Trans. Francis Golffing. New York: Doubleday, 1956.

Nestle, Joan, ed. *The Persistent Desire: A Femme/Butch Reader.* Boston: Alyson, 1992.

———. *A Restricted Country.* Ithaca. Firebrand, 1987.

Nunokawa, Jeff. "*In Memoriam* and the Extinction of the Homosexual." *English Literary History* 58, no. 2 (1991): 427–438.

O'Connor, Noreen and Joanna Ryan. *Wild Desires and Mistaken Identities: Lesbianism and Psychoanalysis.* New York: Columbia University Press, 1993.

Oikawa, Mona, Dionne Falconer, and Ann Decter. *Resist: Essays Against a Homophobic Culture.* Ontario: Women's Press, 1994.

Orlando, Lisa. "Power Plays: Coming to Terms With Lesbian S/M." *Village Voice,* 26 July 1983, pp. 39–40.

Outrageous Women: A Journal of Woman-to-Woman S/M, vol. 1, no. 1 through vol. 3, no. 3 (1984–1987).

Pagel, David. " 'Rearwards': An Irreverent Assault on Culture." *Los Angeles Times,* 22 August 1991, Home Ed., part F10, col. 1.

Parachini, Allan, and Joe Velazquez. "Federal Funding of Controversial Art Defended." *Los Angeles Times,* 6 March 1990, Home Ed., part F, p. 1.

Pavis, Patrice. "Production, Reception, and the Social Context." In *On Referring in Literature,* ed. Anna Whiteside and Michael Issacharoff, pp. 122–137. Bloomington: Indiana University Press, 1987.

Penelope, Julia ed. *Out of the Class Closet: Lesbians Speak.* Freedom, Calif.: Crossing Press, 1994.

Phelan, Peggy. *Unmarked: The Politics of Performance.* New York: Routledge, 1993.

Phelan, Shane. *Identity Politics: Lesbian Feminism and the Limits of Community.* Philadelphia: Temple University Press, 1989.

Plant, Richard. *The Pink Triangle: The Nazi War Against Homosexuals.* New York: Holt, 1986.

"The Power and the Pride." *Newsweek*, 21 June 1993, pp. 54–60.

Queen, Carol. "Exploring Erotic Personas," *Taste of Latex* 13 (Spring 1996): 11–13.

Radway, Janice A. *Reading the Romance: Women, Patriarchy, and Popular Literature.* Chapel Hill and London: University of North Carolina Press, 1984.

Randall, Margaret. *This Is About Incest.* New York: Firebrand, 1987.

Rajchman, John. *Truth and Eros: Foucault, Lacan, and the Question of Ethics.* New York: Routledge, 1991.

Reik, Theodor. *Masochism in Modern Man.* Trans. Margaret H. Beigel. New York: Farrar, Straus, 1941.

Reti, Irene, ed. *Unleashing Feminism: Critiquing Lesbian Sadomasochism in the Gay Nineties.* Santa Cruz: Her Books, 1993.

Rhoads, Heather. "Cruel Crusade: The Hollywood War Against Lesbians and Gays." *Progressive* 18 (March 1993): 18–23.

Rich, Frank. "Dance of Death: Arlene Croce Sits this One out." *New York Times*, 8 January 1995, section 4, p. 19.

——. "Trail of Lies." *New York Times*, 4 July 1994, p. 17.

Rich, Ruby B. "Feminism and Sexuality in the 1980s." *Feminist Studies* 12, no. 3 (1986): 525–561.

Riviere, Joan. "Womanliness As A Masquerade." (1929). Reprinted in *Formations of Fantasy*, ed. Victor Burgin, James Donald, and Cora Kaplan, pp. 35–44. London: Methuen, 1986.

Roof, Judith. *A Lure of Knowledge: Lesbian Sexuality and Theory.* New York: Columbia University Press, 1991.

Ross, Andrew. *No Respect: Intellectuals and Popular Culture.* New York and London: Routledge, 1989.

Rowe, Michael. "We're As American As You Can Get." *Harvard Gay and Lesbian Review* 2, no. 1 (Winter 1995): 5–10.

Rubin, Gayle. "The Leather Menace: Comments on Politics and S/M." In *Coming to Power: Writings and Graphics on Lesbian S/M*, ed. Samois, pp. 192–227. Boston: Alyson, 1982.

——. "Thinking Sex: Notes for a Radical Theory of the Politics of Sexuality." In *Pleasure and Danger: Exploring Female Sexuality*, ed. Carole Vance, pp. 267–319. Boston: Routledge, 1982.

Russell, Diana E. H., ed. *Making Violence Sexy: Feminist Views on Pornography.* Buckingham: Open University Press, 1993.

Sacher-Masoch, Leopold. *Venus in Furs.* New York: Zone, 1989.

Samois, ed. *Coming to Power: Writings and Graphics on Lesbian S/M.* Boston: Alyson, 1982.

——. *What Color Is Your Handkerchief? A Lesbian S/M Sexuality Reader.* Berkeley: Samois, 1979.

Saylor, Douglas B. *The Sadomasochistic Homotext: Readings in Sade, Balzac, and Proust.* New York: P. Lang, 1993.

Scarry, Elaine. *The Body in Pain: The Making and Unmaking of the World.* New York: Oxford University Press, 1985.

Schleifer, Ronald. "The Space and Dialogue of Desire: Lacan, Greimas, and Narrative Temporality." In *Lacan and Narration: The Psychoanalytic Difference in Narrative Theory*, ed. Robert Con Davis, pp. 871–890. Baltimore and London: Johns Hopkins University Press, 1983.

Scholder, Amy, and Ira Silverberg, eds. *High Risk: An Anthology of Forbidden Writings*. New York: Plume, 1991.

Schor, Naomi. "This Essentialism Which Is Not One" *differences: A Journal of Feminist Cultural Studies* 1, no. 2 (1989): 38–58.

Schrim, Janet. "Lesbian S/M: Two Perspectives." *Gay Community News*, 9 May 1981, pp. 8–9.

Sedgwick, Eve Kosofsky. *Epistemology of the Closet*. Berkeley: University of California Press, 1991.

———. "A Poem is Being Written." *Representations* 17 (Winter 1987): 110–143. Reprinted in Sedgwick, *Tendencies*, Durham: Duke University Press, 1993.

———. "Queer Performativity: Henry James's *The Art of the Novel*." *GLQ: A Journal of Gay and Lesbian Studies* 1, no. 1 (1993): 1–15.

———. and Adam Frank. "Shame in the Cybernetic Fold: Reading Silvan Tomkins." *Critical Inquiry* 21, no. 2 (Winter 1995): 496–522.

———. *Tendencies*. Durham: Duke University Press, 1993.

Seltzer, Mark. *Bodies and Machines*. New York and London: Routledge, 1992.

"The Sex Issue." *Heresies: A Feminist Publication on Art and Politics* 3, no. 4 (1981).

Sexton, Anne. *Live or Die*. Boston: Houghton Mifflin Company, 1966.

Silverman, Kaja. *Male Subjectivity at the Margins*. New York: Routledge, 1992.

Sinden, Donald. *The Everyman Book of Theatrical Anecdotes*. London and Melbourne: Dent, 1987.

Smith, Anna Marie. "The Imaginary Inclusion of the Assimilable 'Good' Homosexual: The British New Right's Representations of Sexuality and Race." *Diacritics* 24, no. 2, special eds. Judith Butler and Biddy Martin (Summer/Fall 1994): 58–70.

Smith, Roberta. "Bob Flanagan, 43, Performer Who Created Art From His Pain." *New York Times*, 6 January 1996, section 1, p. 26.

Smyth, Cherry. "Crossing the Tracks." *Perversions* 1 (Winter 1994): 42–53.

———. ed. *Damn Fine Art*. London: Cassell, 1996.

———. *Lesbians Talk Queer Notions*. London: Scarlet, 1992.

———. "The Pleasure Threshold: Looking at Lesbian Pornography on Film." *Feminist Review*, no.34 (Spring 1990): 152–160.

Snitow, Ann Barr, and Sharon Thompson. *Powers of Desire: The Politics of Sexuality*. New York: Monthly Review, 1983.

Solomon, Alisa. "Dykotomies." *Village Voice*, 26 June 1990, pp. 39–40.

Solomon, Robert C., and Kathleen M. Higgins, eds. *The Philosophy of Erotic Love*. Lawrence: University of Kansas Press, 1991.

Sommer, Dorris. " 'Not Just a Personal Story': Women's Testimonies and the Plural Self." In *Life/lines: Theorizing Women's Autobiography*, ed. Bella Brodzki and Celeste Schenck, pp. 107–130. Ithaca: Cornell University Press, 1988.

Spivak, Gayatri. "Subaltern Studies: Deconstructing Historiography." In *In Other Worlds: Essays in Cultural Politics*, pp. 197–221. New York: Methuen, 1987.

Stamps, Wickie. "Stormy Leather: Leatherdykes and Leathermen Talk About Their Lives and Lusts." *Gay Community News* 16, no. 35 (March 1989): 19–25.

Stanley, Ellis. "Misogyny in Drag." *Off Our Backs* (February 1981): 27.

Steiner, Wendy. *The Scandal of Pleasure: Art in the Age of Fundamentalism.* Chicago: University of Chicago Press, 1995.

Sterling, Jasmine, "The Sex Wars Rage On." *Bad Attitude* 7, no. 1 (December/January 1991): 2.

Stewart, Susan. "The Marquis de Meese." *Critical Inquiry* 15, no. 1 (Autumn 1988): 162–192.

Stoller, Robert J., M.D. *Pain and Passion: A Psychoanalyst Explores the World of S & M.* New York and London: Plenum, 1991.

Taormino, Tristan, ed. *Best Lesbian Erotica 1996*, selected and introduced by Heather Lewis. Pittsburgh: Cleis, 1996.

Taylor, Valerie. *Journey to Fulfillment.* Tallahassee: Naiad, 1982.

Terdiman, Richard. *Present Modernity and the Past Memory Crisis.* Ithaca: Cornell University Press, 1993.

Thompson, Bill. *Sadomasochism: Painful Pleasure or Pleasurable Play?* New York: Cassell, 1995.

Thompson, Mark, ed. *Leatherfolk: Radical Sex, People, Politics and Practice.* Boston: Alyson, 1991.

Toolin, Cynthia. "Attitudes Toward Pornography: What Have the Feminists Missed?" *Journal of Popular Culture* 17, no. 2 (Fall 1983): 167–174.

Townsend, Larry. *The Leatherman's Handbook.* Vols. 1 and 2. New York: Le Salon International, 1972.

Trebay, Guy. "Ron Athey's Slice of Life." *Village Voice*, 1 November 1994, p. 38.

——. "Taking Pains: Bob Flanagan's S/M Cures." *Village Voice*, 4 October 1994, p. 22.

Trebilcot, Joyce. *Dyke Ideas: Process, Politics, Daily Life.* Albany: State University of New York Press, 1994.

Trites, Allison A. *The New Testament Concept of Witness.* Cambridge: Cambridge University Press, 1977.

Tucker, Scott. "Gender, Fucking, and Utopia." *Social Text* 9, no. 27 (1990): 3–34.

Tucker, Scott. "Radical Feminism and Gay Male Porn." *New York Native*, July, 1983, pp. 18–31.

Vance, Carole, ed. *Pleasure and Danger: Exploring Female Sexuality.* Boston: Routledge, 1984.

Valverde, Mariana. "Feminism Meets Fist-Fucking: Getting Lost in Lesbian S & M." *Body Politic* 43 (February 1980): photocopy from Lesbian Herstory Archives, no page number.

Wardrop, S. "The Heroine Is Being Beaten: Freud, Sadomasochism, and Reading the Romance." *Style* 29, no. 3 (Fall 1995): 459–473.

Warland, Betsy, ed. *Inversions: Writing by Dykes, Queers, and Lesbians.* Vancouver: Press Gang, 1991.

Warner, Michael, ed. *Fear of a Queer Planet: Queer Politics and Social Theory.* Minneapolis: University of Minnesota, 1993.

Watson, Julia. "Unspeakable Differences: The Politics of Gender in Lesbian and Heterosexual Women's Autobiographies."In *De/Colonizing the Subject: The Politics of Gender in Women's Autobiography*, eds. Sidonie Smith and Julia Watson, pp. 139–168. Minneapolis: University of Minnesota Press, 1992.

Wechsler, Nancy. "Gayle Rubin and Pat Califia Talk About Sadomasochism: Fears, Facts, Fantasies." *Gay Community News*, 15 August 1981, pp. 6–8.

Welsh, L. *Bad Habits*. New York: Masquerade, 1992.

———. *Private Lessons*. New York: Masquerade, 1993.

Weinberg, Thomas S. "Sadomasochism in the United States: A Review of Recent Sociological Literature." *Journal of Sex Research* 23 (February 1987): 50–69.

Weinberg, Thomas, and G. W. Levi Kamel, eds. *S and M: Studies in Sadomasochism*. New York: Prometheus, 1983.

Wertheim, Ann. "Daddy's Little Girl." *On Our Backs* 7, no. 5 (May/June 1991): 28–29, 40–41.

West, Celeste. *A Lesbian Love Advisor*. San Francisco: Cleis, 1989.

Williams, Bernard. *Shame and Necessity*. Berkeley: University of California Press, 1993.

Williams, Linda. *Hard Core: Power, Pleasure, and the Frenzy of the Visible*. Berkeley: University of California Press, 1989.

Wilson, Angelia R., ed. *A Simple Matter of Justice?: Theorizing Lesbian and Gay Politics*. London: Cassell, 1995.

Wilson, M. Lee. "Female Homosexuals Need for Dominance and Endurance." *Psychological Reports* 55 (1984): 79–82.

Wilton, Tamsin. *Lesbian Studies: Setting an Agenda*. London and New York: Routledge, 1995.

Wisechild, Louise M. *The Obsidian Mirror: An Adult Healing from Incest*. Seattle: Seal, 1993.

Wittig, Monique. *The Lesbian Body*. Trans. David Le Vay. Boston: Beacon Press, 1986.

———. *The Straight Mind and Other Essays*. Boston: Beacon, 1992.

Wolf, Deborah Goleman. *The Lesbian Community*. Berkley and Los Angeles: University of California Press, 1979.

Wolff, Charlotte. *Love Between Women*. New York: Harper and Row, 1971.

Wood, Roy F. "The Conquering Strength." *Drummer* 74 (May 1984): 25–30.

Young-Bruehl, Elizabeth. *Anna Freud*. New York: Summit, 1988.

Yingling, Thomas. "How the Eye is Caste: Robert Mapplethorpe and the Limits of Controversy." *Discourse* 12, no. 2 (Spring/Summer 1990): 3–28.

Yanagisako, Sylvia, and Delaney, Carol. *Naturalizing Power*. New York and London: Routledge, 1995.

Young, James E. *Writing and Rewriting the Holocaust: Narrative and the Consequences of Interpretation*. Bloomington and Indianapolis: Indiana University Press, 1988.

Zawinski, Andrena. "Letter to Editors." *Off Our Backs* (February 1981): 28.

Zita, Jacquelyn N. "Pornography and the Male Imaginary." *Enclitic* 9, nos. 1–2 (1987): 28–44.

Žižek, Slavoj. *Enjoy Your Symptom! Jacques Lacan in Hollywood and Out*. New York and London: Routledge, 1992.

———. "Hidden Prohibitions and the Pleasure Principle: An Interview." Interviewed by Josefina Ayerza, *Flash Art* 25, no. 163 (March/April 1992): 68–70.

———. *The Sublime Object of Ideology.* London: Verso, 1989.

———. *Tarrying With the Negative: Kant, Hegel,and the Critique of Ideology.* Durham: Duke University Press, 1993.

Index

Between Men ~ Between Women
LESBIAN AND GAY STUDIES
Lillian Faderman and Larry Gross, Editors

Claudia Schoppmann, *Days of Masquerade: Life Stories of Lesbians During the Third Reich*

Alan Sinfield, *The Wilde Century: Effeminacy, Oscar Wilde, and the Queer Moment*

Jane McIntosh Snyder, *Lesbian Desire in the Lyrics of Sappho*

Chris Straayer, *Deviant Eyes, Deviant Bodies: Sexual Re-Orientations in Film and Video*

Dwayne C. Turner, *Risky Sex: Gay Men and HIV Prevention*

Thomas Waugh, *Hard to Imagine: Gay Male Eroticism in Photography and Film from Their Beginnings to Stonewall*

Kath Weston, *Families We Choose: Lesbians, Gays, Kinship*

Kath Weston, *Render Me, Gender Me: Lesbians Talk Sex, Class, Color, Nation, Studmuffins . . .*

Carter Wilson, *Hidden in the Blood: A Personal Investigation of AIDS in the Yucatán*

Jacquelyn Zita, *Body Talk: Philosophical Reflections on Sex and Gender*

CPSIA information can be obtained
at www.ICGtesting.com
Printed in the USA
JSHW031021070222
22641JS00001B/43

9 780231 084031